BOUND TO LEAD

BOUND TO LEAD

The Changing Nature of American Power

JOSEPH S. NYE, JR.

BasicBooks
A Division of HarperCollins*Publishers*

Library of Congress Cataloging-in-Publication Data

Nye, Joseph S.
   Bound to lead: the changing nature of American
power/Joseph S. Nye, Jr.
      p.   cm.
   Includes bibliographical references.
   ISBN 0–465–00177–7 (cloth)
   ISBN 0–465–00744–9 (paper)
   1. United States—Foreign relations—1945-
2. World politics—1945-   . 3. Power (Social
sciences). 4. Geopolitics—United States—History—20th
century. I. Title.
E840.N94   1990
973.92—dc20   89-43099

To Bob Bowie, Stanley Hoffmann
and Bob Keohane

great teachers, critics, friends

Contents

PART II
New Challengers?

PART III
New Challenges

Preface to the
Paperback Edition

In our planet's geology, the great tectonic plates shift slowly until a tension builds that we experience as an earthquake. World politics is sometimes similar. For the last forty years, world order rested on the seemingly stable bipolar structure of power that followed World War II. However, economic, social, and political strains were building beneath the surface. The first earthquakes were felt with the Eastern European revolutions of 1989. And it is unlikely that all the tremors are over. The "second Russian Revolution" is still in its early stages. Foretelling its shape a decade from now is as difficult as it would have been in 1789 to imagine the future of France.

Saddam Hussein's invasion of Kuwait in August 1990 was another major tremor. Ironically, Saddam correctly appraised the waning power of his Soviet ally, and in a February 1990 speech in Amman, Jordan, he described the United States as the country that "will maintain its superiority as a superpower without an equal to compete with it."[1] Yet he drew the conclusion that he could safely attack Kuwait. Consistent with the diffusion of power described in chapter 6, the nature of the post–Cold War world order remains fluid and full of surprises.

A happier sense of surprise was conveyed by Czech President Vaclav Havel when he addressed the American Congress. Remarking on the rapid changes in the world, the former playwright said that four months out of prison and two months into his presidency, he observed that even playwrights, who have to cram a whole human life or an entire historical era into a two-hour play, could scarcely understand the contemporary rapidity of political change. "And if it gives us trouble," Havel continued, "think of the trouble it must give to political scientists who spend their whole lives studying the realm of the probable."[2]

Several significant changes have occurred since this book was first published in April 1990, but fortunately they are consistent with its main thesis. Soviet power has declined and its empire collapsed more rapidly than expected, but that is an acceleration of the trend described in chapter 4. Germany has reunified much more rapidly than expected, but the key question, as explained in chapter 5, remains the pace of European integration. Alone, a unified Germany remains only one-quarter the size of the United States. The American economy slipped into a recession that will produce gloomy economic numbers for a time, but dips in the business cycle are to be expected. Recession is not a good indication of long-run trends unless it leads to prolonged depression.

The American response to the Persian Gulf crisis

demonstrated, as this book argues, that the United States remains the only country with significant hard and soft power resources. But the long-term effects of the Gulf crisis depend less upon those American resources than upon the lessons that the American public draws from the experience. History suggests caution, for in the 1920s and the early 1970s, the American public chose not to make use of its formidable power resources for international leadership. Then as now, the key uncertainties about America's future role in the world revolved around domestic politics.

In 1988, Paul Kennedy's best-selling *The Rise and Fall of the Great Powers* captured a public mood of anxiety about American decline at the end of the Reagan era. Reviewing *Bound to Lead* in June 1990, Kennedy distinguished between two schools of thought about America's future. Declinists, such as he, believe that America's position relative to the rest of the world will continue to worsen. Revivalists (the label he assigns to me) are "not purblind optimists, but they believe either that the talk of America's 'decline' has gone too far, or that, while things are indeed wrong, they can be corrected."[3] That is a fair assessment of the thesis of this book.

Before the Gulf crisis, the belief in decline had already colored interpretations of current events. A striking case in point was *Lignes d'Horizon*, a book published in 1990 in Paris, written by Jacques Attali, a key adviser to President Mitterrand and the director of the new multilateral bank for Eastern Europe, who argues that the American decline is so steep that the future will be dominated by a European bloc and a

Japanese-led Pacific bloc.[4] At a more mundane level, a front-page article in the *New York Times* claimed that President Bush's inability to dominate the 1990 Houston Summit of the advanced industrial nations was a sign of slipping American power. Such accounts show little sense of history for, as described in chapter 8, when economic summitry began in the mid-1970s, the United States was similarly unable to dominate. By exaggerating American dominance in the past, declinists and their followers in the press find it easy to diminish America's present.

Similar problems plague declinist efforts to prove domestic social decay. Without question, some problems, such as drug abuse, violent crime, and the crisis in secondary education, are worse today than they were thirty years ago. But others, such as institutionalized racism or the position of women in society, are better. Still others are hard to evaluate.

The same can be said of the economic picture. Important industrial sectors such as consumer electronics and automobiles have slipped badly. The household savings rate dropped from 8 percent in the 1970s to 5 percent in the 1980s, and the government deficit subtracted another 3 percent. Since gross investment stayed roughly the same, the missing savings were made up by capital imports that transformed the United States into the world's largest debtor in absolute terms.

The declinists stress this negative side of the ledger, but there is another side. During the 1980s, the American economy grew by 2.5 percent a year, above its historical average of 2 percent over the past century.

Contrary to Attali's view of the United States as merely "Japan's granary," industry contributed the same one-fifth of the gross national product that it had in the 1970s. Productivity in manufacturing rose by 3.5 percent per year in the 1980s, and absolute productivity (product per worker) remained higher than in Japan or Germany. The United States remains in the forefront of such high-tech industries as aircraft, chemicals, biotechnology, software, and computers. Moreover, some economists believe that the slower 1 percent rate of growth of overall labor productivity (that is, in all sectors) is an underestimate that reflects the difficulty of measuring productivity increases in the service sector.

These seemingly contradictory facts can be aggregated by looking at the American share of the world product. As shown in chapter 3, for the last decade and a half, the American share of world product has held stable at about 23 percent of the total. In fact, if one uses purchasing power parities, which correct the current exchange rate of currencies for what the money will buy in a local economy, the American share of world product, and of the product of the seven summit nations, actually increased in the 1980s.

Kennedy has written that the end of the Cold War reduced "the significance of the one measure of national power in which the United States had a clear advantage over other countries"—the military.[5] But this not only ignores American economic, scientific, cultural, and ideological strengths, it also misunderstands the past and present roles of military power. One reason the United States was unable to boss around its allies in the past was that it was never a fully hegemonic power. Its military strength was balanced by Soviet military strength, and Europe and Japan sometimes prevailed over the United States in intra-alliance bargaining because of Washington's greater concern about the Soviet Union.

The end of the Cold War reduced but did not eliminate the role of military force. In Asia, many cleavages have nothing to do with the Cold War. Many Europeans welcome the continued presence of a United States four times the size of Germany. Even if reduced, the American security guarantee remains of value to Europe and Japan as insurance against the uncertain future of the second Russian Revolution. And if the allies value an American insurance policy more than the United States does, that may do more for American bargaining power, ironically, than much larger forces did at the height of the Cold War.

Moreover, when Iraqi tanks rolled into Kuwait, they damaged another aspect of the declinist argument: the view that the world had entered a multipolar era in which economic power replaced military power. They also exposed the one-dimensional nature of the power of Germany and Japan.

Some believe that the very existence of a debate about American decline calls the health of the country into question. Kennedy finds uncanny echoes of concerns in Edwardian Britain, and notes the view that a strong man does not worry about his health. He faults the revivalists for being ahistorical in their optimism.[6] But if concern about decline is proof of its presence, then the United States has been finished since the start. As discussed in the introduction to this book, the founding fathers were already worrying about decline in the eighteenth century. The theme returned in the 1890s with the closing of the American frontier. More recently, in the 1950s the Soviet launch of Sputnik was taken as a sign of relative American decline, as was the oil crisis of 1973.

A more plausible view is that American political moods swing more rapidly than underlying reality warrants. The latest bout of declinism may reflect a natural reaction to the exaggerations of the 1980s, to the decline of particular industrial sectors, to rapid social change, and perhaps to the loss of the certainties of the Cold War. In addition, the pendulum of American attitudes often swings to a generational rhythm. A dispassionate observer looking at the greed, shortsightedness, and weak political leadership of America in the 1920s might wrongly have concluded that the country was in a long-term decline.

The United States cannot stand alone as the world's policeman or, as one politician put it, "the world's 911." As argued in chapter 8, Americans need to develop better approaches to multilateral burden sharing to deal with issues arising out of the diffusion of power. Yet the United States is the largest country in the international system in both hard and soft power resources, and if the largest power does not lead in organizing multilateral action, no one will.

Over the long term, America's hard and soft power resources will depend upon addressing the difficult domestic issues of the budget deficit, the savings rate, and our educational system, which I describe in chapter 7. On the optimistic side, one can cite the size of the American market, its flexibility and entrepreneurial resources, and the greater openness of the United States than Europe or Japan to immigration in the face of declining demographic changes. On the other hand, without improved education and investment, such resources will be wasted.

Military strength depends on a strong economic base. Cultural and ideological appeal depend on maintaining a healthy and open society. But there is no objective reason Americans cannot afford both social security and international security. Unlike Britain in 1914, the United States remains both the world's largest economy and its largest military power. If declinist writings persuade the public to support domestic reforms, that will be all to the good. But if they persuade Americans to become more protectionist and to draw back from international leadership on the grounds that a declining power can't afford it, they may create a self-fulfilling fallacy. The moral for a post–Cold War world is to beware of historians bearing false analogies.

Preface

Americans are worried about national decline. Many believe that the country is overextended and should reduce its external commitments. But in a world of growing interdependence among nations, this advice is the wrong answer, and U.S. decline is the wrong question. Not only is the premise debatable, but it diverts our attention away from the *real* question: How is power changing in modern international politics? Traditional theories about the rise and fall of great powers could lead Americans to pursue the wrong strategies in the new politics of the twenty-first century.

For two decades, I have taught Harvard undergraduates about international politics. I tell them that before they can understand change in politics, they must first grasp the traditional theories about power that date back to ancient Greece. However, I also tell them that the traditional view will allow them to understand only half the story of contemporary international politics. And when opinion makers and public officials become mired in historically traditional views and base policies on analogies about decline, the problem is no longer academic.

My concern about the current American debate over decline is not merely parochial. Given the size of the United States, most other nations have an interest in Americans understanding their role. If the most powerful country fails to lead, the consequences for the rest of the world may be disastrous. Typically, periods of anxiety about the decline and rise of nations have been periods of tension and miscalculation. In a world with more than 50,000 nuclear weapons, such miscalculations could be fatal to more than just the United States.

Bound to Lead has grown out of my long-standing concern about how to understand change in world politics, and more immediately out of the Avoiding Nuclear War Project at Harvard's Center for Science and International Affairs. Financed by the Carnegie Corporation, the project has one strand devoted to understanding the long-term conditions for international stability. In 1988, Graham T. Allison, Albert Carnesale, and I edited *Fateful Visions,* a collection of essays on the long-term nuclear future. Although that book raises a number of questions about the decline of Soviet power and the implications for stability of shifting from a bipolar to a multipolar world, it says little about the United States. *Bound to Lead* develops the same theme but in the context of the current public debate about American decline. I was also stimulated by Paul Kennedy's history of *The Rise and Fall of the Great Powers.* While I disagree with some of his conclusions, I found his book challenging. My tribute is that I have taken his work seriously.

I am endebted to a surprisingly large number of people for such a small book. David Hamburg and Fritz Mosher of the Carnegie Corporation and Clint Smith of the Hewlett Foundation provided financial and moral support. Teaching a graduate seminar with Stephan Haggard helped hone my realization of the inadequacy of the prevalent theories of war and change in world politics. My students and research fellows did much to educate me. Ralph Dahrendorf provided a wonderful setting for a month of rewriting at St. Antony's College in Oxford.

I wish to thank the many people who made important comments on earlier drafts of the manuscript: John Alic, Graham Allison, Robert Art, Benina Berger-Gould, James Blight, Robert Bowie, Harvey Brooks, Albert Carnesale, Houchang Chehabi, Richard Cooper, Ralph Dahrendorf, Michael Doyle, Richard Eichenberg, Peter Feaver, Thomas Graham, John Hall, Stanley Hoffmann, Samuel Huntington, Helge Hveem, William Jarosz, Teresa Johnson, Peter Katzenstein, Stephen Kelman, Paul Kennedy, Robert Keohane, Martin Kessler, Yuen Foong Khong, Sean Lynn-Jones, Lisa Martin, Kerry McNamara, Molly Nye, Patrick O'Brien, Robert O'Neill, Robert Paarlberg, Adam Roberts, Henry Rosovsky, Eugene Skolnikoff, Roger Smith, David Spiro, Lawrence Summers, Raymond Vernon, Ezra Vogel, and David Welch.

I also benefited greatly from the intelligence, skill, and goodwill of three excellent assistants, Veronica McClure, Kathleen O'Reilly, and Melissa Bauman.

I am especially grateful to my colleagues Robert R. Bowie, Stanley Hoffmann, and Robert O. Keohane, for their help in shaping this book before and during the writing. And, as with everything, Molly Harding Nye lived and shared this book with me.

The rare occasions when one stops and acknowledges one's debts to others are humbling, but rewarding. What a blessing to be surrounded by so many good people! I hope these pages are some repayment.

The Debate About Decline

In 1941, *Life* magazine proclaimed this "the American century."[1] The United States emerged from World War II with its armies victorious and the dollar impregnable. Historian Arnold Toynbee argued that the United States had to succeed Britain as the leader of the world.[2] President Truman accepted that challenge in 1947, when the United States replaced waning British aid to Greece and Turkey. By the mid-1960s, Undersecretary of State Eugene Rostow claimed that "the United States has now occupied the role of chief policeman for the free world for about twenty years. The office has required diplomatic and military exertions of us in a long series of conflicts—from Iran, Lebanon, Turkey, and Greece to Berlin, Korea, Cuba, and Vietnam."[3] At the same time, Harvard Professor Samuel Huntington argued that "by the year 2000 it should be clear retrospectively that the dominant feature of international politics during the thirty years after World War II was the expansion of American power."[4]

By the 1970s, however, *Business Week* declared that "the colossus that emerged after World War II" was "clearly facing a crisis of the decay of power."[5] The United States had suffered defeat in Vietnam, an oil embargo, and rising inflation at home. In the 1980s, America slid from the position of the world's largest creditor to that of a net debtor. Its share of world product slipped from 33 percent of the total in 1950 to 23 percent in the 1980s. Its share of world exports fell from 17 percent in 1950 to 10 percent in 1988, and its share of world monetary reserves dropped even more dramatically, from 50 to 9 percent.[6]

By 1989, half the American public believed that the nation was in decline. Only one in five Americans believed that the United States was the top economic power, even though it remained by far the world's largest economy. After President Reagan's military build-up in the 1980s, only a fifth of the people believed that the United States was ahead of the Soviet Union in overall military strength. About a third of the public believed that the country's nuclear arsenal was weaker than that of the Soviet Union, and half believed that the United States was behind in conventional military strength.[7] A rash of books and articles published in the 1980s described the decline of nations, and American decline in particular.

Comparisons of Britain and the United States now emphasize the negative rather than the positive. "Today America is where Britain was around the turn of the century," wrote MIT economist Lester Thurow in 1985. "Rome lasted a thousand years, the British Empire about 200; why are we slipping after about 50 years?"[8]

Others find the United States position in the 1980s so reminiscent of the British decline in the late nineteenth century that "rather than investigating whether a situation of hegemonic decline and economic crisis exists, it is now possible to examine what effects this situation has had."[9]

Some scholars suggest that the American situation is typical of the imperial overstretch that has occurred throughout history. A growing nation builds its military power to protect its expanding economic interests, but eventually the cost of projecting military power saps its strength and the nation is replaced by another rising economic power. Immanuel Wallerstein sees overstretch as "a regular happening," with decline starting in Venice around 1500, in Holland around 1660, in Britain around 1873, and in America around 1967. "The basic reason was the same: the overall productivity edge relative to that of the closest rival states . . . had begun to fritter away because of aging plant (in the loosest sense of this term) and rising comparative costs of the factors of production, combined with the high economic costs of political and military imperium which led to rising taxation levels."[10] Paul Kennedy, in his bestselling book *The Rise and Fall of the Great Powers*, writes that "the difficulties experienced by contemporary societies which are militarily top-heavy merely repeat those which, in their time, affected Phillip II's Spain, Nicholas II's Russia, and Hitler's Germany."[11]

Such historical analogies suggest that major U.S. foreign policy changes are needed. Kennedy, for example, believes that "our overcommitments in foreign policy can be reduced,"[12] whereas political scientist David Calleo attributes America's fiscal deficit to its "comparatively large military expenditures." Calleo suggests

withdrawing troops from Europe, and "selective proliferation" of nuclear weapons to our allies.[13] Walter Mead
believes that America's decline will continue.[14] Others
also conclude that the United States needs to reduce its
international commitments in accordance with its
diminishing strength.[15]

I argue, however, that these historical analogies are
misleading and the diagnosis wrong. Policies of
retrenchment are premature and, ironically, they could
produce the very weakening of American power they
are supposed to avert. Withdrawal from international
commitments might reduce American influence overseas without necessarily strengthening the domestic
economy. Further, the nations of the world have
become so inextricably intertwined that efforts to draw
back would be difficult at best.

But before one can attempt to shape policies on the
basis of historical analogies and theories of decline, it is
essential to have an accurate assessment of America's
current position. This assessment can be based on an
examination of these four issues: (1) What is America's
current power position? (2) How is it changing? (3) What
has caused the changes? and (4) What are the appropriate responses? These concerns, which must be dealt
with separately, are often mixed together in historical
analogies and grand theories of decline. Moreover, contrary to many of the decline assertions cited earlier, the
answers to these questions are not solely pessimistic;
they often show a more positive view of the U.S. position at the end of the twentieth century.

In this introduction, I explain the terms of the contemporary debate about decline and discuss its importance.
Part I is about the nature of power in the past—chapter
1 investigates the history of hegemonic or dominant pow-

ers, chapter 2 challenges the validity of currently popular comparisons of Victorian Britain and modern America, and chapter 3 examines in detail the extent and nature of U.S. power after World War II to the present. In part II, chapters 4 and 5 question the ability of potential challengers—the Soviet Union, China, Europe, and Japan— to supersede the United States as the world's leading power. Although this book concludes that the United States will remain the leading power, part III explains why this conclusion, which is based on traditional power analysis, in no way permits American complacency. Chapter 6 examines the changing nature of power in the modern world, and chapter 7 explains the new challenges that such changes present to our society. Finally, chapter 8 outlines a new strategic vision for dealing with the problems of future decades.

CRITICAL QUESTIONS

There is no doubt that the United States is less powerful now at the end of the twentieth century than it was in mid-century. Even conservative estimates show that the U.S. share of global product has declined from more than a third of the total after World War II to a little more than a fifth in the 1980s.[16] However, there is less agreement on what these numbers mean.

One problem in assessing U.S. decline is the "World War II effect." Unlike the other great powers, the United States was strengthened by the war. It was not bombed or invaded, and it built impressive military forces and a powerful industrial base. Other nations involved in the war were devastated. In this sense, U.S. economic preponderance in the 1950s was anomalous.

But like the boy on the block who dominates while others have the flu, American preponderance was bound to erode as other nations regained their economic health. Further, the recovery of Europe and Japan was an explicit goal of the U.S. policy of containing Soviet expansion. Much of the relative decline since the 1950s, then, is simply a return to normal after the artificial effect of World War II.

IS DECLINE CONTINUING?

Paul Kennedy argues that U.S. decline has been continuous: "The U.S. share of world GNP, which declined naturally since 1945, has declined much more quickly than it should have over the last few years." David Calleo is even more alarmist: "Thanks to economic strain and mismanagement, relative decline has begun to turn absolute."[17]

However, other investigations do not support the case for continuous decline in America's share of the world product. Charles Wolf of the Rand Corporation notes that "if a more appropriate and representative base year is used—say, the mid-1960s (or even a pre-World War II year such as 1938)—the remarkable fact is that the U.S. economy's share of the global product was about the same 'then' as it is 'now': about 22% to 24%."[18] Herbert Block's careful estimates of shares of world product date the fading of the World War II effect on the United States somewhat later than Wolf does, but the result is the same. Block estimates that the United States represented about a quarter of world product in the early twentieth century and about a third in 1950. He claims that the postwar American share of world product declined until 1974 and then stabilized. Similarly, the American Council on Competitiveness finds that the U.S. share of world product has held constant at 23 percent since the mid-1970s, and that its share of the product of the major industrial democracies actually increased slightly in the 1980s. The Central Intelligence Agency, using numbers that reflect the purchasing power of different currencies, reports that the American share of world product increased slightly from 25 percent in 1975 to 26 percent in 1988.[19]

The results of these studies conflict with the view that American decline has been either precipitous or continuous. They suggest instead that the World War II effect lasted for about a quarter century and that most of the decline worked its way through the system by the mid-1970s and then stabilized. In contrast, those who support the view of continuous decline challenge the use of global product as an indicator. They prefer other indices, claiming that GNP estimates are crude aggregates that change too slowly.[20]

CHANGING YARDSTICKS

How should we measure power in a changing world? Throughout the centuries, statesmen and other observers have mistakenly perceived the metric of power. For example, seventeenth-century mercantilist theorists, who focused on Spain's reserves of gold and silver bullion from the mines in the Western Hemisphere, would not have predicted Holland's commercial rise or the strength of France derived from larger population and improved administrative structures. In the eighteenth century, those who focused on France's population and rural industry would have missed the rise of Britain due to its political stability and favorable conditions for the Industrial Revolution. In 1900, American writer Brooks Adams used the control of metals and minerals as an index of future military and economic power; he predicted the decline of Britain and the ascendancy of Russia and China.[21]

However, raw materials and heavy industry are less critical indices of economic power today than are information and professional and technical services. According to sociologist Daniel Bell, the first technological revolution happened two hundred years ago, with the advent of steam-powered transportation and factory machine production. The second technological revolution arrived a century ago, when the spread of electricity and chemistry allowed the production of synthetics and plastics. The third technological revolution, underway today, joins computers and telecommunications to produce television imagery, voice telephone, digital computer data, and facsimile transmission.[22] These new technologies offer a unified but complex system of services from interlinked computers and electronic mail to information storage and retrieval. The information revolution is changing the notion of markets; no longer geographic places, they have become global networks. Speed and flexibility of response to new information is becoming increasingly important. If Bell is correct, the appropriate indicators of power today are related to manufacturing and services in the information industries.

The information revolution is having very different effects on different nations. The centralized planning systems of the Soviet Union and China lack the flexibility needed for an information-based economy. The European economies have been slower than the United States and Japan in adapting to the new environment. Japan has made the most rapid gains in high-technology exports, but these gains have come more at the expense of the rest of the world than of the U.S. share, which dropped only slightly over the decade 1980-1990. In chapter 3, I look more closely at indices at several levels of aggregation—from GNP to the detail of a specific industry—to compare how various nations have fared.

IMPERIAL OVERSTRETCH?

Although imperial overstretch is a frequently cited cause of the change in America's power position, the facts do not support the theory. According to the overstretch theory, "the Great Power is likely to find itself spending much *more* on defense than it did two generations earlier, and yet still discover that the world is a less secure environment."[23] However, even after President Reagan's military build-up, the current U.S. defense outlay is only about 6 percent of GNP; in the Eisenhower and Kennedy administrations, it was near 10 percent. Further, the U.S. defense burden is not at all like that of Spain or France in their last days of grandeur. Philip II's Spain devoted three-fourths of all government expenditure to war and war debt.[24] The France of Louis XIV and the Russia of Peter the Great devoted, respectively, 75 and 85 percent of their revenues to war and the military establishment.[25] In the United States today, just about 27 percent of the federal budget is spent on defense (including veterans' benefits). And unlike the historical examples, America's overseas commitments do not involve the occupation and control of conquered territories.

Paul Kennedy has argued that our net defense burden is greater today because the United States has a lower share of world product than it did previously. He likens the United States to an aging man carrying a pack up a hill, less able to carry the burden than before.

But, as figure I.1 shows, the ratio of America's defense burden to its share of world product has not increased over time and is even lower now than it was in the 1950s. Although such ratios of aggregates are sometimes unreliable, they still cast doubt on analogies about increasing burdens. Indeed, contrary to the theory of imperial overstretch, the U.S. defense burden today is lighter than it was in the 1950s, and the political burdens of American commitments are lighter today than during the Vietnam War. Some theorists of imperial overstretch assume that defense spending is harmful to the economy, noting that Japan spends a bit more than 1 percent of its GNP on defense and has a higher rate of economic growth than the United States. However, such simple correlations are misleading. South Korea and the People's Republic of China, for example, spent more of their GNP on defense than did the United States in the late 1970s and early 1980s, yet both had even higher economic growth rates than Japan. Moreover, while defense spending has had some negative effects, it also has had some positive effects on the U.S. economy. Few careful and balanced economic studies show conclusively that defense spending had a significant negative *net* impact on the economy.[26] A priori assumptions about the effects of defense spending cannot rescue the theory of imperial overstretch from its fatal problem: it simply does not fit the facts of the American position at the end of the twentieth century.

PRIOR DEBATES

The debate about America's current position in the world is confusing not only because of fuzzy concepts

FIGURE I.1

Ratio of Defense Burden to Share of World Product, United States (1955–1988)

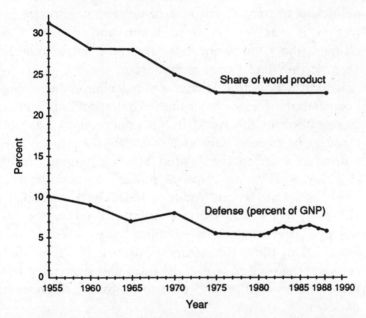

SOURCE: Herbert Block, *The Planetary Product in 1980: A Creative Pause?* (Washington, D.C.: U.S. Department of State, Bureau of Public Affairs, 1981), pp. 74–77, 86–87; Central Intelligence Agency, *Handbook of Economic Statistics, 1988* (Washington, D.C., 1988), pp. 12, 22, 24; Council on Competiveness, *Competiveness Index* (Washington, D.C., 1988), app. II.

and numbers, but also because of emotional factors. The idea of decline touches a raw nerve in American politics. Some people react emotionally against discussions of decline because of national pride. But it is counterintuitive and ahistorical to believe that the United States should have the dominant share of world product or power forever. American power has clearly declined since 1945, and even if the decline has largely halted, some continued erosion would be natural. The appropriate American response to the changing international environment should not rest on an exaggeration of American power. Thus, it is foolish for politicians to treat discussions of decline as unpatriotic, just as it was for those in Spain and Britain who claimed they too were not like past great powers because they had "a superior system."[27]

Unfortunately, the debate about decline is becoming polarized along ideological lines. Understanding America's position in the world is too important to leave to ideology or to loose historical analogies. All too often, journalists refer to the United States emerging "from World War II as an imperial power" or describe the 1950s as a time when "America bestrode the world."[28] However, as we shall see in chapter 3, even at its postwar peak, the power of the United States was far more limited than these exaggerations suggest. Analyses that compare the present with a mythical past depreciate the present U.S. position and contribute to the impression of decline.

Concern about decline would be good for the United States if it cut through complacency and prodded Americans to deal with some of the serious domestic issues outlined in chapter 7. On the other hand, Samuel Popkin has found that excessive anxiety about decline may turn American opinion toward nationalistic and protectionist policies that would constrain our ability to cope with issues created by growing international interdependence.[29] Thus, there is no virtue in either overstatement or understatement of American strength. The former leads to failure to adapt, the latter to "cures" that do more harm than the disease.

There is a long history of concern about decline in Western thought. It can be found, for example, in the works of eighteenth-century European writers Rousseau, Montesquieu, Burke, and Gibbon. The idea of decline, particularly as it relates to the history of Rome, even worried the founders of the American Republic.[30] Recently, Samuel Huntington identified five phases of what he calls "declinism" in postwar America: (1) after the Soviets launched Sputnik in 1957; (2) after Nixon's announcement of multipolarity in the late 1960s; (3) at the time of the oil embargo in 1973; (4) after Soviet expansion in the late 1970s; and (5) after the onset of Reagan's fiscal and trade deficits in the late 1980s. Huntington suggests that such recurring worries may be "better indications of American psychology than of American power."[31]

There is also a history of premature and misleading predictions of decline. Many eighteenth-century British leaders lamented Britain's decline as a result of losing the American colonies. Horace Walpole foresaw Britain's reduction "to a miserable little island, and from a mighty empire . . . [to] as insignificant a country as Denmark or Sardinia."[32] These predictions, colored by the eighteenth-century view of colonial commerce, failed to foresee the new industrial base of power in the Victorian era that gave Britain a second century. Yet at the height of Britain's ascendency in 1865, Matthew Arnold saw "an imminent danger of England losing immeasurably in all ways, declining into a sort of greater Holland."[33] In 1878, former Prime Minister William Gladstone worried that "America is passing us by as if in a canter."[34] At the turn of the century, as we shall see in chapter 2, Britons debated how to appraise their global position but they were unable to reach a consensus or to draw policy conclusions.

THE CONCEPT OF DECLINE

Decline is a tricky word because it bundles together two quite different concepts: a decrease in external power and internal deterioration or decay. However, a country may experience decline in one sense, but not in the other. For example, the seventeenth-century Netherlands flourished internally but declined in power because other nations became stronger. Spain, on the other hand, lost external power in part because it suffered an absolute economic decline from the 1620s to the 1680s.[35] Or, like Venice, a country may reach its internal cultural peak after outside factors (the shift of trade routes) initiated its decline as an economic power. At the beginning of this century, Vienna was a cultural capital even as the Austrian Empire declined politically.

Obviously, the two concepts of decline are related. Internal deterioration can contribute to loss of external power, but often it is difficult to identify which internal changes were the major causes of power loss and when they occurred. At latest count, scholars have advanced more than two hundred alleged causes of the decline of Rome and still disagree on dates.[36] The Romans themselves often saw their world in despairing terms; some of them began to worry about decline as early as 133 B.C., six centuries before the conventional date for the Fall of Rome. From A.D. 300 to 450—the period that modern historians identify as declining—the Roman economy was demonstrably healthy. Financial problems contributed to the gradual paralysis of the state, but commerce and manufacturing were lively.[37] As one historian concludes, "the 'Rome that declines' is thus not one single thing but many things, and the search for any one cause across the board is futile. So, too, is the search for any one period in which all aspects of Roman civilization were much changed."[38] The eastern half of the Roman Empire survived under increasingly precarious conditions for nearly another thousand years after Roman armies became unable to protect the western provinces. The Western Empire was not the victim of a rising challenger state. It succumbed to the long-term pressure of invading migratory tribes: "In any straight fight they could, and they usually did, defeat superior numbers of Germans. . . . What they could not do was cope indefinitely with this kind of enemy."[39]

Power is relative, depending in part on what is happening at home and more so on what is happening outside. An empire may survive for a long time after aspects of civilization begin to decay at home if outside challengers are weak. Although civic corruption and loss of administrative and military efficiency may have allowed nomadic tribes to sack Rome, its external challengers were weak. The Fall of Rome in A.D. 476 occurred two centuries after the onset of major corruption in its government and deterioration of its military.

A nation may also decline in power relative to other nations because it chooses not to use the power resources at its disposal. For instance, early eighteenth-century France allowed its naval and fiscal resources to stagnate relative to Britain's, but unlike Spain in the previous century, the French decline was only temporary. The stagnation in French war potential did not represent an absolute decline, as the subsequent Napoleonic Empire proved. Yet in terms of basic resources, "one could argue that France's ability to expand militarily was greater in 1750 than it would be in 1805."[40] The difference was in the results of leadership and policy choices. A more recent example is the United States. Emerging from World War I as a potentially dominant global power, it nonetheless chose a policy of isolationism that made it a secondary player in world political events. American influence was lower in 1928 than in 1918, but not because it had lost power resources.

Absolute decline, in which there is a loss of critical power resources or of the ability to use one's own resources effectively, is less common than relative decline in which the power resources of others grow greater or are used more effectively. Neither type of decline requires nor implies domestic decay. As Raymond Aron suggests, "[d]ecadence implies value judgments. . . . Decline simply describes a power relationship."[41] Such external power relationships are the concern of this book. Although in chapter 7 I examine how internal changes affect power relationships, the main focus of this book is on the external dimensions of power, not value judgments about the quality of American civilization at the end of the twentieth century.

DOES IT MATTER?

Some suggest that the current debate on American decline should be regarded as a register of mass psychology and popular fads rather than an analysis of power.[42] Others ask why Americans should worry about power. Why not focus solely on wealth and live as well as Swedes or Canadians? The short answer is that the United States is not in the same geopolitical position as Sweden or Canada. It cannot afford a free ride in world politics. If the largest country in a world of nation-states abdicates leadership (as the United States did in the 1920s), the results can be disastrous for all. In an assessment of the debate about American decline, British scholar Susan Strange concludes that "we are all in agreement . . . on the critical nature of the present end-of-century decade. We share a common perception that mankind . . . is standing at a fork in the road. . . . In the last resort, it may be that this common concern is more significant than the differences of interpretation."[43]

DECLINE AND WAR

Perceptions of change in the relative power of nations are of critical importance to understanding the relationship between decline and war. One of the oldest generalizations about international politics attributes the onset of major wars to shifts in power among the leading nations. Thus Thucydides accounted for the onset of the Peloponnesian War which destroyed the power of ancient Athens. The history of the interstate system since 1500 is punctuated by severe wars in which one country struggled to surpass another as the leading state.[44] If, as Robert Gilpin argues, "international politics has not changed fundamentally over the millennia," the implications for the future are bleak.[45] And if fears about shifting power precipitate a major war in a world with 50,000 nuclear weapons, history as we know it may end.

Psychology plays a large role in initiating war as well. It was not merely the rise of Athenian power but also Sparta's fear of that rise that caused the Peloponnesian War. Some historians argue that misperception played a role; ironically, Athenian expansion may actually have tapered off shortly before the onset of the war.[46] World War I is another striking example. Its immediate precipitant was the punitive response of the Austro-Hungarian gov-

ernment to an act of terrorism. The rashness of the Austrian response was affected by the fear that their empire
was in decline and they had no good alternative. The
Germans gave their Austrian allies a blank check in 1914
partly because they saw little risk of war and partly because they feared growing Russian strength. Some key
officials felt it better to risk war with Russia in 1914 than
to face it later. Britain, in turn, intervened because it
feared rising German dominance on the continent. Fear
of decline played a significant role in the risks that leaders
took. In Gilpin's words, "the outbreaks of hegemonic
struggles have most frequently been triggered by fears of
ultimate decline and the perceived erosion of power."[47]
Some who apply such theories to modern times believe
that "a period of increasing war could be expected around
2000–2030."[48]

Of course, such concerns may be too alarmist. There
are no iron laws of history. People can learn from their
mistakes, and the awesome destructive power of nuclear
weapons is a new stimulant to learning.[49] There is no
need for a declining Soviet Union to repeat the role of
Austria-Hungary, or for the United States to play Britain, or for modern Japan to be like prewar Japan. But
indeterminacy cuts both ways. Dangers persist, and prudent diplomatic calculations may become more difficult
when fundamental assumptions are shaken. Historians
have attributed the current unprecedented "long peace"
among the major powers to fear of nuclear war and to
the stability of the bipolar system, in which two nations
have dominated the balance of power.[50]

THE END OF BIPOLARITY?

Theorists and political leaders have heralded the
emergence of a multipolar system for nearly two dec-

ades. Mikhail Gorbachev's reforms and the changes in Eastern Europe have led to discussion of the end of the Cold War. What such changes mean for stability is not clear. A reduction in the intensity of U.S.-Soviet conflict is indeed welcomed, but political leaders have had no experience managing a truly multipolar balance of power in the nuclear age. How these leaders learn and respond to new situations will be affected by their perception of opportunities and dangers, including fears of decline. For instance, what would it mean for stability if a Japanese leader grew tired of guiding a mercantile nation and concluded "there's no glory in an abacus, so I vote for grandeur";[51] or if Soviet leaders saw nationalism eroding their country; or if Germans seek to unite the three German-speaking states?

Current changes are taking place in a world that is built on the outcome of the last hegemonic war, which ended in 1945 with the division of Germany. That division temporarily answered the German question that plagued Europe since Bismarck created a state in the center of Europe that, to be strong enough to defend itself simultaneously on two fronts, was also so strong that it frightened its neighbors. In Asia, 1945 meant the end of Japan's bid for military hegemony over the western Pacific, and the adoption of a new commercially oriented approach to international affairs in close alliance with the United States.

The United States did not seek a territorial empire or a hegemony that would keep the losing nations of 1945 in servile positions. Instead, it stimulated their economic revival and strategic partnership to balance Soviet power. To the extent that the United States has had a grand strategy for foreign policy over the past forty years, it has been to promote economic prosperity and political stability in Western Europe and Japan and to maintain close alliances with them. As George Kennan pointed out, after the war, only a few areas in the world had the industrial and technological creativity to affect deeply the global balance of power: the United States, the Soviet Union, Western Europe, and Japan.[52] Of these, Europe and Japan are close geographically to the Soviet Union. That they are close to America *politically* has been profoundly important to the global balance of power for forty years.

Because the geopolitical world still rests on the tectonic plates of 1945, a rapid shifting of those plates may call for dramatic new strategies. But if the changes are incremental, a radical shift of strategy may do more harm than good. Any strategic assessment must begin with an appraisal of U.S. power in terms of traditional power resources. This assessment is the focus of parts I and II of this book.

CONTINUITY AND CHANGE

As we shall see in part III, a good assessment of power must go beyond traditional geopolitics. If we focus too heavily on power transitions among leading states, the historical analogies may mislead us about the nature of other changes that are occurring in world politics. The end of this century will be very different from its beginning. The American problem now is not one of decline like Britain's or of challenge by a rising contender like Germany. The United States is likely to remain the leading power, yet it will have to cope with unprecedented problems of interdependence that no great power can solve by itself. Many of the new issues in international politics—ecology, drugs, AIDS, terrorism—involve a diffusion of power away from states to private actors and require organizing states for cooperative responses. The classical geopolitical agenda of international security among independent nations will continue alongside these new problems of transnational interdependence. A good strategy must focus on both aspects simultaneously. If our analyses are cast solely in terms of the power transitions of the past, we will overlook what is new about the future.

Theories and historical analogies are not just academic; they color our view of the world.[53] As we shall see in chapter 3, the United States was not as powerful in the postwar period as is implied by those who speak of American "hegemony" or "empire." The natural decline after 1945 is often exaggerated by comparison with a mythical past, when America allegedly "bestrode the world." In fact, the World War II effect had largely worked its way through the international system by the early 1970s. As C. William Maynes points out, the loss of nuclear superiority, the end of self-sufficiency in oil, and the challenge to the dollar can be dated back to the Nixon administration.[54] At that time, some critical adjustments took place, including the withdrawal from Vietnam and the end of convertibility of the dollar into gold. While there has been some relative decline of power in specific sectors since then, the American position has changed much less in the past decade and a half than it did in the earlier period of supposed hegemony. Further, as part II demonstrates, no country is at this time well positioned to challenge the United States for global leadership.

Lest Americans become complacent, however, it is important to emphasize that the traditional focus of statesmen and scholars on the rise and fall of nations and on new challengers and old hegemons neglects to account for a critical new dimension of world politics—the growth of transnational interdependence and the diffusion of power to smaller states and private actors. As we will see in part III, no great power, not even the United States, is placed well enough to deal with these issues alone. One positive message of this book is that American leadership is likely to continue well into the next century. But another message—the changing nature of power—is equally important. Too much concern about a decline of power in traditional terms, or too much complacency about the status quo, may cause Americans to overlook the importance of the changing nature of power and, as a result, to pursue the wrong strategies as they enter the twenty-first century.

PART I

POWER IN THE PAST

Power Transitions

Power in international politics is like the weather. Everyone talks about it, but few understand it. Just as farmers and meteorologists try to forecast storms, so do statesmen and analysts try to understand the dynamics of major changes in the distribution of power among nations. Power transitions affect the fortunes of individual nations, and are often associated with the cataclysmic storms of world war. But before we can examine theories of hegemonic transition—that is, some of the leading efforts to predict big changes in the international political weather—we first need to recognize some basic distinctions among the terms *power, balance of power,* and *hegemony.*

POWER

Power, like love, is easier to experience than to define or measure. Power is the ability to achieve one's purposes or goals. The dictionary tells us that it is the ability to do things and to control others. Robert Dahl, a leading political scientist, defines power as the ability to get others to do what they otherwise would not do.[1] But when we measure power in terms of the changed behavior of others, we have to know their preferences. Otherwise, we may be as mistaken about our power as was the fox who thought he was hurting Brer Rabbit when he threw him into the briar patch. Knowing in advance how other people or nations would behave in the absence of our efforts is often difficult.

The behavioral definition of power may be useful to analysts and historians who devote considerable time to reconstructing the past, but to practical politicans and leaders it often seems too ephemeral. Because the ability to control others is often associated with the possession of certain resources, political leaders commonly define power as the possession of resources. These resources include population, territory, natural resources, economic size, military forces, and political stability among others.[2] The virtue of this definition is that it makes power appear more concrete, measurable, and predictable than does the behavioral definition. Power in this sense means holding the high cards in the international poker game. A basic rule of poker is that if your opponent is showing cards that can beat anything you hold, fold your hand. If you know you will lose a war, don't start it.

Some wars, however, have been started by the eventual losers, which suggests that political leaders sometimes take risks or make mistakes. Often the opponent's cards are not all showing in the game of international politics. As in poker, playing skills, such as bluff and deception, can make a big difference. Even when there is no deception, mistakes can be made about which power resources are most relevant in particular situations (for example, France and Britain had more tanks than Hitler in 1940, but Hitler had greater maneuverability and a better military strategy). On the other hand, in long wars when there is time to mobilize, depth of territory and the size of an economy become more important, as the Soviet Union and the United States demonstrated in World War II.

Power conversion is a basic problem that arises when we think of power in terms of resources. Some countries are better than others at converting their resources into effective influence, just as some skilled card players win despite being dealt weak hands. Power conversion is the capacity to convert potential power, as measured by resources, to realized power, as measured by the changed behavior of others. Thus, one has to know about a country's skill at power conversion as well as its possession of power resources to predict outcomes correctly.

Another problem is determining which resources provide the best basis for power in any particular context. In earlier periods, power resources were easier to judge. According to historian A. J. P. Taylor, traditionally "the test of a Great Power is . . . the test of strength for war."[3] For example, in the agrarian economies of eighteenth-century Europe, population was a critical power resource because it provided a base for taxes and recruitment of infantry. In population, France dominated Western Europe. Thus, at the end of the Napoleonic Wars, Prussia presented its fellow victors at the Congress of Vienna with a precise plan for its own reconstruction in order to maintain the balance of power. Its plan listed the territories and populations it had lost since 1805, and the territories and populations it would need to regain equivalent numbers.[4] In the pre-nationalist period, it did not much matter that many of the people in those provinces did not speak German or feel themselves to be German. However, within half a century, nationalist sentiments mattered very much. Germany's seizure of Alsace-Lorraine from France in 1870, for example, made hope of any future alliance with France impossible.

Another change that occurred during the nineteenth century was the growing importance of industry and rail systems that made rapid mobilization possible. In the 1860s, Bismarck's Germany pioneered the use of railways to transport armies for quick victories. Although Russia had always had greater population resources than the rest of Europe, they were difficult to mobilize. The growth of the rail system in Western Russia at the beginning of the twentieth century was one of the reasons the Germans feared rising Russian power in 1914. Further, the spread of rail systems on the Continent helped deprive Britain of the luxury of concentrating on naval power. There was no longer time, should it prove necessary, to insert an army to prevent another great power from dominating the Continent.

The application of industrial technology to warfare has long had a powerful impact. Advanced science and technology have been particularly critical power resources since the beginning of the nuclear age in 1945. But the power derived from nuclear weapons has proven to be so awesome and destructive that its actual application is muscle-bound. Nuclear war is simply too costly. More generally, there are many situations where any use of force may be inappropriate or too costly. In 1853, for example, Commodore Perry could threaten to bombard Japan if it did not open its ports for supplies and trade, but it is hard to imagine that the United States could effectively threaten force to open Japanese markets today.

THE CHANGING SOURCES OF POWER

Some observers have argued that the sources of power are, in general, moving away from the emphasis on military force and conquest that marked earlier eras. In assessing international power today, factors such as technology, education, and economic growth are becoming more important, whereas geography, population, and raw materials are becoming less important. Kenneth Waltz argues that a 5-percent rate of economic growth in the United States for three years would add more to American strength than does our alliance with Britain.[5] Richard Rosecrance argues that since 1945, the world has been poised between a territorial system composed of states that view power in terms of land mass, and a trading system "based in states which recognize that self-sufficiency is an illusion." In the past, says Rosecrance, "it was cheaper to seize another state's territory by force than to develop the sophisticated economic and trading apparatus needed to derive benefit from commercial exchange with it."[6]

If so, perhaps we are in a "Japanese period" in world politics. Japan has certainly done far better with its strategy as a trading state after 1945 than it did with its military strategy to create a Greater East Asian Co-Prosperity Sphere in the 1930s. But Japan's security vis-à-vis its large military neighbors—China and the Soviet Union—depends heavily on U.S. protection. In short, even if we can define power clearly, it still has become more difficult to be clear about the relationship of particular resources to it. Thus, we cannot leap too quickly to the conclusion that all trends favor economic power or countries like Japan.

Like other forms of power, economic power cannot be measured simply in terms of tangible resources. Intangible aspects also matter. For example, outcomes generally depend on bargaining, and bargaining depends on relative costs in particular situations and skill in converting potential power into effects. Relative costs are determined not only by the total amount of measurable economic resources of a country but also by the degree of its interdependence in a relationship. If, for example, the United States and Japan depend on each other but one is less dependent than the other, that asymmetry is a source of power. The United States may be less vulnerable than Japan if the relationship breaks down, and it may use that threat as a source of power.[7] Thus, as we shall see in chapters 5 and 6, an assessment of Japanese and American power must look not only at shares of resources but also at the relative vulnerabilities of both countries.

Another consideration is that most large countries today find military force more costly to apply than in previous centuries. This has resulted from the dangers of nuclear escalation, the difficulty of ruling nationalistically awakened populations in otherwise weak states, the danger of rupturing profitable relations on other issues, and the public opposition in Western democracies to prolonged and expensive military conflicts. Even so, the increased cost of military force does not mean that it will be ruled out. To the contrary, in an anarchic system of states where there is no higher government to settle conflicts and where the ultimate recourse is self-help, this could never happen. In some cases, the stakes may justify a costly use of force. And, as recent episodes in Grenada and Libya have shown, not all uses of force by great powers involve high costs.[8]

Even if the direct use of force were banned among a group of countries, military force would still play an important political role. For example, the American military role in deterring threats to allies, or of assuring access to a crucial resource such as oil in the Persian Gulf, means that the provision of protective force can be used in bargaining situations. Sometimes the linkage may be direct; more often it is a factor not mentioned openly but present in the back of statesmen's minds.

In addition, there is the consideration that is sometimes called "the second face of power."[9] Getting other states to change might be called the directive or commanding method of exercising power. Command power can rest on inducements ("carrots") or threats ("sticks"). But there is also an indirect way to exercise power. A country may achieve the outcomes it prefers in world politics because other countries want to follow it or have agreed to a system that produces such effects. In this sense, it is just as important to set the agenda and structure the situations in world politics as it is to get others to change in particular situations. This aspect of power—that is, getting others to want what you want—might be called indirect or co-optive power behavior. It is in contrast to the active command power behavior of getting others to do what you want.[10] Co-optive power can rest on the attraction of one's ideas or on the ability to set the political agenda in a way that shapes the preferences that others express. Parents of teenagers know that if they have structured their children's beliefs and preferences, their power will be greater and will last longer than if they had relied only on active control. Similarly, political leaders and philosophers have long understood the power that comes from setting the agenda and determining the framework of a debate. The ability to establish preferences tends to be associated with intangible power resources such as culture, ideology, and institutions. This dimension can be thought of as soft power, in contrast to the hard command power usually associated with tangible resources like military and economic strength.[11]

Robert Cox argues that the nineteenth-century *Pax Britannica* and the twentieth-century *Pax Americana* were effective because they created liberal international economic orders, in which certain types of economic relations were privileged over others and liberal international rules and institutions were broadly accepted. Following the insights of the Italian thinker Antonio Gramsci, Cox argues that the most critical feature for a dominant country is the ability to obtain a broad measure of consent on general principles—principles that ensure the supremacy of the leading state and dominant social classes—and at the same time to offer some prospect of satisfaction to the less powerful. Cox identifies Britain from 1845 to 1875 and the United States from 1945 to 1967 as such countries.[12] Although we may not agree with his terminology or dates, Cox has touched a major point: Soft co-optive power is just as important as hard command power. If a state can make its power legitimate in the eyes of others, it will encounter less resistance to its wishes. If its culture and ideology are attractive, others will more willingly follow. If it can establish international norms that are consistent with its society, it will be less likely to have to change. If it can help support institutions that encour-

age other states to channel or limit their activities in
ways the dominant state prefers, it may not need as
many costly exercises of coercive or hard power in bargaining situations. In short, the universalism of a country's culture and its ability to establish a set of favorable
rules and institutions that govern areas of international
activity are critical sources of power.[13] As we shall
see in greater detail in chapter 6, these soft sources
of power are becoming more important in world politics today.

Such considerations question the conclusion that the
world is about to enter a Japanese era in world politics.
The nature of power is changing and some of the
changes will favor Japan, but some of them may favor
the United States even more. In command power,
Japan's economic strength is increasing, but it remains
vulnerable in terms of raw materials and relatively weak
in terms of military force. And in co-optive power,
Japan's culture is highly insular and it has yet to develop
a major voice in international institutions. The United
States, on the other hand, has a universalistic popular
culture and a major role in international institutions.
Although such factors may change in the future, they
raise an important question about the present situation:
What resources are the most important sources of
power today? A look at the five-century-old modern
state system shows that different power resources played
critical roles in different periods (see table 1.1). The
sources of power are never static and, as we shall see in
chapter 6, they continue to change in today's world.

In an age of information-based economies and transnational interdependence, power is becoming less transferable, less tangible, and less coercive. However, the
transformation of power is incomplete. The twenty-first

TABLE 1.1
Leading States and Major Power Resources, 1500s–1900s

Period	Leading State	Major Resources
Sixteenth century	Spain	Gold bullion, colonial trade, mercenary armies, dynastic ties
Seventeenth century	Netherlands	Trade, capital markets, navy
Eighteenth century	France	Population, rural industry, public administration, army
Nineteenth century	Britain	Industry, political cohesion, finance and credit, navy, liberal norms, island location (easy to defend)
Twentieth century	United States	Economic scale, scientific and technical leadership, universalistic culture, military forces and alliances, liberal international regimes, hub of transnational communications

century will certainly see a greater role for informational and institutional power, but military force will remain an important factor. Economic scale, both in markets and in natural resources, will also remain important. As the service sector grows within modern economies, the distinction between services and manufacturing will continue to blur. Information will become more plentiful, and the critical resource will be the organizational capacity for rapid and flexible response. Political cohesion will remain important, as will a universalistic popular culture. On some of these dimensions of power, the United States is well endowed; on others, questions arise. But even larger questions arise for the other major contenders—Europe, Japan, the Soviet Union, and China—as we shall see in part II. But first we need to look at the patterns in the distribution of power—balances and hegemonies, how they have changed over history, and what that implies for the position of the United States.

BALANCE OF POWER

International relations is far from a precise science. Conditions in various periods always differ in significant details, and human behavior reflects personal choices. Moreover, theorists often suffer from writing in the midst of events, rather than viewing them from a distance. Thus, powerful theories—those that are both simple and accurate—are rare. Yet political leaders (and those who seek to explain behavior) must generalize in order to chart a path through the apparent chaos of changing events. One of the longest-standing and most frequently used concepts is balance of power, which eighteenth-century philosopher David Hume called "a constant rule of prudent politics."[14] For centuries, balance of power has been the starting point for realistic discussions of international politics.

To an extent, balance of power is a useful predictor of how states will behave; that is, states will align in a manner that will prevent any one state from developing a preponderance of power. This is based on two assumptions: (1) that states exist in an anarchic system with no higher government and (2) that political leaders will act first to reduce risks to the independence of their states. The policy of balancing power helps to explain why in modern times a large state cannot grow forever into a world empire. States seek to increase their powers through internal growth and external alliances. Balance of power predicts that if one state appears to grow too strong, others will ally against it so to avoid threats to their own independence. This behavior, then, will preserve the structure of the system of states.

However, not all balance-of-power predictions are so obvious. For example, this theory implies that professions of ideological faith will be poor predictors of behavior. But despite Britain's criticism of the notorious Stalin–Hitler pact of 1939, it was quick to make an alliance with Stalin's Soviet Union in 1941. As Winston Churchill explained at the time, "If I learned that Hitler had invaded Hell, I would manage to say something good about the Devil in the House of Commons."[15] Further, balance of power does not mean that political leaders must maximize the power of their own states in the short run. Bandwagoning—that is, joining the stronger rather than the weaker side—might produce more immediate spoils. As Mussolini discovered in his ill-fated pact with Hitler, the danger in bandwagoning is that independence may be threatened by the stronger ally in the long term. Thus, to say that states will act to balance power is a strong generalization in international relations, but it is far from being a perfect predictor.

Proximity and perceptions of threat also affect the way in which balancing of power is played out.[16] A small state like Finland, for instance, cannot afford to try to balance Soviet power. Instead, it seeks to preserve its independence through neutrality. Balance of power and the proposition that "the enemy of my enemy is my friend" help to explain the larger contours of current world politics, but only when proximity and perceptions are considered. The United States was by far the strongest power after 1945. A mechanical application of power balance might seem to predict an alliance against the United States. In fact, Europe and

Japan allied with the United States because the Soviet Union, while weaker in overall power, posed a proximate threat to its neighbors. Geography and psychology are both important factors in geopolitics.

The term *balance of power* is sometimes used not as a prediction of policy but as a description of how power is distributed. In the latter case, it is more accurate to refer to the distribution of power. In other instances, though, the term is used to refer to an evenly balanced distribution of power, like a pair of hanging scales. The problem with this usage is that the ambiguities of measuring power make it difficult to determine when an equal balance exists. In fact, the major concerns in world politics tend to arise from inequalities of power, and particularly from major changes in the unequal distribution of power.

HEGEMONY IN MODERN HISTORY

No matter how power is measured, an equal distribution of power among major states is relatively rare. More often the processes of uneven growth, which realists consider a basic law of international politics, mean that some states will be rising and others declining. These transitions in the distribution of power stimulate statesmen to form alliances, to build armies, and to take risks that balance or check rising powers. But the balancing of power does not always prevent the emergence of a dominant state. Theories of hegemony and power transition try to explain why some states that become preponderant later lose that preponderance.

As far back as ancient Greece, observers attempting to explain the causes of major world wars have cited the uncertainties associated with the transition of power. Shifts in the international distribution of power create the conditions likely to lead to the most important wars.[17] However, while power transitions provide useful warning about periods of heightened risk, there is no iron law of hegemonic war. If there were, Britain and the United States would have gone to war at the beginning of this century, when the Americans surpassed the British in economic and naval power in the Western Hemisphere. Instead, when the United States backed Venezuela in its boundary dispute with British Guyana in 1895, British leaders appeased the rising American power instead of going to war with it.[18]

When power is distributed unevenly, political leaders and theorists use terms such as *empire* and *hegemony*. Although there have been many empires in history, those in the modern world have not encompassed all major countries. Even the British Empire at the beginning of this century encompassed only a quarter of the world's population and Britain was just one of a half-dozen major powers in the global balance of power. The term *hegemony* is applied to a variety of situations in which one state appears to have considerably more power than others. For example, for years China accused the Soviet Union of seeking hegemony in Asia. When Soviet leader Mikhail Gorbachev and Chinese leader Deng Xiaoping met in 1989, they pledged that "neither side will seek hegemony in any form anywhere in the world."[19]

Although the word comes from the ancient Greek and refers to the dominance of one state over others in the system, it is used in diverse and confused ways. Part of the problem is that unequal distribution of power is a matter of degree, and there is no general agreement on how much inequality and what types of power constitute hegemony. All too often, hegemony is used to refer to different behaviors and degrees of control, which obscures rather than clarifies the analysis. For example, Charles Doran cites aggressive military power, while Robert Keohane looks at preponderance in economic resources. Robert Gilpin sometimes uses the terms *imperial* and *hegemonic* interchangeably to refer to a situation in which "a single powerful state controls or dominates the lesser states in the system."[20] British hegemony in the nineteenth century is commonly cited even though Britain ranked third behind the United States and Russia in GNP and third behind Russia and France in military expenditures at the peak of its relative power around 1870. Britain was first in the more limited domains of manufacturing, trade, finance, and naval power.[21] Yet theorists often contend that "full hegemony requires productive, commercial, and financial as well as political and military power."[22]

Joshua Goldstein usefully defines hegemony as "being able to dictate, or at least dominate, the rules and arrangements by which international relations, political and economic, are conducted. . . . Economic hegemony implies the ability to center the world economy around itself. Political hegemony means being able to dominate the world militarily."[23] However, there are still two important questions to be answered with regard to how the term *hegemony* is used. First, what is the scope of the hegemon's control? In the modern world, a situation in which one country can dictate political and economic arrangements has been extremely rare. Most examples have been regional, such as Soviet power in Eastern Europe, American influence in the Caribbean, and India's control over its small neighbors—Sikkim,

Bhutan, and Nepal.[24] In addition, one can find instances in which one country was able to set the rules and arrangements governing specific issues in world politics, such as the American role in money or trade in the early postwar years. But as chapters 2 and 3 show, there has been no global, system-wide hegemon during the past two centuries. Contrary to the myths about *Pax Britannica* and *Pax Americana,* British and American hegemonies have been regional and issue-specific rather than general.

Second, we must ask what types of power resources are necessary to produce a hegemonic degree of control. Is military power necessary? Or is it enough to have preponderance in economic resources? How do the two types of power relate to each other? Obviously, the answers to such questions can tell us a great deal about the future world, in which Japan may be an economic giant and a military dwarf while the Soviet Union may fall into the opposite situation. And, as we shall see in chapter 3, a careful look at the interplay of military and economic power raises doubt about the degree of American hegemony in the postwar period.[25]

THEORIES OF HEGEMONIC TRANSITION AND STABILITY

The focus of this book is more on general hegemony than on regional or issue hegemony. General hegemony is the concern of theories and analogies about the instability and dangers supposedly caused by hegemonic transitions. Thus I will focus on the extent to which the United States was able to use its preponderant military or economic resources to maintain the essential rules and norms governing interstate relations in the postwar period. But before we turn to the American experience, we should first look at how theorists of hegemonic transition have categorized history.

Classical concerns about hegemony among leaders and philosophers focus on military power and "conflicts precipitated by the military effort of one dominant actor to expand well beyond the arbitrary security confines set by tradition, historical accident, or coercive pressures."[26] In this approach, hegemony is preponderance arising out of military expansion, such as the efforts of Louis XIV, Napoleon, or Hitler to dominate world politics. The important point is that, except for brief periods, none of the attempted military hegemonies in modern times has succeeded (see table 1.2). No modern state has been able to develop sufficient military power to transform the balance of power into a long-lived hegemony in which one state could dominate the world militarily.

More recently, many political scientists have focused on economic power as a source of hegemonic control. Some define hegemonic economic power in terms of resources; that is, preponderance in control over raw materials, sources of capital, markets, and production of goods. Others use the behavioral definition in which a

TABLE 1.2
Modern Efforts at Military Hegemony

State Attempting Hegemony	Ensuing Hegemonic War	New Order After War
Habsburg Spain	Thirty Years' War, 1618–1648	Peace of Westphalia, 1648
Louis XIV's France	Wars of Louis XIV	Treaty of Utrecht, 1713
Napoleon's France	1792–1815	Congress of Vienna, 1815
Germany (and Japan)	1914–1945	United Nations, 1945

SOURCE: Charles F. Doran, *The Politics of Assimilation: Hegemony and Its Aftermath* (Baltimore: Johns Hopkins University Press, 1971), pp. 19–20.

hegemon is a state able to set the rules and arrangements for the global economy. Robert Gilpin, a leading theorist of hegemonic transition, sees Britain and America, having created and enforced the rules of a liberal economic order, as the successive hegemons since the Industrial Revolution.[27] Some political economists argue that world economic stability requires a single stabilizer and that periods of such stability have coincided with periods of hegemony. In this view, *Pax Britannica* and *Pax Americana* were the periods when Britain and the United States were strong enough to create and enforce the rules for a liberal international economic order in the nineteenth and twentieth centuries. For example, it is often argued that economic stability "historically has occurred when there has been a sole hegemonic power; Britain from 1815 to World War I and the United States from 1945 to around 1970. . . . With a sole hegemonic power, the rules of the game can be established and enforced. Lesser countries have little choice but to go along. Without a hegemonic power, conflict is the order of the day."[28] Such theories of hegemonic stability and decline are often used to predict that the United States will follow the experience of Great Britain, and that instability will ensue. Goldstein, for example, argues that "we are moving toward the 'weak hegemony' end of the spectrum and . . . this seems to increase the danger of hegemonic war."[29]

I argue, however, that the theory of hegemonic stability and transition will not tell us as much about the future of the United States. Theorists of hegemonic stability generally fail to spell out the causal connections between military and economic power and hegemony. As already noted, nineteenth-century Britain was not militarily dominant nor was it the world's largest economy, and yet Britain is portrayed by Gilpin and others as hegemonic. Did Britain's military weakness at that time allow the United States and Russia, the two larger economies, to remain mostly outside the liberal system of free trade? Or, to take a twentieth-century puzzle, did a liberal international economy depend on postwar American military strength or only on its economic power? Are both conditions necessary today, or have modern nations learned to cooperate through international institutions?

One radical school of political economists, the neo-Marxists, have attempted to answer similar questions about the relationship between economic and military hegemony, but their theories are unconvincing. For example, Immanuel Wallerstein defines hegemony as a situation in which power is so unbalanced that

> one power can largely impose its rules and its wishes (at the very least by effective veto power) in the economic, political, military, diplomatic, and even cultural arenas. The material base of such power lies in the ability of enterprises domiciled in that power to operate more efficiently in all three major economic arenas—agro-industrial production, commerce, and finance.[30]

According to Wallerstein, hegemony is rare and "refers to that short interval in which there is simultaneously advantage in all three economic domains." At such times, the other major powers become *"de facto* client states." Wallerstein claims there have been only three modern instances of hegemony—in the Netherlands, 1620–1650; in Britain, 1815–1873; and in the United States, 1945–1967 (see table 1.3). He argues that "in each case, the hegemony was secured by a thirty-year-long world war," after which a new order followed—the

Peace of Westphalia after 1648; the Concert of Europe after 1815; and the United Nations–Bretton Woods system after 1945.[31] According to this theory, the United States will follow the Dutch and the British path to decline.

The neo-Marxist view of hegemony is unconvincing and a poor predictor of future events because it superficially links military and economic hegemony and has many loose ends. For example, contrary to Wallerstein's theory, the Thirty Years' War *coincided* with Dutch hegemony, and Dutch decline began with the Peace of Westphalia. The Dutch were not militarily strong enough to stand up to the British on the sea and could barely defend themselves against the French on land, "despite their trade-derived wealth."[32] Further, although Wallerstein argues that British hegemony began after the Napoleonic Wars, he is not clear about how the new order in the balance of power—that is, the nineteenth-century Concert of Europe—related to Britain's supposed ability to impose a global free-trade system. For example, Louis XIV's France, which many historians view as the dominant military power in the second half of the seventeenth century, is excluded from Wallerstein's schema altogether. Thus, the neo-Marxist historical analogies seem forced into a Procrustean ideological bed, while other cases are left out of bed altogether.

TABLE 1.3

A Neo-Marxist View of Hegemony

Hegemony	World War Securing Hegemony	Period of Dominance	Decline
Dutch	Thirty Years' War, 1618–1648	1620–1650	1650–1672
British	Napoleonic Wars, 1792–1815	1815–1873	1873–1896
American	World Wars I and II, 1914–1945	1945–1967	1967–

SOURCE: Immanuel Wallerstein, *The Politics of the World Economy* (New York: Cambridge University Press, 1984), pp. 41–42.

Others have attempted to organize past periods of hegemony into century-long cycles. In 1919, British geopolitician Sir Halford Mackinder argued that unequal growth among nations tends to produce a hegemonic world war about every hundred years.[33] More recently, political scientist George Modelski proposed a hundred-year cyclical view of changes in world leadership (see table 1.4). In this view, a long cycle begins with a major global war. A single state then emerges as the new world power and legitimizes its preponderance with postwar peace treaties. (Preponderance is defined as having at least half the resources available for global order-keeping.) The new leader supplies security and order for the international system. In time, though, the leader loses legitimacy, and deconcentration of power leads to another global war. The new leader that emerges from that war may not be the state that challenged the old leader but one of the more innovative allies in the winning coalition (as, not Germany, but the United States replaced Britain). According to Modelski's theory, the United States began its decline in 1973.[34] If his assumptions are correct, it may be Japan and not the Soviet Union that will most effectively challenge the United States in the future.

TABLE 1.4

Long Cycles of World Leadership

Cycle	Global War	Preponderance	Decline
1494–1580	1494–1516	Portugal, 1516–1540	1540–1580
1580–1688	1580–1609	Netherlands, 1609–1640	1640–1688
1688–1792	1688–1713	Britain, 1714–1740	1740–1792
1792–1914	1792–1815	Britain, 1815–1850	1850–1914
1914–	1914–1945	United States, 1945–1973	1973–

SOURCE: George Modelski, *Long Cycles in World Politics* (Seattle: University of Washington Press, 1987), pp. 40, 42, 44, 102, 131, 147.

Modelski and his followers suggest that the processes of decline are associated with long waves in the global economy. They associate a period of rising prices and resource scarcities with loss of power, and concentration of power with falling prices, resource abundance, and economic innovation.[35] However, in linking economic and political cycles, these theorists become enmeshed in the controversy surrounding long cycle theory. Many economists are skeptical about the empirical evidence for alleged long economic waves and about dating historical waves by those who use the concept.[36]

Further, we cannot rely on the long-cycle theory to predict accurately the American future. Modelski's treatment of political history is at best puzzling. For example, he ranks sixteenth-century Portugal as a hegemon rather than Spain, even though Spain controlled a richer overseas empire. Likewise, Britain is ranked as a hegemon from 1714 to 1740, even though eighteenth-century France was the larger military power. Modelski's categories are odd in part because he uses naval power as the sine qua non of global power, which results in a truncated view of military and diplomatic history. Although naval power was more important for countries that relied on overseas possessions, the balance in Europe depended on the armies on the continent. Britain could not afford to ignore its armies on land and rely solely on its naval power. To preserve the balance of power, Britain had to be heavily involved in land wars on the European continent at the beginning of the eighteenth, nineteenth, and twentieth centuries. More specifically, Modelski underrates the Spanish navy in the sixteenth century as well as the French navy, which outnumbered Britain's, in the late seventeenth century.[37] Some major wars, such as the Thirty Years' War and the Anglo-French wars of the eighteenth century, are excluded altogether from Modelski's organization of history.

Vague definitions and arbitrary schematizations alert us to the inadequacies of such grand theories of hegemony and decline. Most theorists of hegemonic transition tend to shape history to their own theories by focusing on particular power resources and ignoring others. Examples include the poorly explained relationship between military and political power and the unclear link between decline and major war. Since there have been wars among the great powers during 60 percent of the years from 1500 to the present, there are plenty of candidates to associate with any given scheme.[38] Even if we consider only the nine general wars that have involved nearly all the great powers and produced high levels of casualties, some of them, such as the Seven Years' War (1755–1763), are not considered hegemonic in any of the schemes. As sociologist Pitirim Sorokin concludes, "no regular periodicity is noticeable."[39] At best, the various schematizations of hegemony and war are only suggestive. They do not provide a reliable basis for predicting the future of American power or for evaluating the risk of world war as we enter the twenty-first century.

As we shall see in chapter 6, the changing nature of world politics and power today makes past instances of hegemonic transition less relevant to our understanding of the future. The devastating consequences of nuclear war, the changing public attitude toward war, and the increase in economic and ecological interdependence make the present world quite different from the past. But before we can look to the future, we need first to establish in the next two chapters a clear understanding of the nature of British and American power in two alleged hegemonies of the past.

2

The British
Analogy

The Great Power is in trouble. A costly intervention in a distant part of the globe disrupted its economy and created doubts about whether it can fulfill its international commitments. Military superiority is lost. Its most powerful rival, the world's largest land power, now has a significant naval force. Forty years ago, the Great Power's economic and industrial capacity was in a class by itself. Now its industrial base is eroding, imports are soaring, and calls for protectionism are rising. It asks its allies to share its burdens but to little avail. Funds are needed to repair the domestic social fabric but no one knows where they will come from. It is uncomfortable being the top nation in a period of relative decline.

Does this scenario describe early twentieth-century Britain or the United States at the end of the century? Paul Kennedy suggests both,[1] and he is not alone in drawing such analogies. Scholars on the Left write of "uncanny resemblances between late Victorian England and the United States today,"[2] and professors at Harvard Business School argue that "starkly put, the question is whether the United States is in the early stages of a decline similar to the United Kingdom."[3]

As we saw in chapter 1, theories of hegemonic stability and transition in the modern world are based mostly on two cases: Victorian Britain and post-1945 America. Robert Gilpin, a leading theorist of hegemonic transition, argues that "the *Pax Britannica* and *Pax Americana*, like the *Pax Romana*, ensured an international system of relative peace and security." Since the Industrial Revolution, the United States and Britain have "succeeded in this hegemonic role partially because they have imposed their will on lesser states and particularly because other states have benefited from and accepted their leadership."[4] The economist Charles Kindleberger argues that a liberal system of free trade has required that one country keep the system open: "For the world economy to be stabilized, there has to be a stabilizer, one stabilizer."[5] But providing order is expensive. Although smaller countries benefit, they cannot be forced to pay their share of the burden. This, in turn, saps the capability and will of the leading state and contributes to decline.

Others have raised serious questions about the theory of hegemonic stability. For instance, the theory is criticized for its assumption that the order created by the large state is a public good that benefits all states. In some cases, the order created by large states does not benefit others. Even when others do benefit, the large state may not be benevolent; it may merely be acting in its own interests and receiving ample rewards.[6] The provision of order in this case would be a source of strength to the state rather than a cause of decline.

The theory is also ambiguous about the relationship between military and economic power. It dates Britain's leadership of the coalition that defeated France and created the new order at the Congress of Vienna at the beginning of the century, whereas most scholars date Britain's economic hegemony at least a half-century later. As Arthur Stein points out, "the golden age of free trade in the nineteenth century began decades after Britain's emergence as a hegemonic power. The return to protectionism started in the latter part of the nineteenth century, when Britain, despite the beginning of a decline in its relative power, was still the hegemon."[7] While Britain enjoyed naval power on the world's peripheries, its military power in Europe was limited and had little relation to its economic policies. It was never powerful enough to impose free trade on the United States or on European countries. Although Britain embraced free trade with the repeal of the Corn Laws in 1846, its decision was unilateral and did not rest on the ability to force other major countries to cut tariffs.[8] In what two British historians call "the imperialism of free trade,"[9] British gunboats occasionally forced poor countries in what would today be termed the Third World to open their ports to trade. But there is a significant difference between coercing distant, less-developed countries and winning the adherence of major European rivals. Timothy McKeown makes the point that French and Prussian tariff reductions in the 1860s were triggered more by liberal ideology and domestic politics than by British pressure.[10]

Like Cinderella's sisters, the theorists of hegemonic stability and transition find the slipper of nineteenth-century history an uncomfortable fit. According to Robert Keohane, "that the theory of hegemonic stability is

supported by only one or at most two cases casts doubt
on its general validity."[11] If the theory of hegemonic
stability and transition really boils down to a poorly
based historical analogy, we must doubt its usefulness
in explaining the current American situation. To understand why the analogy is misleading, we need to look
more closely at the British experience.

HOW STRONG WAS GREAT BRITAIN?

Between 1689 and 1815, Britain and France fought
seven major wars. France was the most populous country in eighteenth-century Europe, with 21.5 million people in 1750, compared to a population of 10.5 million
in the British Isles.[12] France also had the largest army,
while Britain's ranked third or lower. The British navy
ranked first in number of ships, but at the time of the
American War of Independence, the French-led naval
coalition considerably outnumbered the British navy.[13]
Even as late as 1830, the French economy was slightly
larger than Britain's, with 14.8 and 14.2 percent, respectively, of Europe's total GNP.[14]

Britain's advantages in the eighteenth century were
in its naval power, its protected island location, and its
more advanced system of credit and public finance
which allowed it greater leeway than France in financ-
ing its military efforts.[15] As it entered the nineteenth
century, Britain maintained these power resources
and gained two others: a growing population (which
quadrupled from 10 to 40 million) and a burgeoning
industrial production. Although British and French
manufacturing production were about equal in 1800, by
the 1850s Britain surpassed France. Britain's GNP rose

nearly 2.5 percent each year during Queen Victoria's reign. In Kennedy's words, "Britain benefited so much from the general economic and geopolitical trends of the post–1815 era that it became a different type of Power from the rest. . . . By the 1860s, however, the further spread of industrialization was beginning to change the balance of world forces once again."[16]

Britain had a relatively easy time in the first half of the nineteenth century. From the defeat of France in 1815 until the unification of Germany in 1870, Britain benefited from a stable balance of power without the dangers of any one country dominating Europe. Moreover, despite occasional threats, there were no serious challenges to British naval supremacy. Until the 1890s, Britain was able to maintain the standard set by Foreign Secretary Lord Castlereagh in 1817 of a navy equal to the next two fleets combined.[17] The empire was ruled in large part through local troops. Thus, the costs of defense averaged about 2.5 to 3 percent of GNP for much of the century, rising briefly to 6 percent during the Boer War.[18] Britain also benefited from relative political stability at home during times when some of its potential rivals were torn by domestic political turmoil. The nation's liberal philosophy of free trade was not accepted by the United States and Russia, the two largest economies in the latter half of the 1800s. And, as we have seen, Britain did not impose its trade philosophy on its continental rivals. Even so, the widespread nineteenth-century belief in a limited governmental role tended to coincide with British liberal preferences.

Despite its sources of power, Britain was not as preponderant in the nineteenth century as is implied by those who speak of *Pax Britannica*. Although it may have had the highest per-capita income (some economic historians suspect that the American level was higher), Britain ranked third (behind Russia and France) with a 14-percent share of Europe's GNP in 1830, and third (behind Russia and Germany) with a 17-percent share in 1913.[19] As table 2.1 shows, Britain had the second largest number of military personnel at the end of the Napoleonic Wars and the fourth largest on the eve of World War I. With the exception of the Boer War, Britain's small volunteer army never exceeded 300,000, a quarter of which was tied down in India.[20]

Britain's leadership in terms of share of world manufacturing production was relatively brief, from 1860 to the 1880s (see table 2.2). Its preponderance was greatest in 1880, but it was overtaken by the United States by 1890 and by Germany early in the twentieth century. However, Britain maintained its leadership in world trade throughout the nineteenth century. In fact, the United States did not surpass Britain's share of world trade until after World War II.[21] (See table 2.3.) But share of world trade is a poor index of power. A low share may reflect a large internal market and a low degree of dependence on the outside world, whereas a high share may represent high vulnerability. As British military planners concluded in 1901, when they debated

TABLE 2.1

Britain's Share of Military Personnel of the Great Powers,
1816–1914

	1816	1830	1860	1880	1900	1914
British rank	2nd	4th	3rd	4th	3rd	4th
Britain as a percentage of the largest (Russia)	36%	17%	41%	27%	54%	39%

SOURCE: Paul Kennedy, *The Rise and Fall of the Great Powers: Economic Change and Military Conflict from 1500 to 2000* (New York: Random House, 1987), pp. 154, 203.

TABLE 2.2

Britain's Share of World Manufacturing Production, 1800–1980

	1800	1830	1860	1880	1900	1913	1939	1953	1980
Share	4.3%	9.5%	19.9%	22.9%	18.5%	13.6%	10.7%	8.6%	4.1%
Rank	2nd	2nd	1st	1st	2nd	3rd	3rd	3rd	6th
Share of largest or	33.0%	30.0%	19.7%	14.7%	23.6%	32.0%	31.4%	44.8%	31.2%
next country	(China)	(China)	(China)	(U.S.)	(U.S.)	(U.S.)	(U.S.)	(U.S.)	(U.S.)

SOURCE: Paul Bairoch, "International Industrialization Levels from 1750 to 1980," *Journal of European Economic History* 11 (1[Spring 1982]): 275, 284; Paul Kennedy, *The Rise and Fall of the Great Powers: Economic Change and Military Conflict from 1500 to 2000* (New York: Random House, 1987), pp. 149, 202.

whether to resist or appease the growing American
naval strength, even if a strengthened navy could defeat
the U.S. fleet, "the vast size of the internal American
market and the country's relatively small dependence on
foreign trade rendered it virtually immune from even
the most complete naval blockade."[22] Similarly, Britain's position as the world's leading exporter of capital
assured an inward flow of dividends, which meant it did
not have to worry about trade deficits, and gave it a nest
egg of foreign assets to finance foreign purchases of war
materials after 1914. But the nation's export of capital
was a mixed blessing. The 8.5 percent of Britain's net
national product that was invested abroad in the eight
years before World War I represented savings not used
for upgrading British industry. In addition, the high
value of the pound hurt the competitiveness of British
industry.[23]

THE DECLINE OF BRITISH POWER

Explaining Britain's decline has almost become an
industry in itself, albeit of cottage scale.[24] A lengthy list
of domestic causes has been adduced. As early as 1898,
Henry Adams believed that "British industry is quite
ruined." But he also believed that "Germany has

TABLE 2.3
British and American Shares of World Trade, 1780–1971

	1780	1820	1860	1880	1913	1938	1948	1971
Britain	12%	27%	25%	23%	16%	14%	12%	7%
United States	2	6	9	10	11	10	16	13

SOURCE: Walt W. Rostow, *The World Economy: History and Prospect* (Austin, Tex.: University of Texas Press, 1978), table II–8.

become a mere province of Russia."[25] In 1900, his brother Brooks Adams wrote that since 1890, "an impression has gained ground that England is losing vitality, that the focus of energy and wealth is shifting, and that, therefore, a period of instability is pending." He blamed, in part, British lethargy and high living, and pointed to the Boer War as an indication that Britain no longer had the willingness to accept casualties in war.[26] (Of course, this was soon disproved by the enormous British losses in World War I.)

World War I showed Britain to be an impressive power. It not only had willing manpower but also an industry capable of being mobilized for war, overseas investments that could finance the purchase of U.S. technology and military supplies, and a navy large enough to ensure control of the Atlantic. In addition, Britain could call on the resources of its empire. Of the 8.6 million British forces in World War I, nearly a third came from overseas (though four-fifths of the expenditure was British).[27] By 1918, Britain had the world's largest air force and navy and the empire had reached its maximum size. In 1921, both popular and informed British opinion agreed with General Jan Smuts of South Africa that the British Empire had "emerged from the War as quite the greatest power on earth."[28]

Yet the war, or more precisely, the thirty-year struggle with Germany, did more to hasten British decline than any other factor. Competing with Germany, rather than possessing an empire, drove up defense spending. It is perhaps too simple to say along with Woody Allen (in the movie Zelig) that the explanation is easy—"Britain owned the world and Germany wanted it." But if Bismarck and his successors had not unified the many German states into a single continental force after 1870 (with a population already larger than Britain's), the British era might have lasted longer. It was Germany, not the pre–1914 empire, that overstretched Britain.

Of course, the British era would not have lasted forever. Even early in the nineteenth century, Alexis de Tocqueville pointed out the enormous potential of the United States and Russia.[29] In 1835, Richard Cobden wrote that "our only chance of national prosperity lies in the timely remodeling of our system, so as to put it as nearly as possible upon an equality with the improved management of the Americans."[30] Cambridge historian Sir John Seely argued in 1883 that federation of the empire was the only way that Britain would be able to compete with Russia and the United States, which were "on an altogether different scale of magnitude." In 1879, former (and future) Prime Minister William Gladstone worried that America "can and probably will wrest from us our commercial superiority."[31]

In short, Britain's relative power was bound to decline because of a number of external factors. The spread of industrialization throughout the world was raising new economic and military competitors. The growing strength of Germany meant that Britain would no longer have a free ride on the continental balance of power. Moreover, as we saw in chapter 1, the spread of railways meant that Britain would no longer have as much time to raise interventionary forces and to transport them to the continent. Also, the distribution of power in the regional balances of the Atlantic and Pacific was shifting because of the growing strength of the United States and Japan. By the turn of the twentieth century, British planners felt they could no longer afford a navy that dominated the Pacific and Western Hemisphere, as well as home waters. Thus, Britain signed an alliance with Japan and appeased the United States with conciliatory measures, including accession to the Panama Canal, which further enhanced American naval strength by allowing the United States to shift its fleet quickly between two oceans. Henceforth, Britain applied the traditional two-power naval standard— that is, a navy equal to the next two contenders—only to its home waters.[32]

A final external cause of the decline of British power was the rise of nationalism, which helped to transform the empire from an asset to a liability. In 1914, London declared war on Germany on behalf of the entire British Empire. But long before post–World War II anticolonial nationalism stripped away Britain's Asian and African colonies, the dominions of Canada, Australia, and New Zealand were resisting rule from London. By the time of the Chanak Crisis with Turkey in 1922, London discovered that it could not automatically count on empire support. After 1926, British military planners no longer considered the British Commonwealth a reliable basis for military plans. Such forces were at best "a possible bonus." Yet, as Correlli Barnett points out, the continued existence of the empire "would pump away from England the military resources she needed for her own war in Europe." American Lend-Lease in 1941 provided those resources, but by 1945, "British power had quietly vanished amidst the stupendous events of the Second World War."[33]

There were also internal causes of the decline of British power. Among the most important were the failure to maintain the productivity of British industry, particularly in new sectors, and the nature and level of education. The two factors were related. "British governing class education was really appropriate to a moment in history that had already vanished. . . . They hardly thought at all of British power in terms of industrial competitiveness, science, technology, or strategy." Britons found the imperial alternative "more attractive than the 'industrial' one because its upper class was dominated by a landowning aristocracy which set the tone for the rest."[34] Although Britain continued to produce entrepreneurs who responded to market incentives, these entrepreneurs focused on the staples of textiles, shipbuilding, and light industry rather than on the new science-based industries. The nation failed to invest in the latest technology in such critical new industries as chemicals, electricity, and precision engineering. "The most sophisticated sectors of the late nineteenth and early twentieth centuries depended far more on applied science. It was in exports from these that Britain was most conspicuously outclassed."[35] In 1913, Britain controlled two-thirds of world exports of manufactures in declining sectors but only one-fifth of exports of expanding sectors.[36] Until 1902, it had no public secondary school system despite public awareness of German educational superiority. Britain had only 7 universities, compared to 22 in Germany and about 700 colleges and technical schools in the United States.[37]

As noted earlier, the increasing economic importance of overseas investment was transforming Britain into a rentier society where financial interests maintained an overvalued currency detrimental to British industry.[38] Overseas investment rose from 0.2 to 5.2 percent of GNP between 1870 and 1913. By 1900, 80 percent of the capital issues on the London market were for overseas investment. By 1914, Britain owned 43 percent of the world stock of investment overseas.[39] As Nobel Laureate Sir W. Arthur Lewis put it in 1978:

Britain was caught in a set of ideological traps. She could not lower costs by cutting wages because of the unions. . . . She could not . . . increase her propensity to export by developing or by paying export subsidies. She could not pioneer in developing new commodities because this now required a scientific base which did not accord with her humanistic snobbery. So instead she invested her savings abroad; the economy decelerated, the average level of unemployment increased, and her young people emigrated.[40]

Finally, Britain had problems with power conversion. Its domestic political process did not allow the full transformation of its potential power resources into effective influence. Aaron Friedberg convincingly shows that the problem was not complacency—to the contrary, there was widespread concern about decline.[41] At the turn of the century, "the press argued that England was behind in scientific organization, in the use of machinery, and the training of workers."[42] But the debate was confused, with little agreement about useful measures or appropriate responses. While return to primacy was impossible after 1900, and Britain did seek out new allies after the Boer War, British elites could have done more to preserve the nation's position and to prepare for coming challenges. British conservatives believed that Britain was financially stretched to its limit and feared the economic effects of raising income taxes. They failed to invest in the forces needed to maintain global naval supremacy and disguised that fact from the public by keeping the same slogans. Thus, the British Empire became dependent on the goodwill of the new regional powers—the United States and Japan. Henceforth, Britain had to avoid embroilment with more than one first-class power in more than one region of the world at a time. Further, it did not implement conscription (as the other major European powers had done after 1871) or pay for an adequate army to help maintain the balance on the continent in the new age of rail mobilization. The 1906 plan for 120,000 troops to assist France proved woefully inadequate in 1914.[43]

The British debate over trade was phrased in terms of polar extremes of protectionism versus free trade. Little attention was given to temporarily protecting critical sectors or to forcing reciprocity on foreign markets. Colonial Secretary Joseph Chamberlain tried to rouse his Conservative colleagues to a more coherent response, but his protectionist scheme would have made things worse. Not surprisingly, it attracted the support of the least competitive elements of British industry.[44] In any event, Chamberlain wound up splitting his party. Prime Minister Arthur Balfour's moderate suggestion of selected retaliatory tariffs to force open foreign markets was lost in the ideological cross fire over free trade, and little attention was paid to the security implications of the sectoral composition of British industry.[45]

Joseph Chamberlain was no more successful in the security area. At a 1902 colonial conference, he failed to persuade the colonies to share the burden of naval costs. His plaint that "the Weary Titan staggers under the too vast orb of its fate"[46] did not pry forth new resources. Nor could Chamberlain convince his conservative colleagues that Britain's burdens were relatively light. In fact, the entire government budget was only 15 percent of GNP (contrasted with nearly 45 percent in modern Britain). And although the Boer War created a deficit from 1899 to 1903, the budget was in surplus thereafter; the national debt in 1907 was not much higher than it had been in the 1880s. A. J. P. Taylor estimates that Britain spent 3.4 percent of its national income on armaments in 1914, compared to 4.6 percent for Germany and 6.3 percent for Russia. Other estimates place Britain ahead of Germany but behind France in its military burden.[47]

So why did Britain decide it could not afford to maintain naval supremacy or an adequate continental expeditionary force? In large part, it was because the adherents of the prevailing economic orthodoxy believed in the negative effects of government spending, and they particularly opposed raising income taxes. Here the analogy to modern American politics is striking. The popular belief that Britain was suffering from imperial overstretch—despite its light defense burden at 3 percent of GNP—caused it not to invest as well as it might have in the domestic and external power resources that could have slowed its decline.[48]

BRITAIN AND AMERICA: MAJOR DIFFERENCES

Even if Britain's leaders had played their domestic cards perfectly, Britain still would have seen a significant decline in power in the twentieth century. A. J. P. Taylor speculates that the impressive growth of German industry would have brought Germany to the mastery of Europe if it had not been for World War I.[49] The industrialization of the United States, Russia, and Japan was bound to shrink Britain's share. Moreover, nationalism would soon erode the empire. In a sense, Britain rose to its leading position because it was on the first wave of the Industrial Revolution in a pre-nationalist era. Yet it is remarkable that such a small country could control a quarter of the world's people in the largest occidental empire since Roman times.

Such special factors in Britain's rise make skeptics wary about the fashionable analogies between Britain's decline and the current situation of the United States. There are at least four major differences in the power positions of Victorian Britain and modern America. The first is the degree of predominance during the period of alleged hegemony. As we have seen, Britain's power resources in the mid-1800s were most impressive in naval force, finance, and manufacturing production. But, as Robert Keohane points out, Britain was never as superior in productivity to the rest of the world as the United States was after 1945. And twentieth-century United States was never as dependent on foreign trade and investment as was nineteenth-century Britain.[50] Further, as Bruce Russett notes, even during its heyday, Britain was not in first place on some critical power resources, as the United States was after 1945 (see table 2.4).[51] In fact, the United States not only ranked higher on more dimensions during its "hegemony" than did Britain, but there are important differences of scale that suggest these rankings will persist longer. Britain, an island the size of a middling Ameri-

TABLE 2.4

British and American Hegemony Compared

	Britain's Rank			United States' Rank	
	1830	1870	1913	1950	1983
GNP	3rd	3rd	4th	1st	1st
Military spending	2nd	3rd	3rd	2nd	1st
Manufacturing	3rd	1st	3rd	1st	1st

SOURCE: Bruce Russett, "The Mysterious Case of Vanishing Hegemony," *International Organization* 39 (Spring 1985): 212.

can state, ruled a quarter of the world. But, as we have seen, the empire quickly fell victim to nationalism and ceased to be a reliable basis for British military plans.

The second major difference between Victorian Britain and modern America is that the United States has been a single, continental-scale economy immune to nationalist disintegration since 1865. Today, American imports account for only 12 percent of GNP in contrast with the British figure of 25 percent in 1914. As table 2.4 shows, even at the peak of its power in the 1870s, Britain had only the third largest economy in the world and it fell to fourth place by 1914. In contrast, the current U.S. GNP is considerably larger than the nearest competitor states. Such differences of scale must be kept in mind when encountering theories of overstretch.

Third, for all the loose talk (and looser definitions) about an American empire, there are important differences between Britain's territorial empire and America's areas of influence. Americans have more choice about types and levels of defense commitments than did Britain. There are more degrees of freedom for all parties. American trade is not as drawn to unsophisticated markets. By 1913, two-thirds of British exports were going to semi-industrial and nonindustrial countries.[52] Some modern historians argue that territorial empire became a net drain on Britain.[53] Whether NATO is considered a forward defense of U.S. borders in which Europeans provide 90 percent of the manpower, or an act of American generosity, it is hard to portray U.S. alliances constituting a similar burden, particularly since the withdrawal of U.S. troops to home bases would not save money unless the units were disbanded. Unlike Edwardian Britain, which had to leave its isolation and cast about for allies at the beginning of the twentieth century, the task for the United States as it enters the twenty-first century will be to renew and update the successful alliances with the great industrial democracies that have been so critical to the global balance of power for the past forty years.

The fourth major difference between the United States and Britain lies in the geopolitical challenges that the two nations face. Most important, Britain faced rising contenders in Germany, the United States, and Russia in 1900. The nearest of those contenders, Germany, had not only surpassed Britain in economic strength but also was becoming militarily dominant and a threat to Britain's supremacy on the European continent. America's external situation today is quite different. Its principal military adversary, the Soviet Union, is the power suffering from imperial overstretch. The Soviet Union dominates an unstable East European empire and its economy has suffered a serious deceleration of the growth that previously allowed Soviet expansion. In addition, Soviet defense is often estimated to be 15 percent of GNP, and some estimates place the costs of defense and empire at more than 20 percent of GNP—some three times higher than the relative burden on the U.S. economy.[54] The British analogy would be proper if Kaiser Wilhelm II's Germany, rather than passing Britain in economic and military strength, had been declining and searching for a breathing spell from its military build-up.

As we will see in part II, none of the other major world powers is now overtaking the United States in military and economic power. Although Western Europe has the skilled population, the GNP, and the improved Common Market coming in 1992, few observers believe that European integration will progress soon to a single government or a single security policy. Similarly, China may become a potential rival of the United States over a much longer term, but China's human and technological infrastructure is much less developed than that of the United States or even the Soviet Union. And while many Americans believe that Japan's economic strength is a greater challenge than Soviet military power, economic competition is not a zero-sum game where one country's gain is its competitor's loss. Thus far, Japan has chosen the strategy of a trading state rather than that of a military power. There is no current analogue to the Kaiser's Germany.

The more interesting comparisons between Victorian Britain and modern America lie in the domestic domain. Here, as we see in chapter 7, there are legitimate causes for concern. Productivity growth in the American economy has fallen to an annual rate of 1.4 percent from its 2.7 percent average annual rate in the first two postwar decades. In the 1980s, net national savings fell to a new low of 2 percent, and gross investment at 17 percent of GNP was only about half of the Japanese level of 30 percent. Civilian research and development was 1.8 percent of GNP in the United States, 2.8 percent in Germany, and 2.6 percent in Japan. Foreign inventors accounted for almost half of U.S. patents in 1987, compared with one-third a decade earlier. Yet even here, one should be wary of too simple comparisons with Britain.[55] Whereas Britain fell behind in leading sectors of chemicals and electricity at the turn of the twentieth century, the United States is today one of the leaders in critical new sectors such as information processing and biotechnology. The United States attracts capital from the rest of the world whereas Britain exported it.

Further, emigration drained talented Britons from their homeland, but immigration continually infuses the United States with new labor and energy.

Perhaps the most interesting domestic comparison is political. Will the United States cope with both its international commitments as the world leader and its need for domestic reforms? Here the British experience suggests caution. As we have seen, the reluctance to raise taxes to pay for leadership is an apt analogy. Aaron Friedberg shows how the political processes of Victorian democracy tended to fragment the national debate. He speculates that centralized countries may have a better chance of coordinating a response to early inklings of relative decline than do liberal democracies. On the other hand, in 1900 Britain's competitors were behind Britain in efforts to integrate national assessments.[56] Fear of decline in Kaiser Wilhelm's centralized political system contributed to the overreaction and war that ultimately deprived Germany of its possible rise to dominance in Europe. The Soviet Union under Brezhnev is a modern case of a centralized autocratic system that failed to respond quickly to warning signals. Thus, even in politics, the jury is still out, and one must be wary of overly simple analogies. With analogy stripped away, we look at the period after 1945 and the alleged hegemony of the United States in the next chapter.

The Postwar
Balance of Power

World War II destroyed the multipolar balance of power and ushered in the age of Soviet–American bipolarity. Even before the war, it was evident that the two nations were beginning to loom larger than the rest. By 1938, the populations of the Soviet Union and the United States were each at least twice as large as that of any of the other great powers. The United States was already the leading industrial power. The Soviet Union had surpassed France and was just behind Britain in its share of world manufacturing. The war then transformed the potential power of the Soviet Union and the United States into actual military power. Some political scientists view the post–World War II balance of power as unique in the history of the international state system. Although earlier there had been balances in which alliances coalesced around two states, such as in the Peloponnesian War and prior to World War I, no two countries have ever stood so far above the rest in terms of their own power resources.[1] Hence the origin of the term *superpower*.

BALANCE OR HEGEMONY?

Was the distribution of power in the late 1940s truly bipolar or was it an American hegemony?[2] In 1943, U.S. armaments production was three times that of Germany, Britain, or the Soviet Union.[3] American GNP surged by 50 percent (in real terms) during the war, whereas the West Europeans lost a quarter of their economies and Soviet economic growth was choked back by a decade.[4] The United States lost 350,000 people to the war; the Soviet Union lost 20 million. As late as 1950, the U.S. economy was three times that of the Soviet Union, five times that of Great Britain, and twenty times that of Japan.[5] At the end of the war, the United States had sixty-nine divisions in Europe and twenty-six in Asia, occupied part of Germany and all of Japan, and had a monopoly of nuclear weapons. Although by 1948 the United States had cut back from 3 million to 100,000 troops in Europe, it still had predominance in many power resources.[6]

Political leaders at the time, however, did not perceive the United States as dominant. Rather, they saw a world in which the Soviet Union and the United States balanced each other's power. The Soviet Union had three major power resources: military force, geographical location, and soft power resources. Its conventional military force was enormous; even after two-thirds of the army was demobilized, the Soviets still had 175 divisions.[7] Its location in the heart of Eurasia positioned it to influence the key political stakes—Europe, China, and Japan—in the postwar contest. Its soft power resources of transnational ideology and the political institutions of communism were attractive to many and gave the Soviets considerable influence in the domestic politics of critical states such as China, Italy, and France. Despite the American economic predominance and nuclear monopoly, the Soviet Union was able to hold a large part of Europe and Asia from American control. In this sense, then, the postwar balance of power was based on asymmetrical resources: U.S. economic power, nuclear force, and liberal ideology versus Soviet conventional forces, geographical location, and Communist ideology and institutions. Certainly American and European leaders did not feel that there was a predominance of Western power. To the contrary, contemporary accounts depict great anxiety about a precarious balance.[8]

Even in the Western world, American influence was often less than the asymmetry in power resources suggests. The United States often had to compromise with its allies. For instance, to hasten their recovery from the war and reduce European and Japanese susceptibility to Communist ideology, Americans tolerated discrimination against U.S. goods. American concern about Communist encroachment also led the United States to ease its pressure on the European allies to dismantle their colonial empires. Thus, the real force behind the dramatic decolonization that occurred in the postwar period was the rise of nationalism, not a new American hegemon.

Ironically, even though the United States had significantly more power resources than Britain had at an equivalent point after the postwar settlement of 1815, the United States was more strongly constrained by the bipolar structure of power than Britain was by the multipolar balance. Had there been no Soviet Union, a general American hegemony might have existed. But the control promised by America's preponderance in economic resources was limited by the realities of the bipolar military balance. The high degree of control implied by references to *Pax Americana* and by the theories of hegemony surveyed in chapter 1 does not hold true under historical scrutiny.

THE VANISHING WORLD WAR II EFFECT

Whatever degree of control the United States had during the period of its greatest concentration of resources, that asymmetry was bound to decline. As we saw in the introductory chapter, the American share of global power resources exaggerated by World War II went through a natural and steady decline during the next quarter century and then stabilized. According to Samuel Huntington, "if hegemony means having 40 percent or more of world economic activity (a percentage Britain never remotely approximated during its hegemonic years), American hegemony disappeared long ago. If 'hegemony' means producing 20–25 percent of the world product and twice as much as any other individual country, American hegemony looks quite secure."[9]

Paul Kennedy also notes the artificial effect of World War II as well as the difference in scale between Britain and the United States. Other things being equal, he believes that geographical size, population, and natural resources suggest that Britain "ought to possess roughly 3 or 4 percent of the world's wealth and power," and the United States "ought to possess perhaps 16 or 18 percent of the world's wealth or power." Kennedy says we are witnessing the ebbing away from the artificial high after World War II "to a more 'natural' share."[10] But, as Kennedy acknowledges, other things are not equal in world politics and there is disagreement about what constitutes a natural share of power resources. Moreover, since power is relative, shares of resources do not tell us much about a country's ability to control outcomes unless we can also determine how the other shares are distributed. It makes a difference if the shares are widely dispersed or concentrated, and if concentrated, whether the rivals are increasing or losing their shares. We will look at what is happening to other countries in later chapters, but first we need to determine the shape of America's postwar decline.

Although there is no question that the slope of American decline was quite steep in the quarter century after the war, the view that recent U.S. decline has been either continuous or precipitous is debatable. Ironically, the decline of U.S. power was steepest from 1950 to 1973, the period often identified as the "period of American hegemony" (see figure 3.1). American decline has been much more difficult to discern from 1973 to the present, which is often labeled the period of U.S. decline. The semantic irony in this does not matter as long as we do not let the labels mislead us about what was actually happening to American power resources during the two periods.

TRENDS IN ECONOMIC POWER RESOURCES

Reliable historical numbers are hard to come by. Because most of the available data are rough estimates at best, we must use them to examine general trends

FIGURE 3.1

The Shape of American Decline, 1900–1987

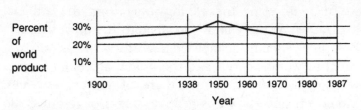

SOURCE: Herbert Block, *The Planetary Product in 1980: A Creative Pause?* (Washington, D.C.: U.S. Dept. of State, Bureau of Public Affairs, 1981), pp. 74–77, 86–87; Simon Kuznets, *Economic Growth and Structure* (New York: W. W. Norton, 1965), p. 144; Council on Competitiveness, *Competitiveness Index* (Washington, D.C.: 1988), app. II.

rather than small changes. Figure 3.1 is based on three authorities: (1) Herbert Block's estimate that early twentieth-century United States accounted for almost a quarter of world product, (2) Simon Kuznets' estimate that the United States represented 25.9 percent of world income in 1938, and (3) the estimate of the Council on Competitiveness that the American share of world product has held steady at 23 percent since the mid-1970s.[11] Alternatively, the approach of the Central Intelligence Agency uses purchasing power parities to correct for how many goods money can buy in different societies; its numbers would cause the curve in figure 3.1 to turn up again in the 1980s. The CIA calculates the American share as falling from 30 percent in 1960 to 25 percent in 1975 and then rising to 26 percent in 1988.[12] We must approach all such figures with suspicion, but it is easier to analyze when the numbers are made explicit rather than left vague. Certainly, figure 3.1 suggests a rather different long-term picture than the image of continuous or rapid decline.

Unfortunately, there is some imprecision in all estimates of world product. For example, it is quite difficult to obtain reliable data on planned economies and less developed countries. GNP reflects population, regardless of whether the people are poor, trained, or employed. With more rapid population growth in the Third World, one should expect the U.S. share of world product to decline over time. Since world product includes services and subsistence agriculture, it may not be as relevant a measure of a country's mobilizable power as share of world manufacturing product. We must be careful, however, not to depreciate the role of services, which account for two-thirds to three-quarters of employment in modern economies. In information-based economies, however, it is often hard to draw a clear line between critical manufacturing and services. For instance, the value in a modern telecommunications switching system lies more in the software than in the hardware.[13] But does a country derive more power from an advantage in manufacturing electronic microchips (Japan) or from holding a clear lead in producing software (United States)? Obviously, both are important. The point is that manufacturing matters, but so do services.[14]

Yet even with these caveats about data, the American share of world manufacturing production has not shown a precipitous decline (see figure 3.2). Contrary to the view that the United States was de-industrializing, manufacturing represented about the same proportion (21 percent) of GNP in the 1980s as it did in the 1970s.[15] Moreover, the U.S. share of world manufactures shows a similar trend. The American postwar preponderance was somewhat greater at nearly 45 percent, and the early postwar decline is thus somewhat steeper. By 1973, however, the American share returned to roughly the 1938 level of 32 percent, and slipped only slightly during the 1970s.[16]

FIGURE 3.2

American Share of World Manufacturing Production,
1913–1980

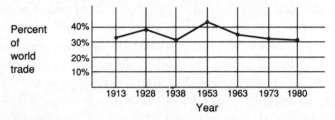

SOURCE: Paul Bairoch, "International Industrialization Levels from 1750 to 1980," *Journal of European Economic History* 11 (2 [Fall 1982]): 275.

Skeptics may argue that the critical indicator of decline is not share of manufacturing production but share of the leading sectors in manufacturing. Perhaps a focus on areas of innovation would give us a clearer picture of continual decline. The idea is plausible, though there are difficulties in reaching agreement on what defines a leading sector and how long it has lasted. One effort by William Thompson compares Britain's share of leading sector industrial activities in the nineteenth century with those of the United States in the twentieth century. On Thompson's measures, Britain emerged from the Napoleonic Wars with a greater than 50 percent share that peaked at 64 percent around 1830, fell below 50 percent in the 1870s, and declined to 15 percent on the eve of World War I. He portrays the American share of leading sector production as reaching 50 percent in 1910, 68 percent in 1920, 57 percent on the eve of World War II, 64 percent in 1950, and declining back to the previous level of 57 percent in 1960. But here again, the more recent years show only slight U.S. decline, from 52 percent in 1970 to 49 percent in 1980. As Thompson warns, however, such aggregate scores are somewhat crude and may disguise the unevenness of sectoral growth patterns.[17]

Another way to analyze the competitiveness in leading sectors is to look at export shares of technology-intensive products.[18] (See table 3.1.) The numbers are similar to those we saw earlier for GNP, although they show a slight decline. The U.S. share of the total declined from 27 percent in 1970 to 23 percent in 1980 and 21 percent in 1986. The United States retained the leading position in world export shares in aircraft, industrial chemicals, agricultural chemicals, engines and turbines, and office and computing machines. It ranked a close second in electrical machinery, plastics, and drugs.[19] Single industries show sharper declines. For example, the United States has virtually left the international television and radio receivers market, and while it still had the largest market share for world electronics in 1988—40 percent compared to Japan's 27 percent—the U.S. share of the world's electronics production was down from 50 percent earlier in the decade.[20]

Obviously, the narrower the focus, the greater the volatility of the indicators. If, for example, we focus solely on Japan, we see that the U.S. share of the joint

TABLE 3.1

World Export Shares of Technology-Intensive Products, 1970–1986

Country	1970	1980	1986
United States	27.0%	22.9%	20.9%
Japan	10.9	14.3	19.8
France	7.1	8.5	7.9
West Germany	16.8	16.3	16.0
Britain	9.8	10.8	9.0

SOURCE: National Science Foundation, *International Science and Technology Update, 1988* (Washington, D.C.: 1989), p. 92.

product of the two countries declined as Japan's share rose. But if we include the American share of the product and exports of the seven industrial countries that hold an economic summit every year, we see that the U.S. share of gross domestic product actually rose slightly in the late 1980s (see table 3.2). In general, though, the indices of economic power at various levels of aggregation are reasonably consistent. They show a relatively sharp decline during the postwar quarter century of supposed U.S. hegemony and relatively moderate change since then.

TRENDS IN MILITARY POWER

Assessing trends in the military balance during the postwar period is more difficult for reasons related to the changing costs of using force, as discussed in chapter 1. Traditionally, war has been the ultimate indicator of national military strength in the prenuclear age. But there has been neither a nuclear nor any other type of war among the great powers for nearly half a century—an unprecedented period in the modern state system.

Nuclear weapons are today the ultimate form of military force. In terms of sheer destructive potential, they

TABLE 3.2

American Share of Seven Summit Economies,
1970–1987

	1970	1980	1987
Share of gross domestic product	48.7%	46.8%	47.3%
Share of exports	24	25	23

SOURCE: Barry P. Bosworth and Robert Z. Lawrence, "America in the World Economy," *Brookings Review* 7 (Winter 1988/89): 43; Council on Competitiveness, *Competitiveness Index* (Washington, D.C.: 1988), app. II.

trump all others. Further, nuclear weapons are the clearest measure of bipolarity. There are five openly declared nuclear weapons states—the United States, the Soviet Union, China, France, and Britain—and four others that are suspected of covertly crossing the threshold of possession—Israel, South Africa, India, and Pakistan. However, the United States and the Soviet Union together account for 98 percent of the estimated 55,000 nuclear weapons in existence today.

However, there is disagreement about the political value of nuclear force and what exactly represents a balance of forces. About equal portions of the American public believe that either the Soviet Union or the United States is ahead in nuclear forces, although public opinion tends to vary more with moods and non-nuclear events than with actual numbers. Similarly, European views of U.S. military strength have fluctuated over the years more in response to political events than to the actual evolution of the military balance.[21] The experts have likewise been divided. Unfortunately, nuclear deterrence theory provides little help. We cannot know, for example, whether China was deterred by nuclear weapons because we cannot determine what China would have done in the absence of nuclear weapons. Some believe that deterrence rests on a delicate balance of terror, in which small differences in the ability of the United States and the Soviet Union to strike each other's weapons first and to have a larger residual force conveys great military power. For example, in the early 1980s, the U.S. Committee on the Present Danger used such arguments to declare that the United States was becoming "number two."[22] Others believe that political leaders do not make such abstract and refined calculations.[23] They argue that Soviet and

American leaders are deterred by the absolute devastation that can be wrought on their countries by any nuclear weapon, rather than by the residual strength of nuclear forces after a first attack on each other's missile silos.

Although history is not conclusive, it does provide some evidence. In 1982, President Reagan and Defense Secretary Weinberger argued that the Soviet Union had "a definite margin of superiority" because of its nuclear counterforce capabilities.[24] During the 1980s, when the Soviets added more accurate strategic warheads, U.S. land-based missiles became more vulnerable to a Soviet first strike. In general, though, the United States did better than the Soviet Union in achieving regional political goals, such as deployment of missiles in Europe and Soviet withdrawal from Afghanistan. Either the Soviets did not have nuclear superiority in the 1980s, or, if they did, the margin was of relatively little value as a power resource.

It is easier to demonstrate that the United States at one time enjoyed nuclear superiority through its monopoly on nuclear weapons until 1949. Yet the initial scarcity of the weapons and concern about their vast destructiveness made American presidents reluctant to use them during the era of U.S. nuclear superiority in the 1950s.[25] Further, American leaders lost any lingering sense of nuclear superiority with the Soviet launching of Sputnik in 1957, which suggested that the U.S. homeland was now vulnerable and that Americans might be behind in a missile gap. Even during the 1962 Cuban Missile Crisis, which some might call the nuclear age's substitute for the traditional showdown of war, something in the order of a seventeen-to-one American nuclear superiority seemed less important to President

Kennedy than the prospect of even a few Soviet nuclear weapons exploding in the United States.[26] While it is sometimes said that the United States "won" the Cuban crisis, the outcome had large elements of compromise. Moreover, American naval and air superiority in the Caribbean probably played a larger role than did nuclear superiority.

It is clear, however, that the Soviet nuclear build-up in the 1960s eliminated American nuclear superiority by the early 1970s. The imprecise term *rough parity* is probably as accurate a description as any for the nuclear balance. It is worth noting that the United States' vulnerability in the late 1950s and its loss of nuclear superiority in the 1960s occurred during the era of supposed American hegemony. The U.S.–Soviet nuclear balance has not shifted dramatically. In the period of supposed posthegemonic decline, as figure 3.3 indicates, the United States continued to lead in number of strategic warheads, as it has throughout the postwar period. The Soviet Union passed the United States in number of strategic delivery systems in 1971, but that relationship remained relatively stable after the early 1970s. Even within the strategic nuclear issue, the situation is best described as a balance of asymmetries. In the view of Chinese analysts in the early 1980s, "to sum up, the Soviet and U.S. military forces each have their strengths and are roughly equal."[27]

The United States also did not enjoy superiority in the size of conventional military forces during its supposed hegemony. As we have seen, the Soviet Union has been superior in the balance of conventional forces in Europe since the final days of World War II. The nature of this conventional imbalance is a matter of heated dispute. Some see a three-to-one advantage in

FIGURE 3.3
United States–Soviet Union Nuclear Balance

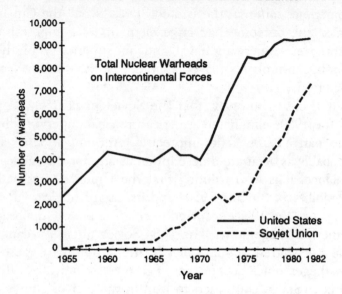

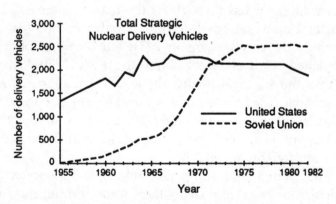

SOURCE: The Harvard Nuclear Study Group, *Living with Nuclear Weapons* (Cambridge, Mass: Harvard University Press, 1983), pp. 74–75.

tanks or armored divisions; others argue that Soviet forces should be discounted for qualitative factors.[28] It is hard to argue, however, that there was an American decline. Until the 1970s, conventional Soviet forces had little ability to move far away from their homeland, whereas the United States, a maritime power, had always enjoyed this capability. Although the construction of a Soviet surface fleet reduced the U.S. lead in mobility and the ability to move forces to distant locations, the Soviets are not close to catching up. Total numbers of naval ships are far less important in this respect than the fact that the United States has fourteen aircraft carriers and the Soviet Union has only four, and these are of a smaller type.[29] In total numbers of military personnel, the Soviet Union has consistently outranked the United States in the postwar period except during the Vietnam War (see table 3.3). However, these figures include Soviet forces that perform internal security and construction work.

Some have attempted to measure a country's military power through its share of global military expenditure. Such indices, however, are not always reliable. Because they measure input rather than output, a country that is technologically inefficient may have to spend more to get a given result. Another major problem is a lack of data on the actual Soviet defense budget. Western intelligence agencies estimate dollar and ruble expenses on the basis of what they see the Soviets fielding and what they think it would cost. But intelligence agencies disagree, and others disagree with the intelligence agencies.[30] At best, then, such estimates are only rough approximations.

Other figures show that the Soviets slightly outspent the United States in military expenditures in the late

TABLE 3.3
Soviet and U.S. Military Personnel, 1963–1987

	1963	1966	1969	1972	1975	1978	1981	1984	1987
United States									
Actual (in thousands)	2700	3090	3460	2320	2098	2033	2168	2244	2279
Percent of world total	12.9	14.2	14.4	9.2	8.2	7.9	7.8	7.7	7.8
Soviet Union									
Actual (in thousands)	3110	2780	3340	3510	4100	4200	4400	4500	4400
Percent of world total	14.9	12.8	13.9	15.8	15.8	16.1	16.0	15.5	15.1

SOURCE: Arms Control and Disarmament Agency, *World Military Expenditures and Arms Transfers* (Washington, D.C.: ACDA, 1963–1989 [annual]).

1940s, but that after the Korean War, U.S. expenditure exceeded the Soviets' until 1962. Following the Cuban Missile Crisis, the Soviets again outspent the United States throughout the 1960s.[31] The recent period is more controversial. The U.S. Arms Control and Disarmament Agency (ACDA) shows the Soviet Union and the United States each with about 30 percent of global military expenditure in 1965. The United States surged ahead during the Vietnam War to a peak in 1968, but then cut its defense budgets in the 1970s when the Soviets did not. Thus, the ACDA data suggest an American decline from 32 percent of world military expenditures in the mid-1960s to 28.4 percent in 1984.[32] Ruth Sivard argues that since 1972, the Soviets outspent the United States in only one year—1975. She estimates American military spending as 35 percent of the total in 1972 and 30 percent in 1983, when it was slightly larger than the Soviet share.[33] (See table 3.4.) To the extent that such estimates are meaningful, they suggest two things: (1) that military bipolarity existed (and continues to exist) in more than just nuclear forces, and (2) that whatever the American experience was in the "hegemonic" 1960s, there is little evidence for U.S. decline in the posthegemonic 1980s.

Another measure of military strength is military technology. Throughout the postwar era, the United States has relied on its advanced technology to counter Soviet advantages in absolute numbers. While technology grows over time, critical military advantages can be derived from maintaining just a few years' lead over other nations. The United States has maintained such an advantage. Its organization of an embargo on export of advanced technology is an example, as is the Soviet Union's efforts to circumvent the embargo. Annual

TABLE 3.4

U.S. and Soviet Shares of World Military Expenditure, 1963–1987

	1963	1966	1969	1972	1975	1978	1981	1984	1987
ACDA Estimates									
United States	36.1%	35.8%	36.2%	26.7%	22.4%	21.1%	23.2%	28.4%	29.1%
Soviet Union	32.4	31.2	31.0	32.2	32.7	33.3	32.3	31.1	29.8
Sivard Estimates									
United States	—	—	—	35.0	27.4	26.1	—	30.8	n. a.
Soviet Union	—	—	—	29.3	28.36	24.6	—	29.3	n. a.

SOURCE: Arms Control and Disarmament Agency, *World Military Expenditures and Arms Transfers* (Washington, D.C.: ACDA, 1963–1989 [annual]); Ruth Leger Sivard, *World Military and Social Expenditures* (Washington, D.C.: World Priorities, 1974–1987 [annual]).

assessments by the U.S. Defense Department (which tends to understate American strength in order to plead for more resources from Congress) give some idea of the large American lead over the Soviet Union in critical military technologies (see table 3.5).

Trends in the various measures of American military power resources are quite similar to those shown by the various measures of U.S. share of global economic resources. The American share of global economic and military power resources declined for the first postwar quarter century. This decline was closely related to the vanishing World War II effect. The pattern of decline produces the semantic irony that American decline was sharpest during the earlier period of alleged hegemony and at best very slight in the period of alleged hegemonic decline. Indeed, some measures show no decline at all in the latter period.

MYTHS OF AMERICAN HEGEMONY

We have looked at the postwar period in the United States in terms of power resources, but how did it look in terms of behavior and outcomes? Many observers casually assume a degree of American influence in the postwar years that simply did not exist. Further, when past hegemony is exaggerated, the present is diminished and the future is more difficult to understand. As the editor of *Punch* is alleged to have replied to someone who complained that his magazine was not as funny as it used to be: "It never was."

As we saw in chapter 1, the term *hegemony* often is applied to situations of unequal power in which one country has a high degree of control over others. When

TABLE 3.5
U.S.–Soviet Balance in Critical Military Technologies, 1980 and 1989[a]

1980: Basic Technologies	U.S. Superior	USSR Superior	U.S./USSR Equal
Aerodynamics/fluid dynamics			X
Automated control	X		
Computers	–X		
Directed energy			X
Electro-optical sensors	X		
Guidance and navigation	X–		
Hydro-acoustics	X		
Intelligence sensors	X		
Manufacturing	X		
Materials (lightweight and high strength)	X–		
Microelectronic materials and integrated circuit manufacture	–X		
Military instrumentation	X		
Nonacoustic submarine detection			X
Nuclear warheads			X
Optics	X–		
Propulsion (aerospace)	X–		
Radar sensors			X
Signal processing	X		
Software	X		
Telecommunications	X		

1989: Basic Technologies	U.S. Superior	USSR Superior	U.S./USSR Equal
Microelectronic circuits and their fabrication	X		
Preparation of Gallium Arsenide (GaAs) and other compound semiconductors	X		
Software producibility	X		
Parallel computer architectures	–X		
Machine intelligence/robotics	X		
Simulation and modeling			X
Integrated optics	X		
Fiber optics	X		
Sensitive radars		X	
Passive sensors			X

TABLE 3.5 (*continued*)

1989: Basic Technologies	U.S. Superior	USSR Superior	U.S./USSR Equal
Automatic target recognition	X		
Phased arrays	X		
Data fusion	X–		
Signature control	X		
Computational fluid dynamics	–X		
Air breathing propulsion	X		
High-power microwaves			X–
Pulsed power	X		
Hypervelocity projectiles	X		
High-temperature/high-strength/ lightweight composite materials	X–		
Superconductivity	X		
Biotechnology materials and processing	X		

ªDashes indicate that the relative technology level is changing significantly in the direction indicated.

SOURCE: U.S. Department of Defense, *Critical Technologies Plan for the Committee on Armed Services, United States Congress* (Washington, D.C.: GPO, 15 Mar. 1989), app. A, pp. A1–A94.

hegemony is used in this way, the type of inequality as well as the scope of control must be specified to avoid confusion. Our interest here is not with regional spheres of influence but with the general type of hegemony that is supposed to be related to stability and the danger of war. Thus, we need to look at the extent to which the United States was able to use its predominant military or economic resources to control interstate relations during the postwar period.

One problem with many portraits of America as a postwar hegemon is a focus on economic aspects to the neglect of military and security dimensions. Robert Cox, for example, refers to a hegemonic *Pax Americana* but focuses almost entirely on economic objectives and instruments.[34] Similarly, Robert Keohane carefully identifies hegemony in terms of economic resources but treats military power merely as necessary "to protect an international political economy from incursions by hostile powers."[35] This one-dimensional view has a distorting effect on our understanding of the postwar period—it exaggerates American power because it focuses on the economic issues in which American power resources were greatest. But, as we have seen, the United States did not possess hegemonic power resources in the military area.

Bipolarity—the existence of Soviet political-military power—severely curtailed overall American power and shaped crucial political trade-offs in the early postwar period. As one careful study of U.S. efforts to regulate its allies' trade during the Cold War concluded, "America's commitment to the alliance proved to be an important source of leverage for the ostensibly weaker West European states. . . . Paradoxically, as the commitment of a hegemonic state to alliance management wanes, its influence over alliance affairs may actually increase."[36] In other words, the political context of the military balance limited U.S. ability to wield its economic power. Richard Cooper notes that during the first two decades after the war, there was a "two-track system" that kept economic and military issues largely separated in day-to-day relations between the United States and its allies.[37] Economic issues were rarely linked explicitly to military ones. But rather than suggesting the irrelevance of the military balance for economic issues during that period, the two-track system suggests its centrality. The United States often subordinated its economic interests during the period of the supposed *Pax Americana* because it was concerned about the high politics of the global balance and the challenge of Soviet power.

The absence of general hegemony helps to explain

the shifts in American bargaining with its allies in the early postwar period. In the lend-lease negotiations during the war, the United States pressed Britain to decolonize and to dismantle preferential tariffs for its colonies. In the negotiations at Bretton Woods to establish new economic institutions at the end of the war, the United States successfully pressed for a more tightly disciplined International Monetary Fund (IMF) than Britain wanted. And in negotiating a loan to Britain in 1946, the United States took a hard line in pressing for convertibility of the British pound. By 1947, however, Americans began to perceive not only the economic weakness of Europe but also the growing threat of Soviet expansion. Containment of Soviet power, the Truman Doctrine on aid to Greece and Turkey, and the Marshall Plan for European economic recovery were all parts of the same new strategy. Subsequently, the United States stopped insisting on convertibility; eased its pressure on the Dutch, French, and British for decolonization and dismantlement of colonial trade preferences; promoted European integration; and accepted discrimination against the dollar. In Asia, the United States brought Japan into the IMF and the General Agreement on Tariffs and Trade (GATT) and provided Japan with access to the American market even though other countries refused to follow suit.

There were good economic and security reasons for several of these changes, and the United States did not always subordinate its short-run economic interests to security concerns. A combination of domestic politics and "resistance to U.S. liberalism by other countries" destroyed the fledgling International Trade Organization, and internal divisions helped prevent the establishment of a public international regime to govern oil.[38] In the 1950s, the United States successfully enlarged an agricultural exception for itself in the GATT. But while there were crosscurrents in the historical stream, it would be hard to explain the transition of the United States from what Robert Keohane calls a rather tight-fisted to a relatively openhanded economic hegemon without taking into account that the United States was never a military hegemon.[39]

Quite unintentionally, America's allies benefited from Stalin's threat and the balance of military power. While the United States would undoubtedly have had to ease its pressure on the Europeans for economic reasons, and American aid was only one of the factors abetting restoration of liberal institutions in Europe,[40] it is unlikely that the U.S. Congress or public would have been as generous in the international redistribution of economic resources were it not for the security threat.[41] As Charles Maier has written about Europe, "the overwhelming difference between 1918 and 1945 was the continuing intervention of the United States and the Soviet Union in their respective spheres of influence."[42] Within its sphere, the United States was far from supreme. "Marshall Aid was not . . . important enough to give the United States sufficient leverage to reconstruct Western Europe according to its own wishes." France and Britain thwarted the development of a strong organization for European economic cooperation. Britain refused to join Europe. In 1957, "instead of a liberal unified Europe came a closely regulated little European common market" with a heavily protected agricultural sector. Western Europe successfully rejected "the economic framework for interdependence which the United States sought to impose on it."[43] This situation was a far cry from the usual image of the American hegemon imposing its liberal policies.

It was a deliberate American policy objective to restore the economic role of its allies in the 1950s, even if it was often done on their terms and at the cost of discrimination and erosion of U.S. postwar economic predominance. By 1958, European recovery had progressed to the point where the Bretton Woods monetary system, long held in abeyance, could be put into practice. But as the world economy returned to a more normal configuration, the United States began to feel the pinch of its already somewhat diminished position. The first sign was President Kennedy's Interest Equalization Tax designed to discourage the export of capital from the United States and to alleviate pressure on the balance of payments in 1963. Then, as its economic preponderance shrank in the mid-1960s, the United States began to depart from the two-track arrangements of the prior decade and appealed to the security concerns of its allies for relief on economic problems. Under President Johnson,

> the United States government not only reminded the West Germans that a continued American military presence was dependent upon West German support of measures to lessen the American balance of payments deficit, West Germany was also pressured to increase its military purchases from the United States and to avoid competitive arrangements with France.[44]

By 1971, with increasing pressure on its balance of payments, Richard Nixon broke the Bretton Woods exchange-rate system that the United States had created, instituted an import surcharge, and refused to continue to exchange gold for dollars. The issue became not whether the United States would impose openness on others but whether it would itself remain an open market and absorb the discrimination it had earlier accepted.[45]

The end of the gold-exchange standard in 1971 is sometimes seen as the end of American hegemony. It is certainly a convenient point, though perhaps a bit late for dating the end of the period when economic hegemony meant relative economic altruism or the tendency to sacrifice economic for security objectives in the two-track approach. In this sense, 1971 reflected the end of the postwar preponderance in economic resources that had allowed the United States to follow an altruistic policy without much difficulty. The United States had given back many of the benefits that it had inadvertently won during World War II, and it began to act more normally; that is, less altruistically. But 1971 did not mean that the world had returned to economic multipolarity. The United States still had far more economic power resources than any other player. The facts that it could change the rules of the game when it felt pinched and that other nations chose to hold dollars after the gold window was closed indicate that the United States still possessed unparalleled economic strength.[46] If hegemonic economic behavior is the ability to change the rules of the international game, then 1971 did not mark the end of U.S. economic hegemony. If hegemonic economic behavior means forcing openness on other states, then the United States did not have great hegemony before 1971. What it did have in the early postwar period was an unnatural share of world product—the World War II effect—which it spent to strengthen its allies in an effort to balance Soviet power in the military area, where there was clearly no hegemony.

According to hegemonic stability theory, the global

economy requires a single predominant power to provide stability; thus, the end of American economic hegemony and the advent of multipolarity should lead to increasing economic instability. Political economists have wrestled with the implications of the theory. Although countries can still choose to cooperate after hegemony,[47] the historical premises of the hegemonic stability theory are questionable. If full hegemony never existed, or if it was weaker than described by political economists who focus only on its economic dimensions, then the difference after hegemony will not be so great. In a study of Cold War trade, Michael Mastanduno notes that "in the era of undisputed American hegemony, U.S. officials were not only unable to determine alliance policy, but found themselves adjusting to the preferences of their allies."[48] However, if we look at all the dimensions of power in the postwar period, we realize that the United States never had full hegemony. The actual processes of influence in the early postwar period are more readily explained by the existence of a military balance of power and perceptions of a Soviet threat, which constrained hegemonic behavior based on American economic preponderance.

SUCCESSES AND FAILURES

As noted earlier, power as a resource is not always readily converted into influence. In terms of behavior, though, what happened to U.S. power over the past decades? This question is not easy to answer because it is often difficult to define or even to identify the causes of success in foreign policy. Success depends in part on how ambitious a country's objectives are, on good fortune, on the actions of others, and on a nation's own efforts. For example, American military assistance, local resistance, and Soviet economic problems all helped to end the Soviet occupation of Afghanistan in 1989. Similarly, although the United States is generally credited with the postwar reconstruction of Europe, Charles Maier calculates that U.S. assistance contributed only 10 to 20 percent of European capital formation in the most critical years. He believes that Europe would not have gone Communist even if the United States had not intervened.[49]

As table 3.6 indicates, the early postwar period in the United States saw some impressive successes but it was also marked by some major failures in military, economic, and institutional issues. Of course, the United States derived influence from its economic preponder-

TABLE 3.6

Several Major U.S. Foreign Policy Efforts, 1945–1960

	Successes	Failures
Political/ military	German and Japanese reintegration; Italian and French elections; Berlin Airlift; covert actions in Iran and Guatemala; troops to Lebanon; Suez withdrawal.	Soviet expansion in East Europe; "loss" of China; Soviets' gain A-bomb; failure to roll back communism in Eastern Europe; "loss" of North Vietnam; Sputnik; "loss" of Cuba
Economic/ social	Marshall Plan; growth, increase in global trade and investment; defeat of 1956 oil embargo	Agricultural trade; economic warfare against USSR; little dismantlement of colonial preferences
Institutions	Bretton Woods; GATT; OEEC; United Nations; NATO	International Trade Organization; oil regime; European Defense Community; collapse of Baghdad Pact

ance. It failed to establish regimes for trade or oil, but fallbacks to the GATT in trade and private company control of oil production and trade were still good for American interests. On rare occasions the United States used its economic power coercively. For instance, when Britain and France invaded Egypt at the time of the 1956 Suez Crisis, withholding oil supplies and opposing an IMF loan to Britain had a decisive effect in accelerating their withdrawal.[50] Certainly the United States has less financial or international institutional power today than it had in 1956. But its period of greatest preponderance in power resources was not one of unblemished success in exercising political influence. In conflicts with Canada, for example, the United States did less well in the 1950s and 1960s than it did between the two world wars.[51] And, as various memoirs attest, the world did not feel hegemonic to American leaders of the time.[52]

MILITARY INFLUENCE

A similar pattern emerges when we look at various attempts by the United States to influence other countries by military force. If the postwar period is divided into two eras—one of supposed U.S. hegemony (1945–1973) and another of supposed U.S. decline (1974–1989)—we see that the United States engaged in nine efforts at coercive nuclear diplomacy in the earlier period and only one in the later era (see table 3.7). Attempts to use U.S. nuclear power to influence Soviet and Chinese behavior involved speeches, alerts, and movements of strategic forces. The United States took such actions in conflicts involving threats to its allies and those in which conventional forces were deemed infeasible.[53]

TABLE 3.7
American Nuclear Threats, 1945–1989

	1945–1973			1974–1989		
	Success	Failure	Uncertain	Success	Failure	Uncertain
High risk	Cuba (1962)		Berlin (1958–1961) Middle East (1973)			Persian Gulf (1980)
Minor risk	Berlin (1948) Korea (1953) Taiwan (1955)		Suez (1956) Lebanon (1958) Taiwan (1958)			

SOURCE: Richard K. Betts, *Nuclear Blackmail and Nuclear Balance* (Washington, D.C.: Brookings Institution, 1987).

Success is difficult to ascertain in these cases because we do not know what the Soviet Union or China really intended to do. Perhaps they were bluffing, or perhaps they had no intentions of doing what the United States feared. For example, in the cases identified as uncertain in table 3.7, neither the Soviet Union nor China gave up any announced objectives. In the four cases listed as successes, the Soviet Union or China backed away from demands that had precipitated or prolonged the con-flict.[54] However, three of the four successful cases involved only minor risk of escalation. Even in the Soviet withdrawal of missiles from Cuba in 1962—the one major success of the earlier period—the American victory was far from clear-cut. The Soviets gained an American pledge that increased the security of a Communist regime ninety miles from the United States and a secret assurance that the United States would even-tually remove American missiles from Turkey. The United States considered three ways to gain the removal of the Soviet missiles—"shoot 'em out with an air strike, squeeze 'em out by a naval blockade, or buy 'em out by a trade." While many people attribute the success to President Kennedy's naval blockade, there was more of the third option than the public realized at the time.[55]

Although it may be tempting to interpret the decline in number of American nuclear threats as an indication of decline in American influence, a careful analysis of the cases shows that American leaders were ambivalent about how much they could rely on their nuclear supe-riority in the earlier period. As Richard Betts concludes, "the arrival of nuclear parity changed the behavior of leaders less than is often assumed." In particular, he notes that the implicit nuclear threats associated with President Carter's 1980 pledge to protect the Persian

Gulf after the Soviet invasion of Afghanistan undercuts the view that parity ended American efforts to manipulate nuclear risk. American efforts to use nuclear influence was affected more by the balance of interests (that is, which side had the higher stakes in the status quo) than by the nuclear balance of power.[56] The decline in the number of U.S. nuclear threats is striking, but it says more about Soviet policies and nuclear learning in both countries than it does about a decline in American power.

Another form of military power is interventions. The incidence of major cases of military intervention in the two periods remains roughly constant (see table 3.8). On average, there was about one every seven or eight years. Some analysts argue that military interventions occur when a hegemon is weakening or drawing inward. If this is true, then the the unchanged incidence of U.S. military intervention suggests no decline. But to count the successes and failures of military interventions with conventional forces in the two periods is meaningless. The Vietnam failure during the supposed hegemonic era outweighs all the rest. Moreover, some observers consider the Korean War a stalemate and President

TABLE 3.8
Major American Military Interventions,
1945–1989

1945–1973		1974–1989	
Success	Failure	Success	Failure
Korea	Vietnam	Grenada	Lebanon
Lebanon			
Dominican Republic			

SOURCE: Herbert K. Tillema, *Appeal to Force: American Military Intervention in the Era of Containment* (New York: Crowell, 1973), chap. 2.

Eisenhower's sending of marines to Lebanon in 1958 an insignificant event. In the later period, President Reagan's successful use of troops to change the situation in Grenada in 1983 involved an exceedingly weak state whose government was in turmoil. Although the number of incidents per year remains the same, the scope of American ambitions was smaller in the later era. There were no more efforts like Vietnam, or even like President Johnson's sending 25,000 troops to the Dominican Republic in 1965. Despite the hostility of the Reagan administration toward the Sandinista government in Nicaragua, the American government stopped short of full-scale military intervention. The reduced number of large-scale interventions reflects the rising costs of major intervention that affected all great powers.

However, it is important not to overestimate the extent of American military intervention in the period of supposed *Pax Americana*. The United States intervened far more often as the regional hegemon of the Caribbean before World War II. The conventional wisdom describes the postwar era as one in which the United States played global police officer, and it is true that there were four military interventions. But just as interesting are the number of times when the United States did not intervene even when serious stakes were at risk. Herbert Tillema identifies 149 such cases (see table 3.9).[57]

As Sherlock Holmes observed, there is much to be learned from dogs that do not bark. Tillema's data show that American efforts to produce favorable outcomes by major military intervention were surprisingly rare in the period of so-called U.S. hegemony. Of course, great powers have other means of influence in addition to

TABLE 3.9
Cases of American Military Nonintervention, 1945-1972

Type	Number	Examples
Communist threat to country of special interest	31	China (1946-1949); Greece (1946-1949); Philippines (1945-1954); Cuba (1956-1959)
Communist threat to other country	13	Algeria (1954-1962); Indonesia (1958-1962); Cyprus (1963-1964)
Communist threat to region	35	Burma (1948-1958); Indochina (1954); Congo (1960-1964); Laos (1959-1962)
Conflict on Communist border	8	Trieste (1946-1953); Tibet (1949-1951)
Conflict in Communist state	9	Hungary (1956); Czechoslovakia (1968); Cuba (1961)
Possible peacekeeping	53	Palestine (1946-1949); India-Pakistan (1965); Nigeria (1966-1969)
Total	149	

SOURCE: Herbert K. Tillema, *Appeal to Force: American Military Intervention in the Era of Containment* (New York: Crowell, 1973), chap. 5.

military force. In some cases, the United States did not intervene militarily because it could obtain favorable outcomes by less costly means such as covert action. In other instances, it may have held back because of domestic moral and political constraints. But in many important cases, the United States did not intervene because of external constraints on American power. As Tillema concludes, "neither extraordinary significance of a threatened nation (as China), nor failure of a covert operation (as in Cuba in 1961), nor humanitarian appeals for intervention to restore peace (as in the Nigerian Civil War of 1966-69) [has] been sufficient to induce American leaders to use military force when a restraint acted on it."[58] If this is a description of military hegemony or *Pax Americana*, the term means far less than is suggested by the theories of hegemonic transition surveyed in chapter 1.

Other ways to wield military influence without overt intervention include the long-standing practice of open or covert support of proxy military forces. Although it is difficult to be certain of the full list of efforts to exercise influence by covert support of proxy forces, table 3.10 lists the major cases that have come to light.

In major publicly known cases, there appears to be no great difference in the incidence or success of covert support for proxy forces in the two periods. In addition, some observers believe that lesser forms of covert intervention in other countries' political processes have diminished as a result of greater publicity at home and congressional oversight. It is impossible, however, to be either precise or certain about such covert political actions.[59]

Another way of wielding military influence is aptly called "force without war"—the use of armed forces to send political signals rather than for military purposes. Barry Blechman and Stephen Kaplan identify 215 inci-

TABLE 3.10

Cases of Covert Support of Proxy Military Forces, 1945–1989

1945–1973		1974–1989		
Success	Failure	Success	Failure	Uncertain
Iran (1953)	Indonesia	Afghanistan	Nicaragua	Cambodia
Guatemala	(1958)	(1980–)	(1981–)	(1984–)
(1954)	Cuba (1961)	Angola		
		(1981–)		

SOURCE: John Prados, *Presidents' Secret Wars: CIA and Pentagon Covert Operations Since World War II* (New York: William Morrow, 1986); Gregory F. Treverton, *Covert Action: The Limits of Intervention in the Postwar World* (New York: Basic Books, 1987).

dents between 1946 and 1975 when the United States used this type of military influence. Nearly half the cases involved only movement of naval forces, while others involved the alerting or movement of ground or air units as well. Blechman and Kaplan argue that these maneuvers contributed to favorable outcomes in three-fourths of the cases in the first six months after an action was taken, but that the effects diminished after three years, when the proportion of sustained favorable outcomes dropped to less than half. Two-thirds of the efforts to use such maneuvers to deter or to assure another country were successful in the long term, but only a fifth of American efforts to compel changes in other countries' behavior had positive outcomes.[60] In other words, even during the period of alleged *Pax Americana,* U.S. efforts to use military threats to compel or induce other nations to change their behavior failed four-fifths of the time.

Blechman and Kaplan's data do not allow a comparison of the two periods of supposed U.S. hegemony and decline. At best, there is anecdotal evidence, such as American naval actions off the coast of Libya, that indicates successful efforts to use force without war in the 1980s. One of their findings, however, is particularly interesting as it relates to how the bipolar balance of power prevented a general American hegemony in the postwar period. The United States was more successful in situations where the Soviet Union was not a participant and less successful in situations with a greater degree of Soviet involvement: "Soviet willingness to use or to threaten force was associated with proportionally fewer positive outcomes."[61] Thus, in terms of deriving political influence from its military forces, outside the Western Hemisphere, American power was not hegemonic but was balanced by Soviet military power.

ECONOMIC SANCTIONS

Another glimpse at the behavioral record of American power is provided by efforts to apply economic sanctions. Threats to withdraw customary trade or financial relations are as old as diplomatic history. Gary Hufbauer and Jeffrey Schott examined 103 cases of economic sanctions between 1914 and 1984. Contrary to the conventional wisdom that economic sanctions never work, they found that in a little over a third of the cases, economic sanctions made at least a modest contribution to realizing a foreign policy goal.[62]

The success and failure rates of U.S. and non-U.S. efforts to influence other states by economic sanctions in the two eras of supposed American hegemony and decline are given in table 3.11. At first glance, there are significant differences between the two periods. The United States did more than twice as well in the earlier period, while the success rate of other countries remained roughly the same over the two periods. However, the United States tried sanctions more often in the later period, which suggests that the diminished success rate may not be due to a decline in power but instead to an increase in ambitions.

Several additional points become clear from a close analysis. First, even during its supposed hegemony, the United States was not successful in its six efforts to bring about major changes or to impair the military effectiveness of other nations. The three rare cases of success at inducing major changes were by nonhegemonic countries. On the other hand, the United States was clearly more successful in destabilization and disrupting other countries' military actions in the earlier than in the later period. The most dramatic fall in the U.S. success rate came when it sought modest policy

TABLE 3.11

Cases of Economic Sanctions by Policy Objective, 1944–1984

Policy Objective	Non-U.S. Cases				U.S. Cases			
	1944–1973		1974–1984		1944–1973		1974–1984	
	Success	Failure	Success	Failure	Success	Failure	Success	Failure
Modest change	3	3	3	4	7	2	6	18
Destabilization	2	2	0	0	7	3	1	3
Disrupt military	0	1	1	1	3	4	0	3
Impair military	0	2	0	0	0	4	0	2
Major change	3	8	0	2	0	2	0	1
Total	8	16	4	7	17	15	7	27

SOURCE: Gary C. Hufbauer and Jeffrey J. Schott, *Economic Sanctions Reconsidered* (Washington, D.C.: Institute for International Economics, 1985), pp. 45–55.

changes by other countries. Most of these modest changes reflected the new and more ambitious U.S. policy agenda of the 1970s: twenty of the twenty-four cases related to human rights or nonproliferation, whereas there were only two and a half such cases in the earlier period. Moreover, the greater success rate of other countries in the later period was similarly related to lower ambitions, since they made only four attempts to use economic sanctions to influence other countries on proliferation and human rights issues.

The differences between the early and later periods in table 3.11 tell as much about the ambitious new human rights agenda of President Carter as they do about diminished power to impose sanctions. In the later period, the United States failed more, but the United States tried more often, particularly on the new global issues. The data are more consistent with a hypothesis of power diffusion related to a new agenda of world politics, which we will discuss in chapter 6, than with a theory of hegemonic decline of a United States pressed by rising challengers.

BALANCE OF POWER IN THE 1990S

According to theories of hegemonic transition and imperial overstretch, a great power becomes exhausted through the protection of its far-flung interests. International commitments sap its strength at home, while rising challengers profit from the public order, global economic growth, and diffusion of the hegemon's technology. Eventually, the hegemon is replaced by a rising challenger which may be a military opponent or one of its former allies. However, such theories, and the general historical analogies that accompany them, do not provide an accurate picture of the situation the United States faces at the end of the twentieth century.

The influence derived from American preponderance in the early postwar years tends to be overrated by theorists of power transition. In terms of resources or behavior, American power is clearly not what it was in the 1950s, but the decline is exaggerated by comparisons with a mythical *Pax Americana* of the past. The United States never enjoyed a general hegemony after the war, so hegemony can be neither lost nor regained in the future. Looking ahead, Soviet military power will persist on the basis of past investments. Even if reform fails to stem Soviet economic decline, Soviet military power will exercise some constraints on American actions. As we will see in chapter 6, major restraints will also arise from the development of transnational interdependence and the diffusion of power. Such changes are not captured by historical analogies about the rise and fall of hegemons and challengers.

However, as table 3.12 shows, the United States remains predominant in traditional power resources at the end of the 1980s. Currently, there are three major states in terms of the basic resources of territory and population—China, the Soviet Union, and the United States—but China's level of development and low per-capita income mean that it has a long way to go to activate the potential power implicit in these basic resources. In terms of military power, the world of the 1990s remains highly bipolar in nuclear arsenals, overall military spending, and the capability of transporting large military forces to distant areas. Space shows the same bipolar pattern, but some might see an American preeminence.[63] Nearly half of the commercial satellites

Ranks and Shares of Traditional Power Resources, 1980s

	United States	Soviet Union	Japan	China	West Germany	Britain	France
Basic Resources							
Population (1989)	4th (4.7%)	3rd (5.5%)	7th (2.4%)	1st (21.1%)	12th (1.2%)	15th (1.1%)	16th (1.1%)
Territory (1989)	4th (7.0%)	1st (12.8%)	— (<1%)	3rd (7.0%)	— (<1%)	— (<1%)	— (<1%)
Economy							
GNP (1985)	1st (27.6%)	2nd (15.1%)	3rd (9.4%)	7th (2.5%)	4th (4.5%)	6th (3.2%)	5th (3.5%)
Manufacturing (1980)	1st (31.5%)	2nd (14.8%)	3rd (9.1%)	5th (5.0%)	4th (5.3%)	6th (4.0%)	7th (3.3%)
High-tech exports (1986)	1st (21.0%)	—	2nd (20.0%)	—	3rd (16%)	4th (9%)	5th (8%)
Merchandise exports (1985)	1st (10.7%)	6th (4.5%)	3rd (9.1%)	15th (1.5%)	2nd (9.6%)	4th (5.3%)	5th (5.1%)
Military							
Nuclear weapons (1989)	1st (tied) (48.0%)	1st (48.0%)	—	5th (<1%)	—	4th (1.0%)	3rd (1.0%)
Military expenditures (1987)	2nd (29.1%)	1st (29.8%)	6th (2.4%)	7th (2.0%)	4th (3.36%)	5th (3.1%)	3rd (3.43%)
Military personnel (1987)	3rd (7.8%)	1st (15.1%)	27th (0.8%)	2nd (12.1%)	14th (1.7%)	20th (1.1%)	11th (1.9%)

SOURCE: Arms Control and Disarmament Agency, *World Military Expenditures and Arms Transfers, 1988* (Washington, D.C: GPO, 1989), table 1; Paul Bairoch, "International Industrialization Levels from 1750–1980," *Journal of European Economic History* 11 (1 [Spring 1982]): 275; Central Intelligence Agency, *World Factbook; The International Data Base* (1989) (Washington, D.C.: 1989).

in space are American. The next largest number belongs to Intelsat, an international organization that is strongly influenced by the United States. If, as some observers believe, "the effective control of space by one state would lead to planet-wide hegemony," the American lead in space resources is significant.[64]

The distribution of economic power resources shows a more complex pattern. It involves two major states, the United States and Japan, and Europe to the extent that the European Community can act as one entity. The most notable feature of the economic distribution is the rise of Japan. Based on the high value of the yen at official exchange rates, Japan has surpassed the Soviet Union as the world's second largest economy. The official exchange rate also makes Japan appear wealthier on a per-capita basis than the United States. When exchange rates are corrected to reflect the purchasing power of currencies in different societies, Japanese per-capita income is about 80 percent of the United States level and 94 percent of the German level. Japan has surpassed France and Britain.[65] In terms of technological resources, the United States, Japan, and Europe play the major roles. Soviet investment in science and technology remains high, but its low share of high-tech exports indicates important lags.

These measurable dimensions of the current distribution of power clearly show that only one country ranks above the others on all four dimensions—the United States. Japan and Europe are not in the top rank in basic and military resources; China is not in the top rank in economic and technological power resources; and the Soviet Union is a dubious contender in technological resources.

However, there are other important dimensions of

power resources that are more intangible and difficult to measure. If a country's culture is attractive, others may voluntarily assimilate its values and preferences. They may also unintentionally provide it with resources. For example, the United States benefits from the use of the English language, its prominence in science and the arts, and its relative openness to foreigners, evidenced by the number of foreign students trained in the United States (some 340,000 in 1987), the inflow of capital seeking a safe haven, and the more than half a million legal immigrants who enter each year.[66] International institutions and norms are another potential source of power, to the extent that they structure other countries' preferences in a manner that accords with that of the dominant power. The United States participates in a large number of international institutions, whose rules and norms in many cases reinforce the liberal views of the United States. In some, like the Bretton Woods institutions, the United States still maintains a large enough voting share to give it a veto. In the United Nations Security Council, the veto is formally prescribed. Its more frequent use in recent years suggests that the United States has less ability to assume that the preferences of other nations in the institution will accord with its preferences. Nonetheless, the institution frequently serves American purposes, and the veto provides protection when it does not.

Alliances are yet another critical institutional resource. When the measurable power resources of the United States, Western Europe, and Japan are aggregated, the military strength of the Soviet Union (and its allies) is effectively countered.[67] To the extent that alliances continue to provide forward defense of American frontiers and increase deterrence through the aggregation of military and economic resources, they are an important source of power. The unequal shape of the Western alliance means that the United States benefits from its position as the hub of alliance diplomacy.

Although the various power resources of the United States give it preponderance at the beginning of the 1990s, this does not mean the distribution of power will continue in America's favor. As we saw at the end of chapter 2 (and will discuss in more detail in chapter 7), there are trends in the American economy and society that could diminish its power resources if left uncorrected. But even if such trends are not reversed, it is important to remember that power is relative. We cannot understand the implications for America's position in the balance of power at the turn of the century until we look at what is happening to the other major countries.

PART II

NEW
CHALLENGERS?

4

Communist Challengers

The United States is undoubtably more powerful at the end of the twentieth century than Britain was at the close of the nineteenth century. Because power is relative, however, the future American position will depend in part on what is happening to potential major challengers. In terms of basic resources and industrial development, there are four potential challengers, two Communist and two capitalist: the Soviet Union, China, the European Community, and Japan. We look at the Communist challengers in this chapter and the capitalist challengers in chapter 5.

THE SOVIET UNION

As shown in chapter 3, the Soviet Union posed the largest challenge to the United States in the postwar period. In basic resources, the Soviet Union has the world's largest territory and third largest population. It is rich in natural resources, including gold and strategic materials, and produces more oil and gas than Saudi Arabia. The Soviets possess nearly half the world's nuclear weapons and rank first in number of military personnel. Throughout much of the postwar period, the Soviet Union has had the world's second largest economy and industrial production. Its investment in scientific research and development grew by nearly 8 percent per year in the 1960s. By the end of that decade, the Soviet research and development community was the largest in the world in number of personnel.[1]

In the 1950s, many people in the West feared that the Soviet Union would surpass the United States as the world's leading power. When Nikita Khrushchev visited the United States in 1959, he boasted that the Soviet Union would overtake the United States by 1970 or 1980 at the latest. Such expectations were written into the 1960 program of the Soviet Communist party and were not removed until 1985. As late as 1976, Leonid Brezhnev told the president of France that communism would dominate the world by 1995.[2]

Soviet leaders used the Marxist term *correlation of forces* to refer to military balance as well as to a general sense of how overall social forces were evolving. It was a vague concept that allowed for a great deal of subjective interpretation, and involved a substantial amount of wishful thinking. In the 1950s, however, there were reasons for the Soviets to believe that the correlation of forces was moving strongly in their favor. Communist ideology and transnational organization had been strengthened in the West by the prestige gained in resisting Hitler. In France and Italy, upwards of a quarter to a third of the electorate voted Communist. In the Third World, communism was associated with the popular movement toward decolonization. The myth of inevitability was strong. The Sino–Soviet split did not openly fracture the movement until the 1960s.[3]

These ideological and organizational sources of power were bolstered by the performance of the Soviet economy, which was growing at nearly 6 percent per year when Khrushchev made his boast. In addition, the heavy Soviet investment in science and technology paid off in 1957, when the Soviet Union became the first nation to launch a satellite into space. Soviet scientists broke the American monopoly on the atomic bomb by 1949, much more quickly than many in the West expected. They exploded a hydrogen bomb in 1953, only one year after the United States and years before Britain and France tested their first thermonuclear weapons.

The Soviets hid the fact that they experienced difficulty building an effective intercontinental ballistic missile. (They apparently had only twenty operational ICBMs at the time of the Cuban Missile Crisis late in 1962.)[4] But from the launching of Sputnik until 1961, many in the West believed that the United States lagged behind the Soviets in what was called a missile gap. In 1960, Khrushchev cut back on conventional forces and launched an ambitious fifteen-year strategic nuclear program. Like Eisenhower before him, Khrushchev was trying to get more bang for the ruble.[5] After Khrushchev was overthrown in 1964, his successors continued his nuclear build-up but reversed his conventional cutback. Leonid Brezhnev inherited a Soviet military with approximately 3.3 million men in 140 divisions (26 foreign-deployed), but bequeathed to his successors 5.5 million men in 208 divisions, including 40 stationed outside the Soviet Union.[6] In addition, Brezhnev began a major naval build-up. By the 1970s, the Soviet Union was able to support wars of national liberation in distant areas. This was a striking contrast to its inability to come to the aid of its clients during the Congo crisis in the early 1960s.

As the United States drew inward after the defeat in Vietnam, the Soviets and their Cuban allies became involved in several African conflicts. Moreover, a number of radical regimes came to power in developing countries and proclaimed their sympathies for the Soviet Union. During the 1970s, the Soviet Union nearly tripled its spending on its East European empire and extended its support to Third World allies. The costs of empire rose from 1 to nearly 3 percent of Soviet GNP.[7] Thus, to many in the West, détente and the arms control treaties of the 1970s were merely tactics to disguise rising Soviet power. Shortly after the 1979 Soviet invasion of Afghanistan, the 1980 American election focused on the issue of rising Soviet power, and President Reagan proclaimed that the Soviets had military superiority.

INDICATIONS OF SOVIET DECLINE

Ironically, just as Western fears of rising Soviet power reached a renewed peak that echoed the 1950s, the erosion of the underlying structure of Soviet strength began to become apparent to some Soviet intellectuals. The secretiveness of the Soviet political system, its lack of effective methods for routine replacement of leaders, and the succession of three dying leaders in the early 1980s prevented the Soviet government from openly acknowledging its problems until Mikhail Gorbachev came to power in 1985. At that time, the Communist party declared the country to be in a "pre-crisis" stage. "By that time," wrote Politburo member Alexander Yakovlev, "it had become perfectly clear that the country was in a state of long-lasting and potentially dangerous stagnation."[8] Since then, the realities and dangers of Soviet decline have been openly discussed. In 1987, Foreign Minister Eduard Shevardnadze warned officials of his ministry that "beyond the borders of the Soviet Union, you and I represent a great country that in the last 15 years has been more and more losing its position as one of the leading industrially developed nations."[9]

Soviet industrialization during the 1930s had been impressive. At 20 percent per year, the Soviet Union had the world's highest growth rates of industrial production. Rapid growth continued in the postwar period with annual rates of growth in GNP ranging between 5 and 6 percent in the first two decades. The Soviet share of world GNP increased from 11 percent in 1950 to 12.3 percent in 1970 (see figure 4.1). After 1970, however, Soviet economic growth began to slow to a rate of 3.7 percent per annum at the beginning and 2.7 percent in the second half of the decade.[10] The Soviet share of world product declined from 12.3 to 11.3 percent. In the 1980s, official figures credit the Soviet Union with an economic growth of about 2 percent a year, but there is considerable dispute about what such numbers mean. One problem is the padding of official statistics in the closed Soviet political system. According to Soviet sources, industrial production has been inflated by up to 3 percent a year.[11] Abel Aganbegyan, a Gorbachev advisor, argues that there was zero growth from 1980 to 1985.[12]   Even more fundamental is the qualitative rather than quantitative nature of Soviet economic

FIGURE 4.1
Soviet Share of World Product, 1950–1980

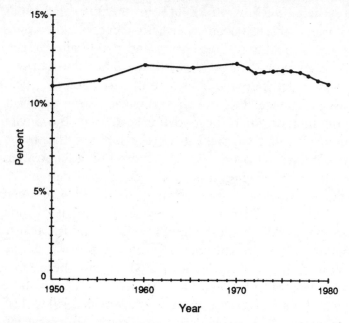

SOURCE: Herbert Block, *The Planetary Product in 1980: A Creative Pause?* (Washington, D.C.: U.S. Department of State, Bureau of Public Affairs, 1981), pp. 76–77.

growth. If, for example, the Soviet central plan produced billions of left shoes but no right shoes, that figure would show up as an increase in national product even though the single left shoes were worthless. The Soviet problem is not quantity but quality of growth.

Stalin's growth model was based on central planning, which made quantity rather than profits the main criterion of a manager's success. Prices were set by planners rather than by markets. The Stalinist economy was successful in mastering relatively unsophisticated technologies and producing basic goods on a massive scale. It was effective in extracting capital from the agricultural sector in the 1930s and using it to build heavy industry. It was also effective in postwar reconstruction when labor was plentiful. However, with a diminishing birthrate and scarce capital, Stalin's model of central planning became less successful.[13]

The biggest problem, however, is that Soviet central planners lack the flexibility to keep up with the quickened pace of technological change in today's information-based economy. They have not come to terms with the third industrial revolution discussed in the introductory chapter. According to Marshall Goldman, "Stalin's growth model eventually became a fetter rather than a facilitator."[14] As computers and microchips become not merely tools of production but embedded in products, the life cycles of products shorten. Many products become obsolete in only a few years, even though the planning system may take much longer to react and may continue toward obsolete goals. The Soviet bureaucracy has been far less flexible than markets in responding to rapid change, and for years "the very word 'market' was practically forbidden."[15]

Stalin's political legacy was yet another hindrance to the Soviet Union. An information-based economy requires broadly shared and freely flowing information to reap maximum gains. Horizontal communication among computers becomes more important than top–down vertical communication. But horizontal communication involves political risks, in that computers can become the equivalent of printing presses. Moreover, telephones can multiply these risks by providing instant communication among computers. Thus, Soviet leaders were reluctant to foster the widespread and free use of personal computers for political reasons. Two simple statistics demonstrate the Soviet disadvantage in the expanding information economy of the 1980s: by the middle of the decade, there were only 50,000 personal computers in the Soviet Union (compared to 30 million in the United States) and only 23 percent of urban and 7 percent of rural homes had telephones.[16] Although this situation made political control easier, it had disastrous economic effects. In the mid-1980s, the Soviets failed to produce a personal computer on a large scale. At the end of the decade, Soviet officials admitted that their computer technology lagged seven to ten years behind the West. Further, lack of freedom for hackers and other informal innovators severely handicapped the development of software. As one Western specialist observes, the Soviets paid a heavy price for central control.[17]

As a result, Soviet industry is not competitive globally. In the view of Soviet economist Nikolai Schmelov, only 7 to 8 percent of Soviet manufacturing meets world standards.[18] Prime Minister Nikolai Ryzhkov revealed that only 29 percent of Soviet machine tools met global standards.[19] In 1988, the chair of the Soviet State Economic Commission lamented the nation's inability to exceed 4 percent of world trade: "in this sphere, we have been unable to become a big foreign trade power."[20] In foreign trade, the Soviet export pattern is similar to that of a developing country, with one raw material—oil—accounting for about 60 percent of hard currency earnings.[21]

Soviet science has also slipped. The massive investments of the 1960s tapered off in the late 1970s. Despite larger numbers of Soviet researchers, studies by the U.S. National Academy of Science judged American science and technology to be superior, although they found the Soviets strong in fundamental fields of physics and mathematics and some applied fields such as metallurgy. But in areas such as biotechnology, Soviet biology was set back until 1965 by the government's support for the crackpot theories of Stalin's favorite biologist, Trofim Lysenko. From 1970 to 1980, the number of Soviet biologists dropped from 4 to 3.6 percent of total scientific research personnel, compared to 18 percent in the United States.[22] Moreover, the emigration of key Soviet scientists has hurt many fields.[23] One careful study of the citations of scientific works has found that the influence of Soviet science diminished in the 1980s.[24]

The Soviet lag in science and technology has not applied as much to space and some military efforts. These two areas are privileged by the central planning system, and have a top priority claim on scarce resources. Yet in an age of "smart weapons" that incorporate microchips and sensors, military technology increasingly depends on an advanced civilian electronics sector. Further, the military priority has added to the problems of the Soviet economy. Until 1989, the Soviet defense budget remained a secret, and there were considerable difficulties in estimating the burden of defense. But by any measure, the concept of imperial overstretch applies to the Soviet Union. Even after Gorbachev announced a figure equivalent to 9 percent of Soviet GNP, Western experts argued that the full costs of Soviet defense were higher. Not only were military space costs not included, but more important, the official budget was based on the subsidized rather than realistic prices that the military paid for inputs. Most estimates of Soviet defense and foreign affairs expenditures range from 12 to 20 percent or more of GNP. Whichever is the real number, it is still two to three times the burden of defense on the American and Chinese economies and ten to fifteen times that on the Japanese economy. In June 1989, Prime Minister Ryzhkov announced a plan to reduce the share of national income devoted to defense by one-third to one-half by 1995.[25]

Results of the large Soviet defense burden include a deficit of about 10 percent of the government budget (more than three times the U.S. level) and hidden inflation over 8 percent in 1989. A Soviet economist argues that the true deficit figure was even higher.[26] The pressures of the military budget may also account in part for the shocking decline in Soviet health standards in the 1970s. The share of health services in the Soviet budget fell between 1965 and 1978. In a situation unique among developed countries, average adult life expectancy in the Soviet Union declined rather than increased. In 1960, life expectancy at age 1 was the same in the Soviet Union as in Western Europe, 71.4 years. By 1980, Western European life expectancy had risen to 73.7 but the Soviet figure had fallen to 69.3.[27] Similarly, infant mortality rates, which had declined for fifty years after the revolution, began to rise again after 1971. In 1974, embarrassed by the statistics, the Soviet government stopped publishing the figures until the Gorbachev era. At that time, the Soviet infant mortality rate stood at 26 per 1,000, compared to 50 for China, 10.6 for the United States, and 6 for Japan.[28]

Agreeing on a net assessment of the current Soviet economy is not easy because of measurement problems and political interests. Scholars argue that American intelligence estimates are too optimistic about the Soviet economy and place too much trust in Soviet official figures.[29] For example, Nicholas Eberstadt contends that the Soviet economy in the mid-1980s was closer to one-third rather than one-half the size of the U.S. economy and that Soviet per-capita output was a quarter of the American level.[30] Swedish economist Anders Aslund argues that "to anyone who has lived in the Soviet Union, it is clear that it is a reasonably well developed Third World country, calling to mind Argentina, Mexico or Portugal in terms of infant mortality, life expectancy, agricultural employment, consumption and other non-military indicators of economic development."[31] Henry Rowen and Vladimir Treml warn that unless there is drastic reform in the Soviet system, "the country is fated to remain economically backward—behind by about a generation (25 to 30 years)—relative to the West. Although such a lag certainly doesn't exist for the military sector today, over time its ability to compete militarily will be in jeopardy."[32] Lest these Western sources sound too biased, it is worth noting the testimony of Soviet leaders. In 1986, Mikhail Gorbachev described the Soviet economy as "very disordered. We lag in all indices."[33] Gorbachev's advisor Abel Aganbegyan believes "we have underestimated the depth of the abyss of stagnation out of which we are now climbing and have underestimated the forces of inertia."[34] Even the special Communist party conference resolution of July 1988 warned that Soviet "scientific and technological progress is yet slow, and the plans for increasing the national income and resource-saving are not fulfilled."[35] Most alarming was Nikolai Shmelov's prediction, made to the Congress of People's Deputies in 1989, that without draconian reforms "we might well have an economic crash within two or three years."[36] Privately, a number of Soviets admit that unless their reforms are successful, the Soviet Union will not remain a leading power in the twenty-first century.

PROSPECTS FOR THE FUTURE

What are the prospects for reform in the Soviet Union? When Gorbachev first came to power in 1985, he followed the footsteps of his mentor Yuri Andropov and achieved some gains in production by stressing greater discipline within the existing structure. But Gorbachev soon realized that greater decentralization and restructuring was necessary. However, the entrenched bureaucrats did not want their power reduced. The head of GOSPLAN, the state planning agency, commented at a 1983 press conference, "under the circumstances, why switch?"[37] In order to bypass the bureaucracy, Gorbachev turned to the media and gave intellectuals greater freedom to dramatize and discuss the need for Soviet reform. He also encouraged greater pluralism in the party and in government institutions.[38] In 1989, the Soviet Union held its first meaningful parliamentary elections in seventy years. But the steps toward economic decentralization and market prices have gone only part way, and the Soviet leadership has been caught in critical dilemmas. The newly elected parliament expressed widespread complaints about the failure of economic reform. Gorbachev's policy of glasnost had greatly outpaced the progress of perestroika.

Price reform is necessary for markets to play a guiding role in economic change, but such reforms in the Soviet Union might double or triple the cost of living and undercut support for Gorbachev's policy. Consumer subsidies already cost the Soviet government some $126 billion per year.[39] There remains an ideological reluctance to permit the visible inequalities of income that go with private entrepreneurship as well as a political reluctance to give enterprise managers significant autonomy from central control. The Soviet leadership tried to steer through these dilemmas with halfway measures, but some intellectuals realized that halfway reforms would not solve their problems. A wry joke that circulated in Moscow during the late 1980s told of Soviet planners trying to decide if they should restructure their traffic patterns according to the more efficient practices of the West. Unable to decide whether to use the American pattern of driving on the right side or the Japanese pattern of driving on the left side, they decide to try a little of each.

Access to Western capital and technology could help to alleviate these Soviet dilemmas, but it cannot resolve them. The Soviet ability to absorb imported technology in the civilian sector has been mixed and often disappointing,[40] and such imports do not touch the basic Soviet problem of adapting an overcentralized system to an information-based economy. The prospects for the success of Gorbachev's reforms remain highly uncertain.

What do these problems imply for the future of Soviet power? As it approaches the end of the twentieth century, the Soviet Union has become a one-dimensional power. Soviet military strength will remain formidable in both nuclear and conventional terms, like a glacier that keeps moving long after the snows have stopped falling. Ed Hewett of The Brookings Institution warns against an exaggeration of Soviet decline: "The USSR will enter the next century . . . about as prosperous and as great as it is now. The important issue . . . will be the direction of change and its momentum."[41] Nonetheless, without economic reform, the Soviet military will begin to lose its technological capability. Marshal Ogarkov, then chief of the Soviet General Staff, pointed out in 1984 that new technologies are leading to smart weapons in an electronic battlefield.[42] Without an advanced scientific and industrial sector, the Soviet military would find it hard to keep up. President Reagan's Strategic Defense Initiative proposal accentuated these concerns. Soviet leaders did not believe that the United States would be able to build a perfect "astrodome" defense but that Reagan's program would widen the gap between the two countries in the fields of advanced sensors and data processing as they apply to a wide range of weapons.

In addition to current economic and future military problems, the Soviets must resolve the question of social cohesion and nationalism. Unlike the United States, China, or Japan, where nationalism reinforces social cohesion, the Soviet Union (like the European Community) experiences nationalism as a corrosive force. While glasnost has not created the nationalities problem, it has given new leeway for its expression.[43] Further, Alexander Motyl argues that the decentralization that is necessary for the Soviet economy exacerbates the problem because it drives local leaders to "objective nationalist behavior. . . . Unless [Gorbachev] is willing to preside over the system's disintegration, recentralization of some kind will be inevitable."[44]

Whether this pessimistic prediction is correct or not, Russians make up roughly half of the Soviet population today, but the higher birthrate of other Soviet nationalities will make Russians a minority in the Soviet Union in the twenty-first century (see table 4.1). Yet Russians dominate in politics, representing 68 percent of the Central Committee of the Communist Party in the early 1980s.[45] With some sixty major language groups and fifteen constituent republics, the growth of ethnicity and nationalistic expression made possible by

TABLE 4.1
Ethnic Composition of the Soviet Union,
1950–2000

	1950	1980	2000 (estimated)
Total Slavic	82%	75%	69%
Percent Russian	57	52	48
Total non-Slavic	18	25	31
Percent Asian	10	16	21

SOURCE: Paul Dibb, *The Soviet Union: The Incomplete Superpower*
(London: Macmillan, 1986), p. 48.

glasnost places an additional burden on the Soviet political system. Ethnic riots have broken out in the Cau-
cuses and Central Asia, and pressures for autonomy
have grown in other areas like the Baltic republics.
Many Russians have responded with increased nationalistic reactions of their own.

As for the power resources of a universalistic ideology, the poor economic and political performance of
communism has greatly eroded the ideology as a source
of power abroad and of cohesion at home. It is a far cry
from the sense in the 1950s of the inevitable victory of
communism. Further, the Soviets are not well placed to
benefit from international institutions as a power
resource. The international Communist movement is
fragmented, and the Soviets have officially recognized
that foreign affairs can no longer rest on a class division
into Socialist and bourgeois camps.[46] The Soviet alliance, the Warsaw Treaty Organization, is an externally
imposed institution of questionable value, and nationalist tendencies are growing stronger in Eastern Europe.
The Soviet economy has not yet adapted enough to
allow full participation in crucial economic institutions
such as GATT and IMF. The one bright point is that
the new thinking in foreign policy and a more flexible

position may allow the Soviets to gain more from their future participation in the United Nations than in the past. Table 4.2 summarizes various judgments about the future prospects of Soviet power.

TABLE 4.2
Past and Future Sources of Soviet Power

Source of Power	Past	Present	Future
Tangible			
Basic resources			
(land and population)	strong	strong	strong
Military	strong	strong	strong
Economic	strong	weak	uncertain
Science/technology	mixed	mixed	mixed
Intangible			
National cohesion	strong	weak	uncertain
Culture/ideology	strong	weak	weak
International institutions	mixed	weak	uncertain

In short, given their basic resources and military strength, it would be a mistake to discount the Soviet Union as a great power in the twenty-first century. As we will see in chapter 6, however, trends in world politics are increasing the importance of the less coercive and less tangible sources of power like national cohesion and ideology. From this perspective, given Soviet economic, technological, political, and ideological problems, the Soviet Union has become a declining rather than a rising challenger to American preeminence. The policy implications of this situation are examined in chapter 8.

CHINA

The Soviet Union has an economy several times the size of China's. At the beginning of the 1980s, the

Soviet Union accounted for 15 percent of world indus-trial production whereas China accounted for only 5 percent. Similarly, China accounted for only 5 percent of world product.[47] But while Soviet growth slowed in the 1980s, China's net material product grew at over 8 percent a year and its per-capita GNP doubled between 1977 and 1987.[48] Projecting such growth into the future, some observers foresee China as the rising challenger to America's global position.

CHINESE ECONOMIC GROWTH

Some economists believe that the official Chinese sta-tistics understate the level of development of the Chinese economy. Dwight Perkins suggests a 1985 fig-ure of $500 per-capita gross domestic product, which is nearly twice the official number.[49] Using the higher esti-mates, the U.S. Commission on Integrated Long-Term Strategy estimates China's national product to be about 40 percent of the Soviet Union's product in 1980. Assuming a Chinese growth rate of 4.7 percent, a Soviet growth rate of 1.6 percent, and a U.S. growth rate of 2.6 percent, the commission projects that Chinese GNP would pass that of the Soviet Union by 2010. It would then be half the level of the U.S. GNP, but only about 10 percent of the American, Japanese, or European lev-els on a per-capita basis. Even if China spends 6 per-cent of its GNP on defense, its military capital stock would still be less than half the Soviet military capital stock in 2010. China's current level is approximately 20 percent of Soviet military capital stock.[50]

The commission's estimates of China's future eco-nomic growth are lower than China's recent perfor-mance, but they are still controversial. Some skeptics feel the estimates exaggerate China's potential, pointing to the low base from which China starts and warning against linear projections. They argue that China is "riddled with infrastructure problems (parts of the country are inaccessible by road, not electrified, have poor sewage, water, and transportation systems); it is a collection of semiautonomous regions with separate languages and cultures, . . . and it will continue to labor under the bureaucratic oppression of a communism in moderate transition."[51] Moreover, political disruptions could interrupt the projected economic growth. Optimists, on the other hand, point out that China's economy more than quadrupled from $67 billion in 1952 to $320 billion in the mid-1970s, despite the loss of 20 million lives to hunger during Mao Tse-tung's "Great Leap Forward" in the late 1950s and of another half-million lives in the Cultural Revolution of the late 1960s.[52] Others support a high-growth projection on the basis of the general pattern of growth in East Asia, suggesting that it is similar to the Protestant ethic that many believe was a stimulus to Europe's economic growth.[53]

Certainly, China has benefited from a number of characteristics not shared by most other developing countries. It has a historical memory of past greatness and it began its postwar development with a moderately well-developed commerce, many large urban centers, and a tradition of literacy related to recruitment for government bureaucracy. Nonetheless, neither these assets nor Confucian culture produced a high rate of growth before World War II. China's per-capita GNP in 1952 was similar to that of Japan in 1886.[54]

The victory of the Communists in 1949 brought China a degree of political cohesion that had eluded it earlier in the century. The importation of the Soviet economic model produced high rates of savings and investment with priority for heavy industry. Mao's efforts to make the Soviet model more egalitarian and regionally decentralized were not successful, but the basic mechanism produced impressive industrial growth. By the mid-1970s, China had an industrial base comparable in scale to those of the Soviet Union and Japan in the early 1960s. Literacy, at about 65 percent, was just below the average of middle-income countries, although less than 2 percent of the labor force had university or secondary education. In 1964, China was the fifth nation to explode a nuclear device, but Chinese technology in general in the late 1970s lagged ten to twenty years behind world levels overall. Sixty percent of the technology employed in Chinese industry in 1980 was completely obsolete by world standards.[55]

Although the inertia of central planning helped to carry China through the politically disruptive years of Mao's Cultural Revolution (1966–1976), Chinese leaders became aware in the latter half of the 1970s that the centralized planning system was not producing rates of growth as high as those in other developing countries in the region. Larger investment of capital was not producing proportionate increases in production.[56] Under Deng Xiaoping, China launched a series of moderate reforms between 1978 and 1984 that expanded opportunities for private and collective ownership in agriculture and in services, offered greater autonomy and incentives to managers, decentralized the management of foreign trade, and established special economic zones in coastal areas to attract foreign investment. After 1984, China pursued a second set of more far-reaching reforms aimed at broadening markets, but their progress was uneven. Double-digit inflation, corruption, and changing income distribution aroused both conservative opposition and liberal demands for political reform. The ensuing protests and repression in 1989 slowed the pace of reform.

In short, China encountered some of the same dilemmas as the Soviet Union in loosening the constraints of the central planning system. Despite the rapid growth of private and collective enterprises, the Chinese economy remained highly regulated with the state sector accounting for about 70 percent of urban employment and industrial production.[57] Not only has the bureaucracy "proven inventive at finding ways to retain considerable power over state enterprises," but "Chinese leaders are also hesitant in allowing the logical implications of past reforms to be realized."[58] On the other hand, Mao never succeeded in destroying the Chinese peasantry in the manner that Stalin did with Soviet farmers. As a result, after Deng's reforms, the Chinese quickly returned to family farming in the 1980s, and this led to impressive gains in agricultural production.[59]

For a few years in the mid-1980s, China actually became a net exporter of grain, though its agricultural production lagged later in the decade. China was also more successful than the Soviet Union in opening its economy to the outside world in the 1980s. It joined the World Bank, the IMF, the Asian Development Bank, and applied for membership in the GATT. China's share of exports in national output grew from 5.6 percent when reforms started in 1978 to 16 percent in 1987. Nearly two-thirds of its exports were manufactured products, particularly textiles. By creating economic zones and open cities along the coast, China attracted $10 billion in direct foreign investment between 1979 and 1987.[60] But like the Soviet Union, the Chinese economy remained heavily autarkic. The currency was inconvertible (with the exception of a few special centers where yuan could be swapped for dollars), and central planners controlled access to critical resources. Domestic industry remained protected behind arbitrary price structures; at least one in eight enterprises lost money but was protected from bankruptcy.[61]

Like the Soviets, success with economic reforms will be essential to Chinese power in the twenty-first century. But reform creates political dilemmas if the structure of political power remains unchanged. The party "hesitates to let the economy develop independent of party interference at all levels of the system." Bureaucrats are better placed to enjoy the opportunities opened by reform, and "that has set in motion a chain reaction eventuating in inflation, corruption, and what is perceived by many to be unjust income distribution."[62] The resulting political disruptions, such as those that occurred in 1989, hinder China's progress.

POWER RESOURCES

In basic resources, China is powerfully endowed, and its potential is still not fully tapped (see table 4.3). Its territory is slightly larger than that of the United States,

TABLE 4.3
Past and Future Sources of Chinese Power

Source of Power	Past	Present	Future
Tangible			
Basic resources			
(land and population)	strong	strong	strong
Military	mixed	mixed	stronger
Economic	weak	mixed	stronger
Science/technology	weak	weak	mixed
Intangible			
National cohesion	mixed	mixed	mixed
Culture/ideology	strong	mixed	uncertain
International institutions	weak	mixed	uncertain

but only 10 percent of its land is arable.[63] China is the world's most populous state with 1.1 billion inhabitants, but currently it has only one-tenth of the U.S. number of university students.[64] In economic terms, China was the fifth largest nation in manufacturing output in the 1980s but remained a minor power in world markets. Despite specifically targeted accomplishments in nuclear weapons and rocketry, Chinese science and technology lagged by a decade or two behind world standards. With a sustained economic growth at twice the rate of the United States, China could reach half the level of American GNP in 2010, but it would remain much poorer on a per-capita basis.

Chinese military power also draws a mixed assessment. Throughout the postwar period, China has been a major regional military power but with little capacity for the global use of force. Although Chinese troops and military assistance helped to thwart the United States in Korea in 1950 and in Vietnam in the 1960s, Chinese military power benefited from geographic proximity in these cases. Yet proximity was often not enough to guarantee success. For example, in 1955 and 1958 the United States was able to prevent China from taking over Taiwan, and China was militarily unsuccessful in its border dispute with the Soviet Union in the late 1960s.

Chinese defense policy rested for many years on a combination of two extremes: (1) finite nuclear deterrence to prevent strategic attack and (2) "peoples' war" to deter or repel invasion by mass mobilization. The first involved high technology; the latter stressed people rather than weapons. China developed a large army of 4.3 million men, but they were poorly equipped. The result was high casualties and a humiliating defeat when

China tried to "teach Vietnam a lesson" by crossing their shared border in 1979. Recently, China has shown an interest in developing more modern general-purpose forces to meet more limited military contingencies than the extremes of nuclear deterrence or mass war.[65] This has involved cutting the armed forces by more than 1 million men and reducing defense expenditures from 12 percent of GNP in 1978 to 5 percent in 1987.[66] At the same time, China has continued gradually to upgrade its military technology, both nuclear and conventional. Its modest military position at the end of the 1980s is summarized in table 4.4.

China's forces show much greater regional than global power capability. Its navy remains primarily coastal, and only eighteen of China's nuclear weapons have a global reach.[67] Despite technical difficulties, China continues slowly to build more nuclear submarines and to enhance the capabilities of its conventional forces. While crucial sectors still lag far behind, China has increased its exports of military equipment to other less-developed countries, becoming by the mid-1980s the fifth largest exporter of weapons to the Third World.[68] With time and continued economic development, China will be able to play a greater global military role, but it has a

TABLE 4.4
Chinese Military Power, 1989

Nuclear forces	250 weapons on 6 ICBMs; 12 SLBMs; 1 submarine; 110 medium-range missiles; 120 medium-range bombers
Conventional forces	3.2 million
Naval forces	115 submarines; 53 destroyers and frigates
Defense expenditure	$12 billion (5 percent of GNP)

SOURCE: International Institute for Strategic Studies, *The Military Balance, 1988–89* (London: IISS, 1988), pp. 146ff.; Central Intelligence Agency, *China: Economic Policy and Performance in 1987* (Washington, D.C.: 1988), p. 17.

long way to go before it approaches the level of the superpowers.

Much of China's global political power in the postwar period was based on the intangibles of ideology and institutions. China's open break from Soviet tutelage in the early 1960s and Mao's challenge to Khrushchev for the mantle of Communist legitimacy made Chinese policy appealing to many postcolonial regimes. Left-wing groups in modern societies were similarly attracted by the egalitarian tone of Maoist ideology. Chinese assistance to overseas parties and governments, while modest, seemed to offer an alternative to the superpowers and the former colonial rulers. When China joined the United Nations in 1971, it acquired a new forum for this global political role. But the excesses of the Cultural Revolution tarnished China's romantic image. Further, the reforms of the post-Mao period not only demonstrated the problems inherent in China's centralized economy but also led to a more pragmatic and regionally oriented foreign policy. While it is exaggerated to say that ideology is dead in China, communism today certainly plays much less of a role in Chinese foreign policy and domestic politics.

China's diminished ideology may lead to problems in national cohesion. Its minority nationalities of 50 million is a small problem in comparison to that of the Soviet Union, but China does have a long tradition of regionalism. Riots have occurred in Tibet. Mao encouraged local self-sufficiency, and the new emphasis on coastal development zones led to friction over income distribution between coastal and interior provinces. In addition, generational change and student protests led to serious political disruption in 1989. The protests and their repression reflected the incompleteness of Chinese reforms. Notwithstanding the disruptions related to economic and political developments, a well-established nationalism is a source of strength for China in contrast to the situation in the Soviet Union.

CONCLUSION

China's huge population and geographical scale ensure it a major role in the increasingly important East Asian region. The extent to which China will become a global power challenging the United States depends on its economic growth and political cohesion. Yet even with good fortune, China has a long way to go. In 1988, before the setbacks of the June 1989 repression, Deng Xiaoping predicted that by 2050 China would be a middle-developed country with a per-capita income in current U.S. dollars of $4,000—about that of Ireland or Puerto Rico today.[69] Two American specialists, Harry Harding and Ed Hewett, note China's advantages in its huge labor pool and its ability to take advantage of relatively inexpensive technologies somewhat behind the leading edge. "Still, even with these advantages, it will take, at a minimum, decades for China to begin to emerge as a serious economic force in the world economy."[70]

Although the Soviet Union is far more industrially developed and technologically advanced than China, "it will take at least two to three decades for Soviet leaders committed to an opening to the world economy to achieve something."[71] Military alliance between the two large Communist states is possible but unlikely. Specific differences along their border are less important than the strength of Chinese nationalism and the Soviet concern about China. Overall, the Communist ideology that seemed so threatening to American power in mid-century appears to be a fetter on America's rivals at the century's end. Thus the Communist countries are not likely to be the rising challengers to American power in the next decades.

5

Allied Challengers

The alliance of Europe and Japan with the United States proved an effective balance to rising Soviet power for forty years. As shown in chapter 3, where American military resources were less than those of the Soviets, America's allies helped make up the difference. But the alliance may not survive in a period of Soviet decline and diminished Soviet threat. As America's replacement of Britain as the leading state has shown, erstwhile allies can become new challengers for predominance. By the late 1980s, American public-opinion polls showed greater concern about economic than military threats to American security.[1] In the early 1970s, President Richard Nixon spoke of a multipolar world, and analysts wrote about an emerging Japanese superstate. Many contemporary commentators feel that these predictions, premature when made, will finally come true in the next decade.[2]

In terms of world product, the most dramatic change in the last quarter century has been the doubling of Japan's share. The rise is even more dramatic if exchange rates are *not* corrected for purchasing power. As figure 5.1 indicates, in the last fifteen years the European Community and Soviet shares of world product declined slightly while Japan's share grew.

THE EUROPEAN COMMUNITY

Not all analysts believe that Japan is the ally most likely to challenge the United States after the turn of the

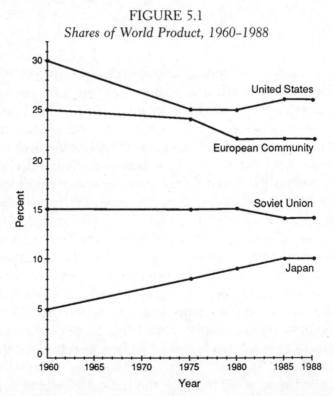

FIGURE 5.1
Shares of World Product, 1960–1988

SOURCE: Central Intelligence Agency, *Handbook of Economic Statistics, 1988* (Washington, D.C.: 1989), table 7 (Organization for Economic Cooperation and Development purchasing price parities were used to correct exchange rates for local standards of living).

century. Samuel P. Huntington argues that if the European Community became politically cohesive, it "would have the population resources, economic wealth, technology, and actual and potential military strength to be the preeminent power of the 21st century." He says that "if the next century is not the American century, it is most likely to be the European century."[3]

Europe's resources are impressive (see table 5.1). Although geographically only a quarter the size of the United States in territory, Europe has a population comparable to that of the United States and twice that of Japan. Its economy is larger than Japan's and only slightly smaller than that of the United States. Further, Europe plays a larger role in world trade. The armed forces of the twelve European Community countries slightly outnumber those of the United States and are ten times larger than those of Japan. Modernization of French and British nuclear forces will yield about 1,200 nuclear weapons in the early 1990s. Moreover, as Europe becomes a prosperous, democratic welfare state, it is "quite possible to conceive of a European ideological appeal comparable to the American one."[4] European culture has long been attractive to the rest of the world. The Europeans also have been important pioneers in international institutions. They have played central roles in the United Nations and international economic institutions, and their European Community has been the source of numerous institutional innovations.

The key question, of course, is whether the European Community will develop enough political cohesion to act as one on a wide range of international issues, or whether it will remain a customs union of twelve nations with strongly different nationalisms and

TABLE 5.1

Basic, Military, and Economic Resources of the European
Community, Japan, and the United States, 1980s–1990s

	European Community	Japan	United States
Basic Resources			
Territory (percent of world)	1.7%	0.3%	7.0%
Population (1987)	324 million	123 million	244 million
Military			
Nuclear weapons (1990s)	1,200	0	25,000
Armed forces	2.6 million	0.24 million	2.2 million
Military expenditure			
(world share, 1985)	10%	2.5%	30%
Economic			
GNP (1987)	$3.8 trillion	$2 trillion	$4.4 trillion
Share of world exports	20%	10%	11%

SOURCE: Central Intelligence Agency, Handbook of World Statistics, 1988 (Washington, D.C.: GPO, 1989); European Community, Basic Statistics of the Community, 25th ed. (Brussels: The Office, 1988); International Institute for Strategic Studies, The Military Balance, 1988–89 (London: IISS, 1988); Arms Control and Disarmament Agency, Military Expenditures and Arms Transfer, 1987 (Washington, D.C.: 1988); Keizai Koho Center, Japan 1989 (Tokyo, 1989).

foreign policies. Further, will Europe's economic slow-down after 1973 be significantly changed by new efforts to perfect the Common Market? In the early 1980s, there was a strong sense of "Europessimism," and fear that Europe's declining share of world product reflected deep cultural and structural problems.

ECONOMIC PROBLEMS

During the first quarter century of the postwar period, Europe grew at a rapid rate of nearly 5 percent each year, more than twice as fast as it did in the nine-teenth century. After 1973, however, its growth rate was halved and then dropped even further in the depressed early 1980s. Growth slowed in all industrial countries after the oil shock of 1973, but "the difference was that in Europe, unemployment kept on rising all through the 1970s and early 1980s," reaching 11 percent in 1986. Unfortunately, Europe had specialized in the medium-technology products that faced heightened competition from Asian producers. "In the information industries that were becoming the locus of global industrial growth, European firms performed poorly."[5] According to a 1984 report to the European Parliament,

> In the early 1970s, Europe was suddenly confronted with a threefold challenge: inflation, the oil shock, and competition from new industries. . . . Europe seemed suddenly to be caught up in the web of its past, adopting what the psychologists might call an escapist posture. It tried to ignore the realities of the new situation by boosting wages at the expense of profits and encouraging consumption at the expense of investment.[6]

The term "Eurosclerosis" was coined to refer to the condition of the European welfare states when government share of GNP averaged 51 percent—in contrast to 38 percent in the United States and 35 percent in Japan—and when there existed a general inability to foster growth and create jobs.[7] By the time the Treaty of Rome marked its twenty-fifth anniversary in 1982, "the Community had reached its nadir. *The Economist* used a grave's headstone for the buried EC [European Community] on its cover."[8] As worrisome as continued high unemployment was Europe's declining position in high technology. While it had the largest share of global exports—20 percent in 1982—its share of high-technology exports dropped from 56 percent in 1970 to 47 percent in 1981. Japan nearly doubled its share of high-tech exports over a similar period.[9] In 1985, "high-tech goods—roughly defined as drugs, chemicals, electronics and telecoms—contributed about 22 percent to the value-added of the European Community's industry. This compares with about 29 percent for America and Japan."[10] Europe in the mid-1980s had the lowest absolute and relative levels of innovative activities of the Western industrial areas.[11] In the words of Michel Albert and James Ball, "we have to look back in history to understand the implications of this sudden sterility, this dramatic eclipsing of Europe. For the first time since the eighteenth century, the major formative initiatives of an industrial revolution are not originating in Europe. Europe is missing out on the third industrial revolution."[12]

This sense of decline and of falling behind Japan and the United States helped to stimulate a European response. Concern about lost momentum had been growing in the late 1970s and early 1980s. Finally, in June 1985, the Commission of the European Community published a proposal, *Completing the Internal Market*, which was approved by the Council of Ministers at the end of the year. The plan involved action on some three hundred measures to remove remaining physical, technical, and fiscal barriers to the movement of goods and persons by 1992. Governments were instructed to end protection of domestic industries by discriminatory procurement, subsidies, licensing, technical specifications, and restrictions on movement. The hope was that a larger market would improve the ability of European firms to compete with those of the United States and Japan. According to an Italian industrialist, "the center of economic and political weight had moved in the past years to the Pacific. Europe had no option but to get together. For Europe, 1992 is a deadline for not being dead."[13]

One of the first effects of the new initiative was to replace the "Europessimism" of the early 1980s with a more optimistic outlook. A study commissioned by the European Community estimated that in 1988 delays caused by borders cost Europe 0.25 percent of gross domestic product; different regulatory restrictions cost 2 percent of GDP; and gains achievable through greater economies of scale were worth 2 to 3.5 percent of GDP. In addition, the study claimed that the European market would gain from greater competition.[14] Others were more skeptical about the scale of the economic benefits from removing remaining barriers to a single market. The economies of scale already available in Europe are adequate in most industries. Some feared that unwieldy large companies would be formed at the European level. Mergers that create "arthritic European champion firms" in place of "sclerotic national champion firms" would not solve Europe's problems.[15] Yet even if the direct economic benefits have been overestimated, the 1992 program has changed both public psychology and private investment decisions in Europe.

POLITICAL INTEGRATION

There are uncertainties about the magnitude of the political and economic effects of the 1992 program. Removal of barriers could merely eliminate governmental interference in free markets, or it could be the first step toward a federalized Europe with a common currency, central bank, common social policies, and a single defense and foreign policy. In 1988, Jacques Delors, the French Socialist president of the European Commission, suggested to the European Parliament that 1992 was a step toward creation of "an embryo European government," which would mean that 80 percent of economic and social decision making would involve Brussels within ten years.[16] But his vision ran contrary to that of Britain's Prime Minister Margaret Thatcher. As her chancellor of the exchequer Nigel Lawson replied in 1989,

> the contrasts between the two rival visions of Europe have become very clear. On the one hand an over-regulated, bureaucratic, protectionist Europe, where uniform standards are enforced by new directives and new regulations from Brussels. . . . On the other hand, there is the vision of a deregulated, free-market open Europe . . . one driven by consumer choice, by transferring sovereignty not to Brussels but to the people.[17]

Between these two polar visions lies a prospect of gradual erosion of national sovereignty. In the view of *The Economist*, "anybody who considers this a lily-livered approach to the building of Europe underestimates the erosion of sovereignty the EEC [European Economic Community] countries are already committed to accept by 1993."[18] The twelve national governments of Europe have agreed to six amendments to the Treaty of Rome that increase the number of issues on which the European Council of Ministers can decide by majority vote rather than requiring unanimity. There is agreement that environmental control and coordination of foreign policy are community matters, and that the ultimate goal is a European Union. The European Parliament, Court, and Commission already have significant powers. But rather than debating visions, Europe is advised to "let reality determine how far these things will lead."[19]

Although a pragmatic approach has carried Europe a long way since 1950, it is less clear that it will carry the twelve nations to federation in the near future. In the late 1940s, after the third major Franco-German war in the seventy years since the unification of Germany, many Europeans realized the need for a new approach but embittered national feelings prohibited serious discussion of federation. The genius of the French planner Jean Monnet showed in his scheme for step-by-step progress in tying the European economies together. In 1950, the Schuman Plan began the integration of the coal and steel industries of six European nations. When more ambitious plans for a European defense community foundered on the shoals of French nationalism and fear of Germany, the six nations in 1957 signed the Treaty of Rome, which provided for gradual development of a Common Market and, less successfully, cooperation in the peaceful development of nuclear energy. The treaty provided for phased reduction of tariffs, a common external tariff, a common agricultural support system, harmonization of many regulations, and coordination of economic policy.[20]

The heart of Monnet's design was the *engrenage* or engagement in which the gradual meshing together of the little wheels of daily social and economic cooperation would eventually turn the bigger wheels of defense and foreign policy. The crucial point was to build on success. In order to preserve gains in areas already integrated, national governments would allow the process to spill over into new areas. At least that was the theory, and it worked until the mid-1960s. In 1965, however, French President Charles de Gaulle set a limit on the development of majority voting and the growth of the bureaucratic powers of the commission in Brussels. The Common Market continued, but the theory of *engrenage* came into question. Further progress could not be accomplished by functionalist stealth but only by agreements in national capitals.

However, this does not belittle the real accomplishments of the European Community. Over thirty years, intracommunity trade in Europe grew from a third to a half of member states' total foreign trade.[21] The Common Agricultural Policy, which accounted for two-thirds of the European Community's budget, was wasteful of resources but it provided social and political stability. The 1950s' proposition that the Common Market was a deal between French agriculture and German industry has been generalized beyond that core pair of countries. A number of joint efforts in technology development and space have met with varying degrees of success, and the Community's expansion to include Greece in 1981 and the Iberian states in 1986 helped to consolidate democratic politics in the southern tier of Europe.

A European monetary system (EMS) was inaugurated in 1979, after failures of monetary coordination earlier in the 1970s, but it did not include Britain and several smaller European countries. The EMS helped to protect its members against some of the wilder fluctuations of the dollar in the 1980s, but it did not represent a central bank or single currency. Like the gold standard in the Bretton Woods system, the EMS character was determined by a central country—West Germany—that did not wish to give up its monetary autonomy. "Germany appears to have pursued its own monetary targets without attempting to cooperate with other countries, while the other countries . . . have followed Germany's policies, changed exchange rates, or imposed capital controls."[22] In 1983, when faced with leaving the EMS or altering its own expansionary policy, the French

Socialist government deliberately chose the discipline of EMS. Since that time, consultations among European central bankers have increased considerably. In 1989, a committee chaired by Jacques Delors recommended a three-stage plan that called for economic and monetary union by establishing a single central bank, a single currency, common monetary policies, and coordinated economic policy.[23] Britain rejected the proposal as too intrusive on its sovereignty, but some increase in monetary coordination could occur without formal change.

While this record is impressive, it does not validate the logic in letting success spill over from one area to another until the little successes mesh with the big wheels of national politics. The European nations coordinate foreign policy initiatives but only to a limited extent. The 1992 project continues in the tradition of technocratic progress and transnational bargains among the corporate leaders in Europe. But there is little evidence that the process has altered mass politics in welfare states, half of whose governments are socialist and half conservative, and whose leaders are geared to totally different electoral cycles. Although there has been some growth of European-wide loyalties, it has not reached a level that can transform electoral and mass politics away from the separate national processes that exist today.[24] Perhaps the functionalist logic will work more clearly in the future than in the past. But in both 1957 and 1985, a combination of internal failure and threats from the external environment led to initiatives that preserved the European idea; they did not radically transform European politics.

Of course, the world outside Europe will continue to change, and some such changes could initiate a dramatic increase in European unity. A change in the role of the United States is often cited as a possibility. The United States has always had mixed effects on European unity. In the early postwar period, the United States encouraged European integration to reduce conflicts, to halt the encroachment of communism, and to make alliance management easier. During the Nixon administration, the United States became more concerned about the directions that an independent Europe might take. But so long as Europeans have been threatened by a Soviet superpower, they have been unwilling to give up the American nuclear guarantee made credible by the presence of U.S. troops in Europe. Dependent in part on the United States for their defense, European leaders have oscillated between the twin fears of American abandonment and being trapped in a superpower war. These fears were stronger in Germany than in Britain or France, for Germany would be on the front line of any Warsaw Pact attack. This situation greatly complicated European defense cooperation.

In principle, the decline in the perceived Soviet threat could reduce the tensions between Atlanticist and Europeanist tendencies among the major nations. In such a world, the United States might decide that it could withdraw its guarantee of the defense of Western Europe, which, in turn, might catalyse a dramatic increase in European unity. While such a possibility exists, it is far from certain for two major reasons. One is uncertainty over the future military role of the Soviet Union. Despite arms reductions and Gorbachev's policy of greater tolerance of change in Eastern Europe, the Soviet Union retains an impressive conventional military capability on the Continent. Faced with the Soviet military capacity, as well as the possible reversal of Gorbachev's new intentions, European leaders are not yet ready to give up their

American insurance policy. In contrast to the 1960s, the strongest suspicions of the Soviet Union and the greatest concern to keep the American presence in Europe in the 1980s are found in France.

Even if Gorbachev's reforms persist, Eastern Europe evolves peacefully toward stability, and the threat from the Soviet Union continues to decline, European desires for an American presence may continue because of the German problem. West Germany is the largest and economically most powerful country in the European Community. In the 1950s, Konrad Adenauer chose to tie the Federal Republic to the West and to defer the likelihood of German reunification to the indefinite future. The prospect of a united Germany following an independent policy in the heart of Europe is sometimes exaggerated, but it remains a source of anxiety. The potential nuclear status of a reunited Germany intensifies such concerns. And so long as these concerns persist in Moscow and in other European capitals, an American presence in Europe can have an important stabilizing effect on fears and expectations.[25] In such a world, East–West détente may not necessarily lead to European defense unity. On the contrary, many West Europeans fear that West German preoccupation with events in Eastern Europe will limit the integration of the European community.

Of course, there are other concerns as well, such as trade frictions leading to tariff wars and eventually to the breakup of NATO. American withdrawal from the defense of Europe would certainly give Western Europe a shock, but its effects are unpredictable. The disappearance of a Soviet threat and withdrawal of American troops could leave behind "a Europe [bound in ways] more akin to the loose ties that bind the Nordic Union, with Europeans following the Scandinavian pattern of pacifism and moralism in international affairs."[26] If so, Europe would not be a new great power.

In any event, European integration is likely to progress gradually rather than dramatically. "If asked, 'In 20 or 30 years, will there be a federal Europe?', most French politicians would, if they were honest, say 'no.' For the foreseeable future, they believe, the Council of Ministers will be the Community's centre of decision-making. . . . Federal Europe is not considered to be around the corner."[27] Such conventional expectations may prove to be wrong, but if the past is any indicator, a federal Europe is a long way off. Even if 1992 lives up to expectations, major political questions remain. In the view of a former official, "the European Community is more likely to continue as a permanent arrangement between states than to emerge as a new state in its own right."[28] While the exaggerated Euro-optimism for 1992 is better than the exaggerated Europessimism of the early 1980s, appraisals of power that do not exaggerate are better yet. If European unity remains elusive, then speculation about Europe as the leading power in the twenty-first century is exaggerated as well.

JAPAN

According to *Newsweek* in 1989, "in banks, boardrooms and government bureaus around the world, the uneasy question is whether Japan is about to become a superpower, supplanting America as the colossus of the Pacific and perhaps even the world's No. 1 nation."[29] The question is not new. In 1970, Herman Kahn predicted that Japan would soon become a nuclear superpower in a multipolar world. He believed that "the 1970s and 1980s will see a transition in the role of Japan in world affairs not unlike the change brought about in European and world affairs in the 1870s by the rise of Prussia."[30] More recently, Daniel Burstein argued that "today Japan needs the United States both for its markets and for military protection. . . . Tomorrow, when Japan no longer needs protection, it will be free to be even more ruthless in its economic competition." Burstein speculates that we may "end up with American and Japanese missiles pointed at each other."[31]

Many Americans and Japanese believe that the United States is in decline. In a 1989 poll reported in the New York Times, 48 percent of the Americans and 49 percent of the Japanese surveyed held that view.[32] However, the Japanese are less confident about the future of Japan. A 1988 poll involving several countries revealed a relative lack of confidence of the Japanese in their country's future. In response to questions about Japan's prospects for the twenty-first century in military power, economic power, and political leadership, fewer Japanese than foreigners expected Japan to become stronger.[33] Many Japanese warn against predicting that a Pax Nipponica will replace Pax Americana. While some write of America as being in a "relentless downhill slide," few see Japan replacing the United States as the great power of the next century. More frequent are descriptions of a "U.S.-centered Pax Consortis" with Japan in a supporting role.[34] As Takashi Inoguchi of Tokyo University put it, "in speaking of the decline of the Roman Empire, Edward Gibbon wryly noted, 'this intolerable situation lasted for about three hundred years.' Pax Americana will probably do likewise."[35] In fact, the Japanese frequently refer to the United States as having sokojikara or "reserve power."[36]

THE GROWTH OF JAPANESE POWER

Japan's past performance is unquestionable. Its power has risen dramatically—in little over a century, Japan changed from a closed, static society to the second largest economy in the world. On the eve of World War I, Japan accounted for 2.5 percent of world industrial production; on the eve of World War II, Japan had reached a 5-percent share analogous to that of France in 1914. Devastated by the war, Japan did not regain its prewar share until 1964, but it then doubled its share in the next decade and a half.[37] From 1950 to 1973, the annual real growth of Japan's GNP "*averaged* 10 percent, probably the highest sustained rate of increase that the world has ever seen."[38] Japan benefited from a large pool of labor ready to move out of agriculture, a literate population, a high savings rate, and the political and social capability to absorb and adapt foreign technology. In the decade following Japan's first postwar recession in 1974, growth slowed to a still respectable 4 percent per year. Further, Japan maintained its high growth by transforming its economy from labor-intensive heavy industry to knowledge-intensive exports despite such shocks as exchange rate and oil price changes.

In 1950, Japan's economy was one-twentieth the size of the American economy; three decades later it had grown to more than half the size of the U.S. economy. In 1988, Japan's per-capita GNP of $19,200, measured in official exchange rates, surpassed the United States for the first time. (When corrected for purchasing power, however, the average Japanese had $13,200 compared to $18,200 for the average American. Such corrections reflect the reality that Americans have twice as many cars per person or twice as much space in their dwellings.)[39] Japan is the world's largest creditor, has the second largest economy, and is the second largest exporter of manufactured goods. It is also the second largest contributor to the United Nations budget and to the International Monetary Fund. The world's ten largest banks (in terms of deposits) are headquartered in Tokyo, and with a foreign aid budget of $10 billion, Japan displaced the United States ($9.2 billion) as the world's largest donor. Further, Japan is the fourth largest direct investor in the United States, and Japanese capital finances a third of the U.S. budget deficit. With a budget of $30 billion, Japan's military expenditures rank third globally, ahead of Britain and France. In technology, Japan is roughly equal with the United States, but ahead in some areas of manufacturing technology.[40]

Since power is relative, Japan's rise in power reflects a decline in American power in the bilateral U.S.-Japan relationship, even though U.S. power has not changed significantly in relation to the rest of the world. As shown earlier in figure 5.1 (p. 142), Japan's share of global product has come from the shares of countries other than the United States, but there has also been a shift in U.S.-Japan power relations. Given Japan's financial role, American leaders have become more sensitive to Japanese opinions. For example, the 1984 collapse in Chicago of the Continental Bank of Illinois occurred in part because the bank made unwise loans to the energy sector, but the collapse was precipitated when frightened Japanese investors withdrew their funds after reading poorly translated news reports based on rumors. More recently, American Treasury Secretary Nicholas Brady suggested that the October 1987 stock-market crash may have been influenced by Japanese sales of U.S. government bonds because of worries about the American currency.[41] Clearly, Japan's financial power has increased.

Nevertheless, the resulting change in U.S.-Japan power relations is sometimes overstated. Daniel Burstein claims that Japanese resentment over the Reagan administration's trade sanctions in April 1987 led Japanese politicians and officials to the idea of a boycott. Lighter than normal purchases of U.S. Treasury bills did push up interest rates in the May 1987 auction, but the evidence for a conspiracy is scant.[42] As *The Economist* points out, all investors, not only the Japanese, were worried about the effect of the American deficit on the value of the dollar, and they required a higher interest premium to cover the added risk. Moreover, "Japanese investors bought a quarter of the auction—not exactly a boycott."[43] Occasionally, Japanese officials question "whether Japan as the largest creditor can and should use its position as leverage for imposing discipline on the debtor nation," but they are also aware of the ways that economic interdependence limits the power of creditors over debtors. "Japanese financial institutions are captives of the American market. When you lend too much money, you have a vital interest in that economy's staying healthy, so you have to cooperate."[44] Another Japanese economist lamented, "the money goes to America because you are fundamentally strong."[45]

However, the increased financial power of Japan has led to some changes in Japanese behavior: "Japan used to leave global politics to the United States. Now it is eager to use its yen aid to become a strategic player itself."[46] With two-thirds of its assistance concentrated in Asia, Japan is emerging as a major power broker in the region.[47] Among the new initiatives, Japan has used its aid to press for reforms in Burma, has asked for a larger vote in international financial institutions, has proposed its own scheme for handling the debts of poor nations, and has provided civilian assistance to UN peacekeeping operations. In the words of one observer, by the late 1980s, "Tokyo is stepping out a bit from Washington's shadow."[48]

Finance and manufacturing, of course, are not the only sources of power. Indeed, Japan's impressive strength in manufacturing may give it less effective influence in the manufacturing area than in the financial area because of its dependence on access to American (and to a lesser degree European) markets. The trade balance in Japan's favor is a poor index of the underlying latent weakness in the Japanese position. In terms of relative vulnerability in the interdependence, Japan is better off in the financial area than in the manufacturing area. Overall, though, "Japan and the other Asian industrialized states are nowhere near as self-sufficient as the United States or even Europe so, as creditors, they will suffer the greater damage to their prospects if world trade contracts under the system's ever-growing burden of uncollectable debt."[49] A balanced appraisal of the relative power positions of the United States and Japan requires a broader assessment.

JAPAN'S POWER RESOURCES

In terms of basic resources, Japan is roughly the size of the state of California. Its insular position eases its defense problems, but the Japanese archipelago is not rich in natural resources. Japan's population is half that of the United States, but 95 percent of the Japanese complete high school compared to 75 percent of Americans. A good deal of Japan's success has been due to the substitution of human skills for missing natural resources. This is likely to become increasingly important as knowledge replaces raw materials as the key economic factor in the information revolution.

Japan remains heavily dependent on imports of raw materials and exports to more populous markets. Closure of foreign markets and disruption of energy imports raise questions of Japan's vulnerability. Although it adapted successfully to the two oil disruptions in the 1970s, it remains 80 percent dependent on imported energy compared to 14 percent for the United States.[50] A continental scale economy is part of what the Japanese mean when they speak of America's power reserve. Many believe that "shortages of land and resources preclude Japan from ever becoming a classic imperialist state."[51]

Perhaps the most striking feature of Japan's power resources is its relative military weakness. During the postwar occupation, the United States introduced a constitution in which "the Japanese people forever renounce war as a sovereign right of the nation." Prime Minister Shigeru Yoshida and his successors turned necessity into a highly successful strategy of remaining lightly armed, relying on an American security guarantee, and focusing on economic growth and exports. Ironically, at the time of the Korean War, the United States tried to persuade Japan to rebuild its military forces to help contain the Soviet Union, but Yoshida successfully resisted the American pressure. Subsequent governments reinforced the Yoshida Doctrine by forswearing the possession or basing of nuclear weapons, forswearing arms exports, and restricting military expenditures to about 1 percent of GNP.[52]

The trading-state strategy has been enormously successful for Japan. However, as a former high-ranking

Japanese official noted, "there will be no free world and no free trading system if the United States does not preserve them for us. . . . The best Japan can aspire to is 'vice-president.' "[53] In the 1980s, Japan gradually increased its military posture, in part as a result of American prodding. Prime Minister Nakasone agreed to share military technology with the United States, brought defense spending slightly above the 1 percent of GNP limit, announced Japan would be responsible for the protection of sea lanes out to 1,000 miles, and increased defense spending by nearly 6 percent per year. When pensions are added (as in NATO accounting), Japan's defense expenditure jumps to third place. In part, this ranking reflects the enormous increase in the value of the yen after 1985. Before that, Japan's budget was eighth in size. The actual forces remain modest, with a 150,000-person "ground self-defense force" and another 90,000 sea and air personnel. By the early 1990s, Japan plans to build 62 destroyers and 430 combat aircraft.[54] Japan's growing capability in military technology gives it bargaining power in this area with the United States as well as with other countries.[55]

Japan's domestic political consensus, however, remains antimilitary. As Motoo Shiina, a parliamentary leader on defense matters, puts it, "When the words 'stronger military' are said, people react negatively."[56] Shimizu Ikutaro, a rare proponent of Japan becoming a nuclear state, laments the prevailing anti-nuclear consensus: "politicians of all persuasions in their utterances in the [National] Diet, university professors in their articles for highbrow periodicals, and newspaper writers in their editorials all endorse this idea, never questioning the legitimacy of the postwar thought that denied Japan its status as a state."[57] A Western correspondent reports that "in the five years I spent in Japan, I did not come across one politician bold enough, or foolish enough, to deliver a pro-nukes speech."[58] To the contrary, some Japanese hoped that President Reagan's Strategic Defense Initiative (SDI) would create a technology that would make nuclear weapons obsolete; for in a world without nuclear weapons, Japan's power would be enhanced.

Of course, strategies can change, and Japan does possess the economic and technical capability to develop a significant strategic and conventional force within a decade. Paul Kennedy believes that those "acquainted with the pattern of 'war and change in world politics' would find it unsurprising if, one day, a different political leadership in Tokyo decided to turn its economic strength into a large degree of military strength."[59] Others, such as Richard Rosecrance and John Mueller, argue that such conventional wisdom fails to take into account the changing nature of world politics at the end of the twentieth century.[60] In this respect, it is worth noting that long lags between economic and military strength have occurred in the past. For instance, the United States became the world's largest economy in the 1870s but it did not become a leading military power until seventy years later. While Japan may change its military strategy some day, it will have to face external as well as internal constraints. Japanese rearmament would stimulate fears and countermeasures by its Asian neighbors, which would limit the gains sought by re-armament. Such a strategy, then, remains unlikely unless Japan is made to feel abandoned by the United States.

Japan's deep-rooted economic strength is impressive. The long-run orientation of its economic leaders, an emphasis on quality, and a detailed knowledge of markets were born in the Meiji period of the nineteenth century.[61] Japan also pioneered in the practices of the "developmental state," in which government targets, assists, and protects infant industries until they are able to compete on a global scale. In the early postwar years, the Ministry of International Trade and Industry (MITI) played an important role, although that role has diminished over time.[62] The result has been an economy marked by a high rate of growth, high savings, lower consumption, and an export imbalance with the rest of the world (see table 5.2).

JAPAN'S FUTURE POWER

Most important about the future of the Japanese economy is whether Japan will be able to move away from its neo-mercantilist strategy rapidly enough to avoid significant retaliation. In 1949, the Japanese slogan was "export or die"; today, it is "import or die."[63] Or, as Peter Drucker notes of Japanese neo-mercantilist policies, "thirty years ago they brilliantly matched the realities of Japan's economy and its needs," but Japan can no longer rely on export-led growth.[64] Externally, the Japanese neo-mercantilist strategy is in danger of stimulating protectionist reactions. Japan has become

TABLE 5.2
Japanese and American Economies, 1980s

	Japan	United States
GNP (1986)	$2 trillion	$4.2 trillion
Growth rate (1982–1986)	3.7%	2.7%
Gross capital formation (percent of GNP)	28%	18%
Private consumption (percent of GNP)	58%	66%
Exports (percent of GNP)	11.5%	7%
Imports (percent of GNP)	7.5%	10%

SOURCE: Keizai Koho Center, *Japan 1989* (Tokyo, 1989), p. 13.

too large a player to have a free ride in the international trading system any longer.

Japan has a two-tiered economy with a highly efficient manufacturing sector and very inefficient protected agriculture and consumer services sectors. Farmers, representing 6 percent of the population, have 18 percent of the vote, which they use to impose high food and land prices.[65] In addition, Japan's inefficient distribution system helps to keep prices high and to dampen consumer demand. "Because of the high cost of domestic nontradables," the Japanese have "much lower overall living standards than their efficiency at producing tradable goods would suggest."[66] High housing prices and an inadequate pension system help to keep personal savings rates high,[67] but an aging Japanese population will add a burden on the economy. The Japanese complain that their universities do not meet American standards of higher education.[68] They argue that educational reforms are needed if Japan is to encourage creativity rather than imitation. Further, although women comprise 40 percent of Japan's work force, their talents are severely underutilized. Japanese leaders believe that management needs to become more internationally oriented in terms of production rather than exports. About 5 percent of Japanese industrial production takes place overseas, in contrast with 20 percent for the United States.[69] According to former MITI official Naohiro Amayo, "if Japan remains forever wedded to traditional Japanese management, that same management style that contributed to the rise of Japan in the 20th century could be the cause of its fall in the 21st century."[70] Other Japanese worry about the rapid aging of the society, the sclerosis of its once flexible elite, and reduced foreign tolerance of Japan's mercantilist policies.

Will Japan change to a post-mercantilist strategy? Some signs are encouraging. Of four political attitudes toward Japanese foreign policy, two remain weak: right-wing nationalism and left-wing neutralism. Of the two positions that compete for the centerground, the internationalists are putting the strongest pressure on the traditional neo-mercantilist position.[71] The internationalist position was set forth in the 1986 report of the Maekawa Commission, chaired by a former governor of the Bank of Japan. The report marked a bureaucratic consensus on turning toward domestic-oriented growth reinforced by the rising exchange rate of the yen. (Ironically, internationalism in Japan means developing the domestic market as a way to reduce large export surpluses.) Although manufactured imports accounted for only 31 percent of Japan's imports in 1985, they rose to 51 percent by 1988.[72] Japan has an impressive tradition of structural adjustment, and the trend today seems to be in the direction of adaptations to maintain Japan's economic strength. The main question will be whether the rate will be fast enough.

However, even if Japan fails to make the changes needed to help maintain the open international economy from which it has benefited, it will still derive power resources from its advanced position in science and technology, although it will not be able to exploit them as well. In several areas, including consumer electronics, communications equipment, and professional instruments, Japan's technology-intensive exports exceed those of the United States, but the United States maintains a substantial lead in aircraft, chemicals, drugs, and computing machines.[73] Table 5.3 summarizes the performances of the United States, Japan, and West Germany in various areas of science and technology. While

TABLE 5.3

Science and Technology Performance (1986–1989)

	United States	Japan	West Germany
Research and development expenditures	$100 billion	$39 billion	$19 billion
Percent of GNP	2.6%	2.9%	2.8%
Nondefense research and development expenditure	$68 billion	$39 billion	$18 billion
Number of scientists	1.4 million	0.4 million	0.1 million
Number of engineers	2.2 million	1.1 million	0.5 million
Share of world scientific literature	35%	7%	6%
Share of U.S. patents	54%	19%	10%
Share of high-tech exports	21%	20%	16%

SOURCE: National Science Foundation, *International Science and Technology Update, 1988* (Washington, D.C.: GPO, 1989), pp. 2, 28, 62, 64, 72, 74, 92, 94.

the United States remains ahead of Japan on all indicators, Japan's growth has been impressive, particularly in applications and exports. From 1973 to 1989, the United States increased its expenditures on research and development from 2.2 percent of GNP to 2.6 percent, but Japan increased its expenditures from 2 to 2.9 percent in those years. Japan's share of patents granted in the United States doubled from 9 percent in 1975 to 19 percent in 1986, whereas the U.S. share of patents slipped from 65 to 54 percent. Japan's share of scientific literature rose only slightly from 5 percent in 1975 to 7 percent in 1984, whereas the U.S. share dipped slightly from 37 to 35 percent.[74]

While some economists raise questions about Japan's economy, the most important questions about Japan's future power focus on its three less-tangible power sources: national cohesion, universalistic culture, and the ability to make use of international institutions. Currently, Japan is a one-dimensional economic power. It will face a number of internal and external problems if it attempts in the future to transform its economic power into military power. However, Japan will be able to extend the political effects of its economic power with much lower costs if it develops its effectiveness in private and public international institutions. For example, in the 1970s, Japanese foreign policy was "hesitant and withdrawn," but participation in the new system of Western summit meetings gradually gave the Japanese new confidence.[75] Thus far, though, Japan has lagged in developing its strength in international institutions.

In terms of national cohesion, Japan is remarkably homogeneous and faces none of the problems of nationalism that limit the power of the European Community and, to a lesser extent, the Soviet Union. Japan is able to achieve high educational standards, in part, because it is a homogeneous, middle-class society: "New entrants to the Japanese work force are generally literate, numerate, and prepared to learn."[76] It enjoyed political stability under the Liberal Democratic party for nearly four decades, although this one-party dominance may have contributed to the recent scandals that have weakened Japan's political leadership. Moreover, the standoff between Japanese political factions and interest groups inhibits change and leads to reliance on foreign pressure to stimulate change. Kent Calder refers to Japan as "a reactive state," and Nakatani Iwao argues that "the pace of change has been slowed and international friction intensified by clannish bureaucrats who, with the support of industry-aligned members of the National Diet, have opposed specific reform measures even while endorsing the idea of reform."[77] Despite these problems, however, Japan has made significant structural changes in the past. Japanese culture has encouraged higher levels of education, improved government-business relations and labor-management cooperation, and a consistent pursuit of long-term goals that have served Japan well in an information-based era. Indeed, Japan has been a pioneer in many of the new forms of industrial organization that are necessary for rapid and flexible use of information.

On the other side of the coin of national cohesion is Japan's cultural insularity. Tokyo University Professor Seizaburo Sato argues that Japan has no strategy for dealing with the outside world: "to be a truly great power, a nation's culture must have relevance to other cultures."[78] James Fallows warns that "Japan's idea that it is separate from the world is its greatest vulnerability," and Clyde Haberman similarly argues that this sense of uniqueness may "paralyze [the] Japanese when they come to grips with the outside world."[79] The point should not be overstated. Uniqueness has not prevented Japan from surveying and learning from the rest of the world, but insularity does limit soft power resources if it alienates other nations and creates awkwardness and hesitation when action is needed.

A Japanese commission argues that internationalization will require (1) removing the constraints on the movement of people, such as the strict barriers to immigration; (2) dropping the Japanese myth of uniqueness; (3) encouraging greater diversity and creativity; (4) a greater tolerance of things foreign; and (5) a more logical style in personal communications.[80] Some of these changes are under way among younger Japanese, but the pace is slower than is needed for effective transformation of Japan's economic power into the ability to wield influence in international institutions.[81] While private Japanese corporations have become increasingly important in world markets, the Japanese government has been slower in establishing its influence in international organizations, and cultural insensitivities have hindered Japan's relations with its Asian neighbors.

For a variety of reasons, then, Japan seems likely to remain a one-dimensional great power rather than a new hegemonic challenger of the United States. Whether Japan's power is gradually transformed into institutional channels that reinforce international stability or into more problematic military directions will depend to a considerable extent on American reactions to Japan's rise and on American willingness to share power in international institutions. Protectionist responses or pressures that offend Japan's national pride could gradually transform the current consensus. Competition with China in Asia might also encourage Japan's domestic interest in military strength. Thus far, however, the new nationalism of Japan's younger urbanized generations is not militaristic; rather, it is "a soft nationalism, born of a mix of callous materialism, self-satisfaction at Japan's economic achievement and a waning of contrition. . . ."[82] Most Japanese do not envision world domination. But this is not the only strand of Japanese nationalism. There is also a more assertive and ethnocentric approach. In 1989, for example, Akio Morita, the head of Sony Corporation, and Shintaro Ishihara, a prominent politician, published a book urging Japan to stand up and say "no" to the United States. They attribute criticism of Japan to foreign racism. Moreover, Japanese journalists report that some editors solicit only articles critical of the United States and resist more balanced accounts of the causes of trade frictions.[83] Which of these views will prevail over the next decade remains an open question. *The Economist* makes a case for the more optimistic outcome:

Pax Nipponica will complement Pax Americana, not supersede it in the way Pax Americana replaced Pax Britannica. Britain's economy was one-seventh the size of America's in 1950; Japan's today is two-thirds the size of America's. More important, the Japanese and American economies have become enmeshed in a way that the British and American ones never were.[84]

In short, the traditional models of power transition and hegemonic change may be profoundly misleading about the end of this century, possibly leading to self-defeating American policy responses. The problem is not that one or the other of America's postwar allies will challenge the United States for hegemony, but that the United States will have to adapt to new patterns of interdependence and new political agendas in the twenty-first century.

PART III

NEW
CHALLENGES

6

The Transformation of Power

What can we say about changes in world power in the coming decades? Since the early 1970s, political leaders and analysts have often used the term multipolarity in a loose and confusing way. If they use it to mean a return to a balance among a number of nations with roughly equal power resources analogous to the pre-1945 period, then this is not likely to be the situation at the turn of the century. In terms of power resources, all the potential challengers except the United States are deficient in some respect (see table 6.1). If economic reforms reverse Soviet decline, if Japan develops a full-fledged nuclear and conventional military capability, or if Europe experiences a dramatic increase in unification, there may be a return to classical multipolarity in

TABLE 6.1

*Power Resources of the Major Contenders, 1990**

Source of Power	United States	Soviet Union	Europe	Japan	China
Tangible					
Basic resources	strong	strong	strong	*medium*	strong
Military	strong	strong	*medium*	*weak*	*medium*
Economic	strong	*medium*	strong	strong	*medium*
Science/technology	strong	*medium*	strong	strong	*weak*
Intangible					
National cohesion	strong	*medium*	*weak*	strong	strong
Universalistic culture	strong	*medium*	strong	*medium*	*medium*
International institutions	strong	*medium*	strong	*medium*	*medium*

*Sources of weakness are italicized.

the twenty-first century. But barring such changes, the United States is likely to retain a full range of power resources considerably greater than those of the other countries, and the Soviet Union may lose its superpower status. In this sense, the coming century may see continued American preponderance. Although many observers believe that the United States will maintain its preeminence in the twenty-first century,[1] this book argues that U.S. hegemony is not likely. Rather, the United States and other countries are likely to see major changes in the sources of power in world politics, which will force them all to face new difficulties in achieving their goals.

INTERDEPENDENCE AND CHANGING POLITICS

As earlier chapters have shown, the United States is likely to retain its superpower status in terms of traditional resources. However, as we saw in chapter 1, proof of power lies not in resources but in the changed behavior of nations. Thus, the critical question for the future United States is not whether it will start the next century as a superpower with the largest supply of resources, but to what extent it will be able to control the political environment and to get other nations to do what it wants. The tasks involved in maintaining super-power status will become more complicated in the coming decades, involving a far broader range of issues and a wider variety of players.

Some trends in world politics suggest that it will be more difficult in the future for *any* great power to control the political environment and to achieve what it wants from others. The problem for the United States will be less the rising challenge of another major power than a general diffusion of power. Whereas nineteenth-century Britain faced new challengers, the twenty-first-century United States will face new challenges.

As world politics becomes more complex, the power of all major states to achieve their purposes will be diminished. To understand what is happening to the United States today, the distinction between power over other countries and power over outcomes must be clear. Although the United States still has leverage over particular countries, it has far less leverage over the more complex system as a whole. It is less well placed to attain unilaterally the goals it prefers, but it is not alone in this situation. All states will have to confront the changing nature of world politics in the future. Such changes, however, are not entirely new. For example, the rapid growth of private actors operating across international borders, whether large corporations or political groups, was widely recognized in the early 1970s. One analyst, Seyom Brown, saw the emergence of "a polyarchy in which nation-states, subnational

groups, and transnational special interests and communities would all be vying for the support and loyalty of
individuals, and conflicts would have to be resolved primarily on the basis of ad hoc bargaining in a shifting
context of power relationships."[2] Even Henry Kissinger,
with his deeply rooted belief in classical balance-of-
power politics, argued in 1975 that "we are entering a
new era. Old international patterns are crumbling. . . .
The world has become interdependent in economics, in
communications, in human aspirations."[3]

By the late 1970s, however, the American mood in
politics had shifted. Iran's seizure of the American
embassy and the Soviet invasion of Afghanistan in 1979
seemed to restore the role of military force and the primacy of the traditional security agenda. Ronald
Reagan's election to the presidency accentuated these
trends in the early 1980s. The U.S. defense budget
increased in real terms for five straight years, arms control was downgraded, and nuclear forces and deterrence
aroused public anxieties. Conventional military force
was used successfully, albeit against the extremely weak
states of Grenada and Libya. The shifting agenda of
world politics discredited the 1970s' concern with interdependence and restored the traditional emphasis on
military power. But the world of the 1980s was not a
return to the 1950s. Public mood shifted more than
power resources. Interdependence in finance and trade
continued to increase rapidly, and trade deficits and
international debt put new pressures on governments.
Despite the political rhetoric of the time, the relations
between the two superpowers did not return to the
Cold War period. In the 1980s, the United States and
Soviet Union had far more contact and communication,
both private and governmental, than had ever existed
in the 1950s.[4]

In a sense, the difference between the 1970s and 1980s was merely the latest oscillation of a recurring argument between realists and liberals over international relations.[5] Realism, with its focus on states' use of military force to balance power in the international system of states, has been the dominant strand, dating back to such classic philosophers as Thucydides, Machiavelli, and Hobbes. The liberal tradition has been the secondary strand, associated with such thinkers as Grotius, Cobden, and Woodrow Wilson. It stresses the impact on states of societal contacts, economic interdependence, and international institutions. In their simplest form, liberal theories of stability have been easily discredited. A high level of trade, for example, did not prevent the great powers from going to war in 1914, and the League of Nations' collective security system did not prevent the outbreak of World War II in 1939. However, the sharp disagreement between the two approaches to international affairs is overstated. Realists tend to take national interests for granted, whereas liberals note how interdependence and international institutions influence states' definitions of their national interests. How states define their national interests and how those interests change have always been weak areas in the realist approach. The latter approach also does not recognize how contacts among different societies can introduce new ideas about national interests.[6]

According to Robert Gilpin, "one must inquire whether or not twentieth-century students of international relations know anything that Thucydides and his fifth-century compatriots did not know about the behavior of states."[7] Gilpin has a point. International politics does not appeal to a higher government to settle its conflicts. In this realm of self-help, force is an ultimate, if expensive, alternative, and those states that ignore military force and balances of power do so at their own peril. Such security dilemmas have existed since the time of Thucydides and they continue today, but modern technology and growth have added new elements of economic and ecological interdependence to the age-old dilemma. After all, Thucydides never worried about global debt, nuclear winter, or the depletion of the world's ozone layer.

CONTINUITY VERSUS CHANGE

The appropriate response to the changes occurring in world politics today is not to discredit the traditional wisdom of realism and its concern for the military balance of power, but to realize its limitations and to supplement it with insights from the liberal approach.

In the traditional realist view, states were the only significant actors in world politics and only a few large states really mattered. But today there are more than three times as many states as there were in 1945. Moreover, other types of actors are becoming increasingly important. Although they lack military power, transnational corporations have enormous economic resources. Twenty corporations today have annual sales greater than the GNPs of eighty states. The annual profits of IBM and Shell, for example, are each larger than the central government budgets of the Philippines, Peru, or Yugoslavia.[8] Multinational corporations are sometimes more relevant to achieving a country's goals than are other states. In terms of economic growth, the annual overseas production by such corporations exceeds the value of international trade.[9] In a regional context, a portrait of the Middle East conflict that did not include the superpowers would be woefully inadequate, as would a description that did not tell of transnational Jewish groups, oil companies, and terrorist organizations. Thus, the issue is not whether state or nonstate actors are more important—states usually are—but that more complex potential coalitions of actors affect outcomes in modern times.

With the changing actors in world politics come their changing goals. In the traditional view, states give priority to military security to avoid threats to their survival. Today, however, states must consider new dimensions of security. National survival is rarely at stake, and most people want to feel secure in more than just survival. Most modern national security policies are designed to ensure economic welfare, group automony, and political status in addition to physical survival within national boundaries. Indeed, some security policies, such as nuclear deterrence, increase the risk to physical survival so that greater enjoyment of the other values may be attained.

National security has become more complicated as threats have shifted from military ones (that is, threats against territorial integrity) to economic and ecological ones. For example, Canadians today are not afraid that U.S. troops will burn Toronto for a second time (as in 1813); they fear that Toronto will be programmed into a backwater by a Texas computer.[10] The forms of vulnerability have increased, and there are trade-offs among policies designed to deal with different vulnerabilities. The United States, for instance, could increase its energy security militarily by developing its rapid deployment force and sending it to the Persian Gulf, but it could also accomplish the same goal by enlarging its strategic petroleum reserve, by imposing a gasoline tax to encourage conservation at home, and by improving cooperation in institutions like the International Energy Agency.

In the traditional view, military force is the dominant instrument of power. Although force remains the ultimate form of power in a self-help system, it has become more costly for modern great powers to use than in earlier centuries. Other instruments such as communications, organizational and institutional skills, and manipulation of interdependence have become important instruments of power. Contrary to some rhetorical flourishes, interdependence does not mean harmony. It is mutual dependence that is often unevenly balanced. The less-dependent or less-vulnerable party in an interdependent relationship can often derive power from threats to manipulate that interdependence. Just as the less enamored of two lovers may use that lesser dependence to manipulate the other, the less vulnerable of two states may use subtle threats to the relationship as a source of power. Interdependence is often balanced differently in different issues, such as security, trade, and finance. Thus, creating and resisting linkages between issues where a nation is either less or more vulnerable than the other becomes part of the power game. Political leaders use international institutions to discourage or promote such linkages; they shop for the forum that best suits their interests in defining the scope of an issue.[11]

As the instruments of power are changing, so are the strategies used to achieve goals. Realists see the goal of security and the instrument of military force as linked by a strategy of balancing power. States wishing to preserve their independence from military threat follow a balancing strategy to limit the relative power of other states. Relative military power is a zero-sum game—one side's gain is necessarily the other's loss. Today, however, economic and ecological issues involve large elements of joint gain that can be achieved only through cooperation. These issues are often critical to the reelection of political leaders. A French president today would not interfere with Germany's increased economic growth because economic interdependence means that German growth is critical to French economic growth. The French decision to forego an independent macroeconomic policy and remain in the European monetary system in the early 1980s is one example of such interdependence. Some believe that this Common Marketization of international politics will become typical.[12] Thus, although balance of power is still an alternative strategy, it is far more limited today than in the past.

Traditional accounts of world politics often refer to an international system that results from the balancing strategies of states. Although to a point we can usefully speak of bipolarity and multipolarity, today different issues in world politics have different distributions of power; that is, different power structures. Military power, particularly at the nuclear level, remains largely bipolar in its distribution. But in trade, where the European Community acts as a unit, power is multipolar. Ocean resources, money, space, shipping, and airlines each have somewhat different distributions of power. The power of states varies as well, as does the significance of nonstate actors in different issues. For example, the politics of the international debt cannot be understood without considering the power of private banks. If military power could be transferred freely across economic and ecological issues, these different structures would not matter, and the overall hierarchy determined by military strength would accurately predict outcomes in world politics. But military power is more costly and less fungible today than in earlier times. Thus, there is more diversity in the hierarchies that characterize different issues. The games of world politics are being played by different actors with different piles of chips at different card tables. They can transfer winnings among tables, but often only at a considerable discount.[13] The military game and the overall structure of the balance of power dominate when the survival of states is clearly at stake, but in much of the agenda of modern world politics, physical survival is not the most pressing issue.

To evaluate American power at the end of the twentieth century, it is necessary to understand the changing nature of world politics. Strong elements of continuity make concern for the traditional military instruments and balance-of-power strategies a necessary condition for a successful policy. But new elements in the modern world contribute to the diffusion of power away from all the great powers. Thus, any successful strategy must incorporate both continuity and change.

POWER DIFFUSION

The great powers of today are less able to use their traditional power resources to achieve their purposes than in the past. On many issues, private actors and small states have become more powerful. At least five trends have contributed to this diffusion of power: economic interdependence, transnational actors, nationalism in weak states, the spread of technology, and changing political issues.[14]

The changing technology of communications and transportation in recent times has had a revolutionary effect on economic interdependence. A century ago, it took two weeks to cross the Atlantic; in 1927, Lindbergh did it in thirty-three hours; today, the Concorde flies across in three hours. Modern telecommunications are instantaneous, and satellites and fiber-optic cables have led to a tenfold increase in overseas telephone calls in the last decade.[15] The declining costs of transportation and communication have revolutionized global markets and accelerated the development of transnational corporations that transfer economic activity across borders. World trade has grown more rapidly than world product, increasing its importance in all major economies. In the United States, trade has more than doubled its role in the economy over the past two decades. Changes in financial markets are even more dramatic. International monetary flows are some twenty-five times the world's average daily trade in goods. The rapid expansion of Eurocurrency and Eurobond markets (that is, currencies held outside their home country) has eroded the capacity of national authorities to control their capital markets. In 1975, foreign exchange markets handled some $10 to $15 billion daily; a decade later, they handled $200 billion daily. "With money pouring across their borders at such unprecedented rates, the capacity of national monetary authorities to influence their national money supplies, to affect their national exchange rates, or even to supervise their banking systems has been reduced to new low levels."[16] Although governments can intervene in such markets, if they do so with a heavy hand they will incur enormous costs in their own economic growth and risk unintended effects. The efforts of the U.S. government in the 1960s to slow the export of capital by U.S.-based multinational firms encouraged those firms to keep and borrow dollars outside the United States. The result was the rapid burgeoning of Eurocurrency markets. As William Woodruff observed, "the integrative role in world finance which London held in the nineteenth century has not passed to Washington. It rests today in the banks of the international capital market and the international money market, and by and large it is outside the jurisdiction of any government."[17] More recently, when the United States and Britain pressed Japan to liberalize its financial regulations, the unintended effect was the unleashing of Japanese financial firms, which led to Tokyo's edging past London as the largest financial market.[18]

In addition to constraining the way states pursue their national interests, transnational actors affect the way such interests are initially defined. Transnational investment creates new interests and complicates the coalitions that contend in world politics. For example, Honda America "is steadily turning into an American carmaker, indeed an American company."[19] It plans to export 50,000 cars annually to Japan in the early 1990s. American politicians are now pressing Europeans to allow access to the European market for Japanese automobiles produced in the United States. In other words, a transnational investment changed an American interest.

The American case is not unique.[20] For years, France restricted Japanese automobiles to 3 percent of the French market (the same percentage as the French automakers' share of the Japanese market) and restricted investment by Japanese companies in France. When Japanese automakers began to establish plants in other European countries that could export to France, the

French government dropped its restrictions on Japanese automakers. A transnational investment changed a long-standing French policy. The diffusion of power to private transnational actors and the resulting complication of national interests is likely to continue, even though it is not well recognized in many comparisons of the power resources of major states.

The process of modernization, urbanization, and increased communication in developing nations has also diffused power from government to private actors.[21] As we saw in chapter 1, military power is more difficult to apply today than in the past because social awakening has increased nationalism in otherwise poor or weak states. This increased social mobilization makes military intervention and external rule more costly. The nineteenth-century great powers carved out and ruled colonial empires with a handful of troops. In 1953, the United States was able to restore the shah of Iran to his throne by a minor covert action. It is hard to imagine, however, how many troops would have been needed to restore the shah in the socially mobilized and nationalistic Iran of 1979. The United States and the Soviet Union found the costs of maintaining troops in Vietnam and Afghanistan unsupportable. In each case, the cause was less an increase in the power of a weaker state than the costliness for outsiders of ruling socially mobilized and nationalistic populations.

Another trend in the diffusion of power is related to a strengthening of weak states. The spread of modern technology has enhanced the capabilities of backward states. While the superpowers have kept a large lead in military technology, the forces that many Third World states can deploy in the 1990s makes regional intervention more costly than in the 1950s. In addition, at least a dozen Third World states have developed significant arms exports: "The proliferation of Third World producers has been paralleled by a widespread desire for diversification among arms recipients in an effort to gain leverage on their major or sole suppliers."[22] When arms are supplied from outside, the supplier often has leverage through technical assistance, spare parts, and replacements. The growth of indigenous arms industries removes that leverage.

In addition, more countries are acquiring sophisticated weapons capabilities. Today, twenty countries have the capability to make chemical weapons, and by 2000 an estimated fifteen Third World nations will be producing their own ballistic missiles.[23] Five states had the bomb when the Nuclear Non-Proliferation Treaty was signed in 1968, and now India, Pakistan, Israel, and South Africa also have some nuclear capability. Brazil, Argentina, and several others might develop military nuclear capabilities within a decade. However, a small nuclear capability will not make these states contenders for global power; in fact, it may increase the risks they face if their neighbors follow suit or if the weapons fall into the hands of rebel groups. Nuclear capability would enhance these states' regional power and increase the potential costs of regional intervention by larger powers.[24] Technology also enhances the power of private groups. For instance, handheld anti-aircraft missiles helped guerrillas in Afghanistan and new plastic explosives are effective tools for terrorists.

The ability of great powers to control their environments despite impressive traditional power resources is also diminished by the changing nature of issues in world politics. Increasingly, the issues today do not simply place one state against another; they are issues in which all states try to control nonstate transnational actors. The solutions to many current issues of transnational interdependence will require collective action and cooperation among states. These include ecological changes (acid rain and global warming), health epidemics (AIDS), illicit trade in drugs, and control of terrorism. Such issues are transnational because they have domestic roots and because they cross international borders. As the nuclear accident at the Soviet reactor in Chernobyl showed, even a domestic issue like the safety of nuclear reactors can suddenly become a transnational issue.

Although force may sometimes play a role, traditional instruments of power are rarely sufficient to deal with the changing issues in world politics. New power resources, such as the capacity for effective communication and for developing and using multilateral institutions, may prove more relevant. Moreover, cooperation will often be required from small, weak states not fully capable of managing their own domestic drug, health, or ecological problems. For example, the United States could not use its traditional power resources to force Peru to curtail the production of cocaine if a weak Peruvian government cannot control private gangs of drug dealers. And, if the American government cannot control the U.S. demand, a transnational market for cocaine will continue. This complexity does not make traditional power resources irrelevant. To the contrary, economic assistance and military force can play roles in coping with terrorism, proliferation, or drugs. But the ability of any great power to control its environment and to achieve what it wants often is not as great as traditional power indicators suggest.

The United States may remain preponderant at the

end of the century, but Americans are unlikely to feel hegemonic. Compared to the 1950s, the U.S. ability to control international financial markets has diminished, America's vulnerability to disruptions in oil markets remains, more countries are potential suppliers of nuclear and military technology, and a host of new transnational problems have arisen. Military and economic power can still be brought to bear on such issues if policies are formulated intelligently. Such policies should not lead to withdrawal from geopolitical alliances, for this would mean giving up a source of influence without reducing interdependence on transnational issues. But the policies should focus more on international institutions, their implications for linkages among issues, and the domestic bases of American strength to deal with transnational interdependence.

POWER REVISITED

Power is becoming less fungible, less coercive, and less tangible. Modern trends and changes in political issues are having significant effects on the nature of power and the resources that produce it. Co-optive behavioral power—getting others to want what you want—and soft power resources—cultural attraction, ideology, and international institutions—are not new. In the early postwar period, the Soviet Union profited greatly from such strategic software as Communist ideology, the myth of inevitability, and transnational Communist institutions. Yet various trends today are making co-optive behavior and soft power resources more important.[25]

DIMINISHED FUNGIBILITY

The fragmented structure of world politics among different issues has made power resources less fungible; that is, less transferable from one issue to another. Money is fungible, in that it can be easily converted from one currency to another. Power has always been less fungible than money, but it is even less so today than in earlier periods.[26] In the eighteenth century, a monarch with a full treasury could purchase infantry, which allowed the conquest of new provinces, which, in turn, could enrich the treasury. That simple process comes close to describing the situation in 1740 when Frederick II of Prussia went to war to seize Austria's province of Silesia. Today, however, the direct use of force for economic gain is generally too costly and dangerous for modern great powers. Even short of aggression, the translation of economic into military power resources may be very costly. For instance, there is no economic obstacle to Japan's developing a major nuclear or conventional force, but the political cost both at home and from the reaction of other countries would be considerable. Militarization might then reduce rather than increase Japan's ability to achieve its purposes.

Because power is a relationship, by definition it implies some context. Diminished fungibility means that specifying the context is increasingly important in estimating the actual power that can be derived from power resources. More than in previous times, one must ask the question, "Power for what?" Yet at the same time, because world politics has only partly changed and the traditional geopolitical agenda remains relevant, some fungibility of military power remains. The protective role of military force is a relevant asset in bargaining among states. One example is the dependence of conservative oil-producing states on the United States for their security, which limited their leverage on the United States during the 1973 oil crisis. The United States still serves as an ultimate guarantor of the military security of Europe and Japan, and that protection creates a power resource in the complex bargaining among its allies. In general, this need for protection makes American influence greater.[27] Even in the new context of a reduced Soviet threat, this resource may be useful as a source of American influence. In the context of the Cold War, the United States often worried about the frailty of its allies and tended to sacrifice some economic interests in the effort to contain the perceived Soviet threat. In the new context, though, if the United States worries less about the Soviet threat than its allies do, it might be able to demand more of its allies.

REDUCED COERCION

Another effect of changing world politics is that power behavior is becoming less coercive, at least among the major states. The present spectrum of coerciveness in the instruments of power ranges from diplomatic notes to economic threats to military coercion. In earlier periods, the costs of coercion were relatively low. Force was acceptable and economies were less interdependent. Early in this century, the United States sent in marines and customs agents to collect debts in some Caribbean countries. But under current conditions, the use of force against small countries like Nicaragua and Panama is more costly.

Manipulation of interdependence under the current conditions is also more costly. Economic interdependence usually carries some benefits in both directions.

Threats to disrupt the relationship, if carried out, could be very expensive. For example, Japan might want the United States to reduce its budget deficit, but a threat to refuse to buy American Treasury bonds would likely disrupt financial markets and have enormously costly effects on Japan as well as on the United States. Because the more threatening and coercive applications of power tend to be more costly, the less threatening types of power resources are becoming more useful.

As we saw in chapter 1, co-optive power is the ability of a nation to structure a situation so that other nations develop preferences or define their interests in ways consistent with one's own nation. This type of power tends to arise from such resources as cultural and ideological attraction as well as the rules and institutions of international regimes.[28] As a European observer notes, American cultural attraction is much greater than Britain's was: "British hegemony did not involve the spread of a way of life for the broad masses, probably only for elite strata of imperialist gentlemen. U.S. hegemony, on the other hand, has included such a distinct way of life."[29] The United States has more co-optive power than other countries in the international system. Institutions governing the international economy, such as the International Montary Fund and the General Agreement on Tariffs and Trade, tend to embody the liberal free-market principles that coincide in large measure with American society and ideology. The United States has "succeeded in creating an institutionalized political framework for world capitalism,"[30] as well as a framework that has permitted the development of transnational corporations. For example, in the 1970s, the United States resisted a restrictive UN code for transnational corporations and instead supported a liberal code within the more sympathetic Organization for Economic Cooperation and Development (OECD). The United States has also pressed for the liberalization of trade in services such as banking, insurance, transportation, advertising, and consulting. In 1985, U.S. pressure persuaded the OECD countries to commit themselves to liberalized transborder data flows.[31]

The international institutions that the United States helped to establish have not merely affected the way other states pursue their interests but also how they understand their own behavior and define their national interests.[32] These international laws and institutions affected domestic politics in Europe and Japan and have helped shape their approaches to international issues. This similarity in definitions of interests between the United States and its allies reduced the degree of potential divergence. Of course, conflicts over interests continue to exist inside international institutions, but the general principles are accepted. And, after all, it is usually easier to haggle over price than over principle. Such regimes do not rest on coercion. A good deal of their success rests on the fact that the United States used them to pursue purposes that others sought as well.

Multinational corporations are another source of co-optive power. Susan Strange argues that U.S. power in the world economy has increased as a result of transnational production: "Washington may have lost some of its authority over the U.S.-based transnationals, but their managers still carry U.S. passports, can be subpoenaed in U.S. courts, and in war or national emergency would obey Washington first. Meanwhile, the U.S. government has gained new authority over a great many foreign corporations operating inside the United States. All of them are acutely aware that the U.S. market is the biggest prize."[33] This power arises in part from the fact that 40 percent of the largest multinational corporations are headquartered in the United States (compared to 16 percent in Japan) and in part from the importance of the American market in any global corporate strategy.[34] Multinational corporations have their own interests, which are often distinct from those of both the home and host countries in which they operate. Steven Kobrin points out that as the operations and strategies of such corporations have become more truly multinational, the ability of the U.S. government to use them as coercive instruments has diminished.[35] Nonetheless, in terms of co-optive power, the origin of multinational firms in the United States has had a number of subtle influences. As Susan Strange asks, "is it more desirable that Americans should wear blue collars and mind the machines or that they should wear white collars and design, direct and finance the whole operation?"[36]

American culture is also a relatively inexpensive and useful soft power resource. Obviously, certain aspects of American culture are unattractive to other peoples, and there is always danger of bias in evaluating cultural sources of power. But American popular culture embodied in products and communications has widespread appeal.[37] Nicaraguan television played American shows even while the government fought American-backed guerrillas. Similarly, Soviet teenagers wear blue jeans and seek American recordings, and Chinese student protesters used a symbol that resembled the Statue of Liberty during the 1989 uprisings. While the Chinese government launched official protests against U.S. interference, Chinese citizens were "as interested as ever in American democracy, American novels, even in break dancing."[38]

Young Japanese who have never been to the United
States wear sports jackets with the names of American
colleges. Of course, there is an element of triviality and
fad in popular behavior, but it is also true that a country
that stands astride popular channels of communication
has more opportunities to get its messages across and to
affect the preferences of others.[39] According to UNESCO
studies, the United States exported seven times more television shows than the next country (Britain) and had the
only global network for film distribution. Although American films account for only 6 or 7 percent of all films
made, they occupy about 50 percent of world screen time.
More generally, in 1981, "the United States was responsible for 80 percent of world-wide transmission and processing of data."[40]

As one British scholar puts it,

> the American language has become the *lingua franca* of the
> global economy and of transnational social and professional
> groups. Whatever the Japanese economy may achieve, the
> Japanese language will never rival English. . . . American
> universities [have] come to dominate learning and the major
> professions not only because they have numbers and
> resources of libraries and finance but also because their work
> is conducted in English. By comparison with this predomi-
> nance in the knowledge structure, any loss of American capa-
> bility in industrial manufacturing is trivial and unimportant.[41]

Japanese consumer products and cuisine have recently
become increasingly fashionable on a global scale. They
seem less associated with an implicit appeal to a broader
set of values, however, than in the case of American
domination of popular communication. In part, this may
reflect the inward orientation of Japanese culture. While
Japan has been extraordinarily successful at accepting
foreign technology, it has been far more reluctant to

accept foreigners. Japan's relations with China, for example, have been hampered by cultural insensitivities.[42] As we saw in chapter 5, many Japanese are concerned about their lack of "internationalization" and the absence of a broader message.

While Americans can also be parochial and inward-oriented, the ethnic openness of the American culture and the political appeal of the American values of democracy and human rights are a source of international influence that European nations have to a lesser degree and Communist countries have largely lost. Compared to Japan and Europe, America's relative openness to immigrants is a source of strength. According to European scholar Ralf Dahrendorf, it is "relevant that millions of people all over the world would wish to live in the United States and that indeed people are prepared to risk their lives in order to get there."[43] Maintaining this appeal is important as well. After President Bush criticized the Chinese government for killing student protesters in China in 1989, "ordinary Chinese have never seemed so supportive of the United States as in the last few days." Newspaper accounts noted that unlike earlier periods, "private attitudes seem to have been detached from official relations."[44] When ideals are an important source of power, the classic distinction between realism and liberalism becomes blurred. The realist who focuses only on the balance of hard power resources will miss the power of transnational ideas.

REDUCED TANGIBILITY

The changing nature of international politics has also made intangible power resources more important. National cohesion, universalistic culture, and international institutions are taking on additional significance. Intangibility also characterizes important aspects of the economic power resources that underlie command power: "Power is passing to the 'information-rich' instead of the 'capital-rich.' Indeed, it is information which unlocks the door giving access to credit, not the mere possession and accumulation of capital."[45]

Information is becoming more and more plentiful, but the flexibility to act first on new information is rare. Information becomes power, especially before it spreads. Thus, a capacity for timely response to new information is a critical power resource. In the context of an information-based economy, raw materials are less important and organizational skills and flexibility are more important. Product cycles are shortening and technology is moving toward "totally flexible production systems, in which the craft-era tradition of custom-tailoring of products" will be incorporated into modern manufacturing plants.[46] Japan has been particularly adept at pioneering such flexible manufacturing processes; the United States and Europe need to do more, and the Soviet Union and China lag seriously behind.

Timely response to information is not only important to manufacturing leadership but also in critical services such as finance, insurance, and transportation. In the past, markets were determined by the limits of transportation and communication between buyers and sellers. Today, however, the "new means of communication allow information on market trends to be immediately accessible to buyers and sellers worldwide."[47] Satellites and fiber-optic cables instantaneously and continuously link people watching little green screens in London, Tokyo, and New York. The fact that the Soviet Union and China do not significantly participate in these transnational credit markets is a serious deficiency in their access to intangible aspects of power. In the 1980s, other governments such as Britain and Japan had to follow American trends in the deregulation of money markets and financial operations to preserve their positions in these important markets.

Intangible changes in knowledge also affect military power. Traditionally, governments have invested in human espionage. Now major powers like the United States and the Soviet Union have continuous photographic and electronic surveillance from space, which provides quick access to a variety of economic, political, and military information. Other nations such as France are beginning to make some low-resolution satellite information commercially available, but the United States leads in high-resolution information.

With time, knowledge and technology will spread. Government secrecy classifications and export regulations on shipments to the Soviet Union, or the restrictions on sensitive technologies essential to nuclear or missile production can slow but not fully stem such flows. Thus, the critical question again is one of time. If the United States can keep its lead time in critical military technologies, it matters less that they will eventually reach the Soviet Union a decade later. And the United States can use the time gained by slowing broader flows of nuclear technology in order to strengthen institutions like the Non-Proliferation Treaty, or by trying to alleviate regional conflicts. Being first in the possession of information is a source of power only if it is coupled with the capability for timely response.

Another intangible aspect of power arises in the context of interdependence. The "power of the debtor" has long been known: If you owe a bank $10,000, the bank has power over you. But if you owe $10 million, you have power over the bank. Thus, if a relationship is beneficial to both parties, the possibility that the weaker side might collapse under pressure limits the power of the ostensibly stronger partner. That is the "power of the weak." Interdependence creates a power situation poorly described by the overt distribution of economic resources. But the ability of the ostensibly stronger state may be limited by the greater organization and concentration of the smaller state. This difference helps to account for Canada's surprising degree of success in bargaining with the United States.[48] If, however, Mexico or some Caribbean states became too weak to deal with internal poverty or domestic problems, transborder flows of migrants, drugs, or contraband might create a new foreign policy agenda for the United States. Similarly, developing countries that cannot prevent destruction of their forests will affect the global climate, yet the very weakness of those states will diminish the power to influence them. Ironically, the current neglect of weak Third World nations may reduce America's future power to influence them on the new transnational issues. The United States will have to devote more attention to the paradoxical power that grows out of political and economic chaos and weakness in poor countries.

POWER CONVERSION CAPABILITIES

A final aspect of power, power conversion capability, takes on a different significance in today's political situation. As noted in chapter 1, there is almost always a gap between a country's potential power—measured by its resources—and its actual or realized power—measured by the changed behavior of other nations and the extent to which others share its preferences. Further, not all potential power can be effectively mobilized and converted to realized power. Prior to 1914, for example, Russia's potential power was greater than its realized power because of its weak physical infrastructure and inefficient political system.

Some countries have been more efficient at power conversion than others. The U.S. political system promotes freedom at the expense of efficiency. In the current information-based economy, which requires timely response to new information, American inefficiencies in power conversion may become overly expensive. As we shall see in chapter 7, domestic changes like improved education and less hierarchical corporations will be needed to improve America's ability to mobilize its power resources. The gap between U.S. preponderance in resources and its ability to achieve its goals will continue to grow if such domestic changes are ignored. Although some gap in power conversion is unavoidable—such as that arising from changes in world politics, altering the mix of resources that produce power— much of the gap will depend on future American policies and choices. As the nature of power in world politics continues to change, the United States will be as well placed as any other nation in terms of the new, intangible sources of power. At the same time, however, the United States will need to adjust to these changes. It will no longer be able to use the Soviet military threat to define its national interest or to spur the conversion of its resources into influence.

There are several ways that the United States can enhance the prospects for achieving its goals under the current conditions of interdependence and power diffusion. One is to be more modest in the selection of its purposes and in defining its national interests. For example, in an age of nationalism, the United States cannot hope to exert great control over the internal policies of other countries. It will never have the resources for control over developing countries that the great powers of earlier times possessed. Further, military intervention will generally be too costly. Instead, U.S. multilateral intervention and diplomatic pressure—such as that used in 1988 to assure fairness in Chile's plebiscite—will be alternative instruments.

The United States also will have to invest more heavily than in the recent past in the soft power resources that help to provide co-optive behavioral power. This includes a greater investment in international institutions and in domestic reforms that will enhance the openness and attractiveness of American political culture. American social performance must become more in accord with professed American ideals, a task more easily urged than accomplished. In addition, the United States will need to be more attentive to transnational interdependence, particularly to how it increases vulnerability to private actors, to manipulation by other wealthy countries, and to the problems of chaos and weakness in poor countries. Transnational issues are closely linked to domestic politics at home and abroad. In order to deal with such issues effectively, Americans will have to become less parochial and more attentive to external changes. Further, U.S. government intervention in transnational issues will require far greater coordination of domestic and foreign policies than in the past.

Finally, the United States will need to develop its ability to adjust domestically to external changes. In a world of transnational interdependence, any attempt by the United States to ignore the influences of external changes would be costly and ultimately futile. The transnational nature of interdependence means that Americans will have to focus more on the domestic bases of their international power.

Domestic
Challenges

A nation can lose power as a result of the rise of other nations or because of its own internal decay. In recent years, there has been growing concern that the United States is suffering from domestic decay, reducing its international competitiveness. Economist Paul McCracken writes that without improvement, "the malady under discussion in the 1990s will be the American Disease."[1] Investment banker Peter Peterson warns Americans that "for some time now the foundations of their economic future have been insidiously weakening."[2] Similarly, former Colorado governor Richard D. Lamm believes that the United States "is not at the cutting edge of competition any more, and while the problem has many roots, to a large extent the United States is a victim of its own institutions." Lamm goes on to cite Arnold Toynbee's warning that the cause of the fall of a great nation "is always *suicide.*"[3]

Certainly, there are serious domestic social problems in the United States; critics cite a great range of problems from drug use to divorce rates. Many Americans lament the loss of the "good old days," and psychological reactions to new social problems probably contribute to a mood of U.S. decline. It is hard to argue with certainty, however, that these social problems are a sign of cultural decay in the United States. Negative cultural changes have to be balanced against such improvements as increased life expectancy, reduced infant mortality rates, the reduction of racial barriers, and improved opportunities for women.[4] It is easy to show decay by comparing the good in the past with the bad in the present. A more convincing argument must compare a balance of social goods and evils today with a similar assessment of the past. After all, nineteenth-century America had deep social problems of racism, inequality, and urban violence.

Even then, different value judgments may lead to different conclusions. For example, increased divorce rates in the United States can be interpreted as an index of social decay or as evidence of increased opportunity for women and men to escape hopeless situations that they previously had to endure. Moreover, it is not clear how such cultural judgments are related to national power. Since international power is the focus of this book, we concentrate here on those aspects of domestic change and politics that are clearly related to international competitiveness and its ability to convert power resources into effective influence.

ECONOMIC SCLEROSIS?

Economic indicators are somewhat easier to interpret than cultural changes; they show that the United States has many economic problems. According to an index constructed by the American Council on Competitiveness, the U.S. economy is slipping. Japan has nearly equaled America's absolute productivity advantage. In 1986, U.S. manufacturing output was $32,000 per employee, only slightly ahead of $31,000 in Japan and $27,000 in Germany. While the United States remains the world's largest exporter of goods and services, its share slipped from 12 to 10 percent between 1972 and 1987. Technological dominance has been lost in several manufacturing sectors and has diminished in others. The annual rate of increase in labor productivity in the U.S. economy, which averaged 2.7 percent in the first two postwar decades, slipped to 1.4 percent in the 1980s. Although the American standard of living is still the highest among the other summit industrial nations, it has grown only one-fourth as fast as the others since 1972, and the American lead over the other nations continues to narrow. The U.S. net savings rate slipped from 7.8 percent in 1979 to 2 percent in 1987. According to *Business Week* in 1987, "the nation is in a growth crisis. . . . Both personal and national agendas that were once unquestioned suddenly seem too expensive."[5]

At the same time, however, the American economy continues to possess a number of strengths. Its growth rate of 2.6 percent over the last two decades is respectable. Also, as we saw in chapter 3, the American share of world product has not declined. The United States retains leadership in many high-technology products as well as in number of multinational corporations. It has a strong science and technology base, a deep-rooted entrepreneurial tradition, and well-developed capital markets. Capital is attracted to the United States because the markets are safe and profitable. And, contrary to conventional wisdom, the American work ethic remains stronger than in many industrialized democracies, with a majority reporting "an inner need to do the best job possible regardless of pay."[6] Thus, the problem again is making a net assessment from contradictory evidence.

In *The Rise and Decline of Nations*, economist Mancur Olson theorizes about the causes of long-term domestic slowdowns. He argues that competitiveness is lost when the arteries of economic growth become clogged by the activities of special interest groups. Olson sees this economic arteriosclerosis occurring more readily in older and more stable societies than in younger or more recently disrupted societies, in that the former type is more likely to suffer a "silting up of the channels of economic progress" as layers of powerful groups protect their special interests from the creative changes of the marketplace. Inefficient producers, trade unions, and bureaucracies reach a series of deals that feather their own nests but curb national efficiency. Olson notes that Germany, Japan, France, and Italy, which "started anew" after 1945, grew more rapidly than Britain and the United States, which were less disrupted by World War II.[7] Critics fault Olson's theory for neglecting other causes that may explain the postwar experience of the industrial economies.[8] However, his ideas direct attention to the question of whether sclerosis has increased in the American economy.

Some observers argue that a greater governmental role in the marketplace is an indicator of sclerosis: as various groups make their deals, they demand more redistribution by the government and more government expenditure. However, the validity of this argument is debatable because government expenditure also involves investment in public goods and because it provides no evidence of economic sclerosis. The average government spending share of GNP for the five largest industrial democracies is 43 percent, compared to 37 percent for the United States. Moreover, this gap has widened somewhat since 1964, when American public spending was 31 percent and other countries averaged 33 percent.[9] Over the past two decades, government participation in the American economy has not increased as much as it has in other advanced industrial countries.

One way that governments protect inefficiency is by guarding against foreign competitors. There are large areas of protected activities in all democracies, such as agriculture in Japan, Europe, and the United States. There has been a change here over the last decade: the percentage of U.S. imports under special protection approximately doubled from 12 percent in 1980 to 23 percent in 1987.[10] Nonetheless, American protectionism is not greater than in other industrial countries.

If the U.S. economy were in fact becoming more sclerotic, there would be a significant slowing of its growth rate. But this is not the case. The average long-term growth of real per-capita income in the United States was 2 percent from 1870 to 1900, 1.7 percent from 1900 to 1925, and 1.9 percent from 1950 to 1980— hardly a sign of economic sclerosis. Robert Lipsey and Irving Kravis conclude that the United States has continued its historical growth rate of roughly 2 percent per annum, and that its growth was even slightly above the long-term average in the 1980s. Thus, the United States' post–World War II fall from top growth rankings among industrial countries cannot be attributed to changes in the American growth rate but instead to an explosion of economic growth in other countries. These countries were catching up from their slower prewar growth rates and enjoying the beneficial effects that lagging economies gain from the diffusion of the leading nation's technology. Fortunately for the United States, gross fixed capital formation, which facilitates the infusion of new technology into the economy, has changed very little. According to Lipsey and Kravis, "it was not the United States that changed its ways, but the rest of the world."[11] This situation has lead to more intense international competition, but it is difficult to show that the competition was caused by economic sclerosis or domestic decay in the United States.

COMPETITIVENESS

The problem for the United States is not so much economic sclerosis or domestic decay but complacency in the face of new external challenges. Even if there has been little decline from the long-run American standards of the past, those standards are not good enough for the future. Current levels of savings, quality of education, and patterns of research, development, and manufacturing will not meet the rising standards of the third industrial revolution, in which knowledge and information play the critical role.

The pace of change has quickened. For example, the cost of information-processing capacity has been declining for decades at the rate of 20 percent a year.[12] Forty percent of all new plant and equipment purchases are for information technology, compared to 20 percent a decade ago.[13] Innovation is continuous and the time is shortening between the introduction of a new product and its obsolescence. According to Ralph Gomory and

Roland Schmitt, "a key factor in the speed of the cycle, as well as in the quality and cost of the product, is the closeness of the tie between development and manufacturing."[14] Even if the United States is not suffering a domestic decline, its domestic problems may continue to slow its adaptation to the higher standards of an information-based economy and hinder its international competitiveness.

If Americans remain complacent about their future performance and focus only on outdated standards, the competitiveness problem will indeed lead to a relative decline of American power as well as lower living standards at home. In 1989, a Massachusetts Institute of Technology Commission on Industrial Productivity argued that parochialism is a serious problem for American industry: "Some American companies still have what it takes to be the best in the world. But many more still do not seem to have recognized that to achieve this status, they will have to make far-reaching changes in the way they do business."[15] In the view of Paul Gray, president of MIT, "the problem was not really understood until sometime in the '80s. And we now have seen efforts to turn this situation around. There's been a transition from a period in which our competitiveness in international markets was declining to one in which we have made changes [that will make] us more competitive."[16] Certainly, competitiveness became an important word in the 1980s. One study found that between 1983 and 1987, the term appeared 5,700 times in the titles of newspaper and magazine articles. Surveys of business leaders and government officials show an intense concern with competitiveness, and public opinion polls show a similar broad awareness.[17] Of course, heightened concern is only the first step toward a solution. Some U.S. policy responses could worsen the problem; for example, "people who are pessimistic about the future of America are most likely to oppose foreign investment and to favor trade restrictions."[18] Ironically, such protectionism would aggravate rather than alleviate the inefficiency that concerns Olson and others. As the MIT Commission points out, the United States must export to pay for the goods it buys and the money it has borrowed from abroad: "Hiding behind the protective walls of tariffs and quotas is not an option; it would impoverish the United States and put at risk the entire international order."[19]

Competitiveness is defined by the President's Commission on Industrial Competitiveness as the ability of a nation to meet the test of free international markets while expanding real incomes at home. It implies a general ability to balance imports and exports over the long term without continual declines in the value of the dollar that cause falling real incomes at home.[20] Competitiveness is a useful measure of America's overall international position, particularly in the manufacturing sector.[21] Further, an information-based economy is not entirely postindustrial, for a wide range of high-skill services from insurance to computer programming remains closely linked to manufacturing. Thus, maintaining a competitive manufacturing sector has an importance far beyond the one-fifth of the economy that manufacturing represents.[22] Improving American competitiveness will require, among other things, greater attention to productivity, research and development, education, and savings.

PRODUCTIVITY

A basic concern about the competitiveness of the American economy is the slowdown in the rate of growth of productivity, from 2.7 percent in 1947–1968 to 1.4 percent in the 1980s. Increased labor productivity, or output per worker, is important because it provides the leeway for higher wages without higher inflation. But an increase in productivity is not necessarily desirable in itself. The United States could increase its average labor productivity by raising minimum wages so that the least productive workers were dismissed. Output per worker would rise, but output per capita would fall.[23] Part of the decline of American productivity growth rates over the last decade and a half reflected the rapid 2-percent annual growth in the labor force as more women and baby boomers entered the job market. In Europe, the strains of the 1970s and 1980s were met by high rates of unemployment, but American wages stayed low enough to keep unemployment down. This meant lower average output per worker in the United States, but "if America's productivity record is just the obverse of keeping employment high, it might not be quite the bad news it seems."[24]

Of course, demographic changes are not the whole story. Another reason the U.S. growth rate in productivity dropped is the lower productivity growth rate in services, which account for 68 percent of GNP and 71 percent of the jobs in the economy. Productivity growth in manufacturing has been much better than in services. Some services, such as haircutting and legal advice, are hard to automate. Improvements in other services, such as banking or insurance, are hard to measure. Official Commerce Department figures for the 1980s show U.S. manufacturing productivity growing at 3.3 percent per year, and manufacturing actually increasing from 21 to 22 percent of GNP. Critics argue that the official figures reflect measurement problems, and that the real growth of manufacturing productivity was 2.8 percent per year.[25] In either case, the data do not support the frequently expressed fears of de-industrialization in the United States. Moreover, estimates of productivity in the service sectors of the economy should be used cautiously.

Another factor contributing to America's declining productivity rates is the tendency of different countries' growth rates to converge over time as late starters catch up with the leaders and exhaust the extra benefits of imported technology. That is, as other countries have moved closer to the United States in their level of development, their rates of productivity growth have tended to decline.[26] The speed of modern communications and the scale of transnational corporations in the postwar era tend to diffuse technology more rapidly and to speed up convergence rates. Economist William Baumol believes that "if we examine our current economic situation in the context of the last century of economic progress, the crisis seems not nearly so severe. [While] our productivity growth rate does require careful attention, there is no basis for the fear that the nation has entered a period of permanent and disastrous decline."[27] But to remain ahead, the United States will have to improve its productivity. Among other things, this will require increased savings and investment, better use of human resources, improved industrial practices, and new technology.[28]

RESEARCH AND DEVELOPMENT

Although difficult to measure, most economists agree that technological innovation plays a major role in a nation's productivity growth. Technology remains an area of impressive American strength, but the United

States has nothing like the enormous lead it held in the early postwar period. Before the war, however, U.S. technology was seldom much better than foreign technology, and in 1940, total expenditure on research and development represented only six-tenths of 1 percent of American GNP.[29] As Harvey Brooks observes, "the U.S. emerged after World War II as the only country that possessed the industrial infrastructure required for the rapid assimilation and commercialization of the new technologies arising out of wartime research and development and out of the subsequent intensive development efforts stimulated by the Cold War."[30]

Not surprisingly, the effects of World War II, particularly the early advantages, diminished over time. For example, while Americans accounted for 65.7 percent of U.S. patents in 1970, their share fell to 54 percent in 1986. Although increased foreign patenting may be an indicator of the growing importance of the American market as well as an index of innovative capability, it is also cause for concern. The American surplus of high-technology exports over imports shrank from $6 billion per year in the early 1970s to less than $1 billion in 1987. As we saw in chapter 3, the American share of high-tech exports dropped from 27 percent of the world total in the early 1970s to 21 percent in 1986.[31] Such changes are not dramatic and they may even be natural, but a surplus in high-tech trade at one time countered the deficit in traditional areas. The return to normal reduces the margin for error in American policies toward science and technology.

The United States remains well in the lead in science, as evidenced by its preponderant share of scientific citations—35 percent of the total in 1987, compared to 7 percent for Japan and 6 percent for Germany. American universities are magnets for scientists and students from around the world. The MIT Commission concludes that the United States is still unarguably the leader in basic research.[32] In terms of competitiveness, America's scientific lead is both good and bad news. On the positive side, the gap between science and technology is diminishing. Japanese patents are not as close to the scientific frontier as are American patents, and the trend toward greater reliance on basic science plays to American strengths.[33] On the negative side is that the more basic the science, the more it is a public good available for anyone to appropriate. Much of the Japanese success in technology has come in manufacturing design and in processes that speed commercialization of innovations. In this regard, the Japanese have the most frequently quoted patents; the American level is above average and the Europeans lag behind.[34]

The United States also leads in research spending. In the 1970s, it scaled back expenditures in research and development but increased them again in the 1980s. In 1988, industry and government each invested $61 billion in research and development, although two-thirds of the federal government's share went to military research. Civilian research and development has been about 1.8 percent of GNP for the past two decades, while Japan and Germany have increased their shares to 2.8 and 2.6 percent, respectively.[35] However, Harvey Brooks questions "whether the ratio of R & D investment to GNP is the proper measure of national innovation effort."[36] Not only does 50 percent of a larger American total go directly to civilian efforts, but there also have been some beneficial spillovers from the military effort in industries such as aircraft and telecommunications. Still, such spillovers are an inefficient means of improving processes for commercialization. Direct investment of funds is a better alternative, and some evidence shows that the flow of technology from military to civilian sectors is less beneficial today than in the past. In areas like electronics, for example, the commercial sector is ahead of the military. In other areas, bureaucratic procedures, high costs, and a tendency toward short-term, mission-oriented contracts slow the transfer of military technology to civilian users.[37] During the Reagan administration, federal research and development expenditures doubled while the civilian portion declined 14 percent in constant dollars.[38] Increased competitiveness will require more efforts in the critical processes of commercialization.

EDUCATION

Another concern is American competitiveness in education. The U.S. expenditure on education is 6.5 percent of GNP, which ranks high among industrial nations. Moreover, the United States enrolls 46 percent of the relevant age group in higher education, compared to 35 percent in Japan, 28 percent in France and Germany, and 21 percent in Britain.[39]

However, the United States has an inadequate return on its investment in education. Whereas 95 percent of Japanese students complete high school, only 75 percent of American students do so. In an information-based economy, the United States will find it costly to waste 25 percent of its human resources. Further, the performance of American students who do complete high school is seriously deficient: only 7 percent of 17-year-olds are adequately prepared for college-level science; 60 percent lack the reading ability to find and explain complex information; and 70 percent cannot write an adequate letter. American students lag seriously behind other nations in science and mathematics as well; at age 14, American students rank 14th out of 17 countries in science education.[40]

It is not surprising that a national study on education spoke of unilateral educational disarmament. As two business leaders describe it, "it is not inconceivable to foresee a second-class future for the United States resulting from a poorly prepared and poorly educated work force, from large and growing numbers of people living in dependency because they are unqualified for the jobs that exist."[41] By the year 2000, the Labor Department estimates that a majority of U.S. jobs will require at least one year of college education.[42] The MIT Commission on Industrial Productivity notes that although American higher education is "the envy of the world," secondary and on-the-job education is "seriously underdeveloped." The educational levels of the past will not suffice in the future because "the role of production workers is shifting from one of passive performance of narrow, repetitive tasks to one of active collaboration in the organization and fine-tuning of production."[43] In this respect, Japan and Germany have superior vocational and on-the-job training.

Another aspect of the problem concerns the education of scientists and engineers. With only half the U.S. population, Japan graduates almost as many first-level engineers as does the United States each year. Although about 8,000 U.S. citizens earned higher technical degrees in 1987, the National Science Foundation projects a need for 18,000 new Ph.D.s in science and engineering at the turn of the century. Currently, a majority of doctorates in engineering in American universities are granted to foreign-born students, and nearly a fifth of all engineers working in the United States are foreign-born. Fortunately, about half of the foreign-born Ph.D. candidates studying in the United States on student visas become members of the U.S. work force. Another positive aspect is that there are few societies as open to renewal by immigration and assimilation of foreign talent as the United States. Immigration and education policies will have to be amended to ensure that we benefit from this potential "brain gain."[44] And not only will it be important to accept those with education, but greater efforts will have to be made to raise the skills of those who arrive without education.

SAVINGS AND DEBT

Concern about American competitiveness is found as well in the issues of savings and debt. By conventional measures, the United States has a strong preference for consumption when compared to other industrial countries. However, a big part of the difference between national savings rates "may be no more than a statistical illusion." Personal savings rates are particularly difficult to calculate and are subject to large errors.[45] The reported U.S. personal savings rate declined from 9.7 percent in the 1970s to 6.7 percent in 1987.[46] As noted earlier, though, Lipsey and Kravis did not find a significant long-term downward trend in levels of gross investment in the American economy. And it is gross investment that brings new capital equipment embodying new technology into the production process. Contrary to conventional measurements, "the United States is close to the average of other developed countries in the degree to which it has used its economy for forward-looking purposes—capital formation in a broad sense." Education and research and development rather than current consumption are investments in the future. Consumer durables, of which automobiles constitute the largest component, in part represent private investment in transportation, which appears as government investment in buses and railroads in other countries. When these factors are included, the U.S. capital formation comes to 30 percent of GNP, compared to an average of 34 percent for ten other industrial countries.[47] If one excludes Japan, where high housing costs and inadequate pensions contribute to an abnormally high savings rate, the United States is close to the historical average of other industrial countries.[48]

However, some consumer durables are consumption goods, and trends in the mid-1980s were in the direction of reduced savings in the United States. During the 1970s, net national savings were 7.9 percent of national income but then slipped to 2.1 percent from 1985 to 1987. During that time, 60 percent of net national investment was financed from abroad. The federal government deficit accounted for part of the problem, but personal consumption also rose because of demographic changes, increased personal wealth, and the substitution of high-interest-yield debt for low-dividend-yield equity by corporations.[49] Demographic trends may begin to alleviate the problem. As baby boomers who did much of the buying become older and more savings conscious, the U.S. personal savings rate will likely rise again. Although there were some signs of increase at the end of the 1980s,[50] a policy to enhance competitiveness would increase incentives for personal savings.

Also important is a reduction of the federal budget deficit, which ballooned from 1 percent of national income in the 1960s to 2 percent in the 1970s and 4.5

percent in the mid-1980s. To a considerable extent, this resulted from the Reagan administration's decision to increase defense expenditures while cutting taxes. In 1987, the budget deficit absorbed two-thirds of net private savings. Although debt is not as important as how the borrowed funds are employed, unfortunately the foreign capital borrowed to finance the deficit did not raise the rate of investment; it financed consumption.[51]

The U.S. budget deficit declined as a percent of GNP at the end of the 1980s, and economists disagree about its real impact. Herbert Stein estimates the cost of the "public spending spree" from 1982 to 1987 at $400 billion in 1982 dollars, or 2 percent of GNP for those five years.[52] Others argue that a deficit of two or three percent of GNP is modest, but they overlook the real costs of being unwilling to tax for what we spent.[53] Reliance on foreign capital markets to finance current expenditures exacerbated the trade deficit, raised problems of international confidence in the dollar, and pushed up interest rates, making the cost of capital higher for American industry.[54] Necessary investment is discouraged when tight monetary policy must compensate for lax fiscal policy. From the view of America's international competitive position, a gradual deficit reduction is the correct choice. It could be achieved at modest levels of macroeconomic cost—the shift of 2 to 3 percent of GNP back to the 1970 level of savings rather than consumption—though at considerable political pain.[55] The fact that the United States is both the richest and most lightly taxed of the OECD nations suggests that the key constraints may be more political than economic.

POLITICAL SCLEROSIS?

The profligacy of the U.S. government's fiscal policies in the 1980s and the difficulty in reaching a consensus on how to reduce the budget deficit have raised questions about the American political system. As indicated in chapter 1, power requires both resources and the ability to convert resources into effective influence. Some observers question whether the American political system is very good at converting potential power into actual influence.

POLITICAL CULTURE AND POWER CONVERSION

American foreign policy-making is a notoriously messy process for reasons rooted in American political culture and institutions. The U.S. Constitution is based on the eighteenth-century liberal view that power is best controlled not by centralization or socialization but by fragmentation and countervailing checks and balances. In foreign policy, the Constitution established an open invitation to the executive and legislative branches to struggle for control.[56] This struggle is complicated by the federal and, in geographic terms, relatively dispersed nature of the political elite; the weakness and poor discipline of the national political parties; the strength and legitimacy of economic, ideological, and ethnic pressure groups; the depth and frequency of political turnover in the executive branch after elections; and the role of the press, almost constitutionally entrenched as a virtual fourth branch of government. All these features are familiar to Americans, but they are alien to most foreign governments.

U.S. institutions are not only complicated, they are

also embedded in a distinctive political culture that
stresses American exceptionalism, moralism, isolation,
and quick solutions to problems. As Dexter Perkins once
observed, this political culture makes U.S. foreign policy
uniquely moralistic and public. In addition, American foreign policy tends to oscillate between inwardly and out-
wardly oriented attitudes, between realistic and moralistic
approaches, and between executive and legislative domination of the process.[57] According to James Schlesinger,
U.S. foreign policy "lacks the steadiness that has been
associated with great powers."[58] This lack of steadiness
has been attributed to various causes. The cultural explanation stresses the optimism and innocence of an isolated
liberal culture, which successively encounters and with-
draws from a harsh outside reality. The geopolitical explanation stresses the extent of the freedom that location
in the Western Hemisphere allowed Americans, except
on rare occasions when intrusion or encirclement looked
possible and stimulated them to respond. The institutional explanation turns to the pluralism and separation
of powers enshrined in the eighteenth-century Constitution, with its invitation to struggle for control of foreign
policy.

A key institutional factor is the constitutional fragmentation and geographical dispersion of power in the United
States. With a far broader and more dispersed political
leadership than the Soviet Union, Japan, or most European countries, the United States takes longer to develop
or to change a consensus on policy. Such lags accentuate
oscillation. To try to shorten them, political leaders often
exaggerate the external threat. One instance of institutional fragmentation is the division of foreign policy powers between the executive and the legislative branches.
This division not only contributes to incoherence but also

the executive must simplify and exaggerate to overcome the inertia of a diverse and loosely structured body of 535 individuals with weak party loyalties. Another institutional factor that contributes to oscillations and inconsistencies is the practice of political appointments far down in the hierarchy of the executive branch. This weakens the ability of career civil servants to pursue a constant policy, and many political appointees hold office for less than two years.

Critics argue that the eighteenth-century formula of separation of power and checks and balances has become a political straitjacket contributing to American decline by preventing the United States from actualizing its potential power. In the early days of the Republic, critics say, the system worked because George Washington's Farewell Address warning against foreign entanglements was heeded. Throughout the nineteenth century, the United States remained aloof from the balance of power in world politics, sheltered by the Atlantic Ocean and the British navy. After the United States played a crucial role in tipping the military balance in World War I, Congress's veto of American entry into the League of Nations curtailed America's potential role in the balance of power and contributed to the global conditions that led to World War II. After 1945, the critics say, the World War II effect left the United States with such vast resources that the inefficiency of the power conversion process did not matter. But the overextension in Vietnam destroyed the political consensus of foreign policy, made Congress and the media more assertive, and caused America to become its own worst enemy.[59] The U.S. government adapted to modern conditions by adding new functions, but "the Madisonian system, rather than having been superseded by a more centralized, internationalized state, has become more labyrinthine as new layers and functions are 'pragmatically' tacked onto the constitutional skeleton. . . . The results are fine during good times, but have drawbacks when choices are difficult, and when coordination and innovation are required."[60]

Proposals have been made to limit the separation of powers, strengthen the presidency by extending its term, and move toward a parliamentary system. Lloyd Cutler, former White House counsel, argues that "in parliamentary terms, one might say that under the U.S. Constitution, it is not now feasible to form a government."[61] Yet major changes have occurred in American government without constitutional amendments, and the functions of government have expanded greatly in the last half century. Cycles of relative assertion between Congress and the presidency antedated the postwar period. And some Europeans wish their parliaments would "become a stronger check on the executive, as Congress is in the United States."[62]

While the American governmental system was designed to maximize liberties rather than efficiency in power conversion, the situation is not as bad as the pessimists charge. There are several problems with their diagnosis. Some write of the postwar hegemony in mythical terms as a period when the United States "wielded virtually unmeasurable military power,"[63] but America's overall surplus of power resources was never so great. Moreover, even during the period of Cold War consensus, there were deep and bitter divisions over such issues as McCarthyism, presidential treaty powers, and foreign policy in China. Ironically, if Congress had acted earlier and more assertively to curtail the executive's power in Vietnam, the worst squandering of power resources in the postwar period might have been prevented. American foreign policy has always been messy and imperfect at power conversion, but history does not support a theory of decline caused or exacerbated by the separation of powers.

RELATIVE GOVERNMENTAL EFFECTIVENESS

Finding flaws in American government is easy, but the relevant issue is how it compares to other governments in the new context of world politics. While technology is not the sole determinant of social change, this book argues that the third industrial revolution is putting a premium on the quick flow of information, flexibility, and innovation—characteristics not generally associated with government bureaucracy in any society. In this regard, part of the strength of American society may rest on the fact that government plays a smaller role than in other industrialized societies. Entrepreneurship is a critical factor, responding to what Joseph Schumpeter called the "creative destruction" of economic change.[64] In a European view, "America has found the iconoclasts and the loners invaluable. Formal old Europe does not produce nearly enough of them. Japan has banished them, all for the sake of the corporate harmony it prizes so much."[65] Further, the government-controlled economies of the Soviet Union and China are at a particular disadvantage in the new context of world politics, both in creating potential power resources and in converting them into actual influence.

The more interesting cases of power conversion are Europe and Japan. Europe has a private sector, but pressure groups are strong within national governments; the complexities of the Brussels process in pre-federal Europe, for example, make American federalism look efficient by comparison. The Japanese political system has been dominated by one party whose division of ministries among its political factions has limited the tenure of each in office and the strength of government. Major scandals over the role of money in politics has further weakened governments: "Much more than in the United States, the political economy in Japan is run by special interest groups, whose interests are protected at the consumer's expense."[66] The result is a two-tiered Japanese economy with an efficient external trading sector and an inefficient domestic services sector.

In terms of external competitiveness, however, Japan has succeeded brilliantly despite the inefficiency of its elected government. Experts explain this success by the fact that Japanese activity is dominated by a career bureaucracy and by businessmen whose long-term focus gives them consistency and determined response in pursuit of the specific national goals over which they have jurisdiction. The Tokyo stock market, large Japanese banks, and Japanese multinational corporations are examples of Japan's new institutional power resources. But the Japanese rise in sectoral power resources, trade surpluses, and share of world product does not mean overall power unless the Japanese government is able to convert it into means of influence. This is where the weakness of Japanese politicians and their lack of an overall strategy matters.

The politicians matter when there is a need to mobilize support for major changes in direction. Japanese government and society work well when a consensus guides the competing bureaucracies and industries. The bureaucratic neo-mercantilist approach led to successful adjustment away from heavy industry in the 1960s, coping with the oil shocks of the 1970s, and, at least in part, more domestic growth after the revaluation of the yen in 1985. But as we saw in chapter 5, a number of thoughtful Japanese worry about the adaptability of their political system to a new context, in which Japan plays a larger role in the world economy and world politics. Japan can no longer expect a free ride, but it is not well organized to control domestic obstacles to international leadership. According to Naohiro Amaya, a former Japanese bureaucrat, "[u]ntil recently, Japan had only to think about how fast it had to go to catch up with the West. Now it has reached the point where it has to think about where it wants to go and how best to get there."[67] Takashi Inoguchi, a leading Japanese political scientist, argues that "Japan's innovative and inventive capacity for the next 10–20 years should not be underestimated," but beyond that period he worries about Japan's ability to respond to demographic changes and demands for social welfare expenditures, as well as its ability to contribute to international public goods. Inoguchi believes that a continuing *Pax Americana* is more likely than a *Pax Nipponica*.[68] And, in a 1989 poll, only 8 percent of Japanese investors expected Japan to overtake the United States as the dominant economic force by the end of this century.[69] Many Japanese are less optimistic than Americans about the ability of the Japanese political system to convert potential power into actual influence in world politics.

Thus, in one sense it is ironic to hear Americans calling for the importation of Japanese governmental methods to make the United States more competitive. It is not clear that the bureaucratic guidance of the Ministry of International Trade and Industry (MITI) is going to be more help than hindrance in the future of Japan. But it is likely that a similar department of trade and industry, trying to pick winners and losers amidst the plural pressures of Washington politics, would do more harm than good. James Fallows quotes an American diplomat, who served in Tokyo, about the mistaken view of importing a Japanese approach: "First we rig politics so that one party is always in power and the big-city votes basically don't count. Then we double the cost of everything else but hold incomes the same. Then we close the borders and start celebrating racial purity. Then we reduce the number of jobs for women by 70 or 80 percent. Then we set up a school system that teaches people not to ask questions."[70] As *The Economist* observes, America "could best serve itself by not copying Japan's mistakes just as Japan is beginning to correct them."[71]

The issue is not whether the American government and society have problems, but that the flaws in the American power-conversion process should not be looked at in isolation. Private institutions, free markets, and social flexibility help alleviate some of these problems, but they do not solve them. Government must provide public goods like security and maintain the legal and environmental conditions for markets to work. It must also provide a redistributive safety net and a sense of social justice. Effective government is essential, but effectiveness is not the same as efficiency. Effectiveness in government must be judged in terms of a political culture that values liberties over efficiency. In terms of ideological power resources, the liberties and human rights that give the United States a political vision and make it attractive to other societies may be worth far more than the inefficiencies they cause. At the same time, however, there are ways to adapt American government to cope better with the changing direction of world politics. One problem is the lack of a long-term perspective, an ever-present problem in democracies. To some extent, as we will see in chapter 8, participation in international institutions helps to provide rules and continuity that counter shifting short-term perspectives. Another problem is parochialism in a world of interdependence. Here the opportunities that the openness of the American political process present for transnational contacts, lobbying, and coalitions may be a hidden virtue. Even so, the increased complexity of the concept of security will require a greater degree of White House coordination among conflicting departments and attention to the economic, ecological, and military aspects of security.[72] The National Security Council can no longer define its role in traditional terms; it must broaden its agenda to include the new dimensions of security.

PRESIDENTIAL LEADERSHIP

Presidential leadership is necessary to explain why certain policies can lead to self-inflicted wounds, whether they be budget deficits, protectionist measures, or curtailment of foreign aid. Effective influence requires a willingness to spend on foreign affairs. Despite a doubling of the U.S. economy between 1960 and 1980, in the latter years the United States spent less on elements of the budget directly concerned with foreign affairs: defense, foreign aid, information, and representation.[73] Further, although defense expenditures increased in the 1980s, American outlays for other aspects of international affairs declined from $13 billion in 1981 to $10 billion in 1988.[74] "We cannot afford it" is the usual argument in a time of budget deficits. But if the United States cut domestic consumption by the 2 percent of GNP that it rose in the 1980s, it could afford both better education at home and the international influence that comes with an effective aid and information program abroad. As the Republican economist Herbert Stein remarks, "[i]t is time to ask the 86 percent of the American people who are not poor to give up some small part of the increase in their consumption in order to fortify the national security, to provide more adequately for the future growth of the national income, to improve the lot of the poor among us."[75]

Leadership means pointing out that the U.S. economy can afford both domestic and international security if Americans are willing to pay for them. Without such leadership, the American ability to convert potential power into actual influence is diminished. A leader who wants to maintain American power at the turn of the century must follow a strategy that rebuilds the domestic bases of American strength while also investing resources to maintain international influence.

Although today the United States faces major social, economic, and political problems, it has faced equal or larger problems in the past. One key to coping successfully with these problems is to remain open to the outside world and adaptable to change. Social flexibility, class fluidity, and economic openness are American advantages compared to Europe and Japan. It would be ironic if fears of American decline led to policies of protectionism, resistance to foreign investment, and curtailment of immigration. Though there have been few signs of long-run economic sclerosis so far, such policies could help to bring it on. However, if the concern about competitiveness leads to new policies on savings, research and development, and education, addressed to the higher standards required by an information-based economy, America's capacity to reinvent itself may again prove a hidden strength. There are some encouraging signs. Americans are becoming more aware of the need to address domestic problems. There have been some improvements in education, though not nearly enough. Scientists and engineers make up 2.8 percent of the U.S. labor force, compared to 2.5 percent in Japan. The American entrepreneurial spirit remains strong. Some U.S. firms are still the best in the world, and foreign sales by America's mid-level firms increased by almost 20 percent a year in the 1980s. Further, the quality of some American products has improved; sales of computer chips to Japan have increased as a result of their improved quality. According to *Fortune* in 1989, "[m]ore than a few U.S. companies—notably in computers, pharmaceuticals and telecommunications—are extending their world-wide leads."[76] Also, foreigners continue to want to invest in the U.S. economy, and foreign students continue to flock to American universities.

On the other hand, the domestic consumption binge continues and political leaders acquiesce while the richest country in the world acts as if it were poor. As the MIT Commission on Industrial Productivity warns, while there is no cause for despair, "the best of the good news in the United States still leaves much to be done."[77] The basic problems will not be solved quickly and sacrifices will be necessary. There are serious domestic problems that Americans must address, even though the system is not sclerotic. Decline is not inevitable, but the wrong choices could bring it on. Even so,

> U.S. growth has been quite respectable by historical stan-
> dards, especially for a leading country. . . . While there is no
> law or single prescription for permanent U.S. leadership, the
> closest major pursuers still have a way to go to catch up
> technologically, and they may find the remaining gap harder

to close than the initial one. In the meantime, the race is benefiting both the leaders and pursuers.[78]

If the international competition leads Americans to overcome their complacency and parochialism and to undertake the necessary domestic reforms, U.S. leadership is likely to continue into the twenty-first century.

8

Future Worlds and American Choices

The institutions of American democracy were not designed to maximize American power in world politics. Most Americans prefer to tolerate the institutional inefficiencies that protect personal liberties rather than to remove them for the sake of pursuing an optimal global strategy. The result is a messy policy process that reflects the Constitution's "invitation to struggle."[1] Nonetheless, the United States has pursued an effective global strategy for more than four decades after World War II. Today, however, that strategy is frayed.

The postwar strategy of the United States had two dimensions; both reflected the lessons of the 1930s. It stressed that an open international economy would prevent the retaliatory closing down of world trade that had exacerbated the Great Depression and contributed to political instability. In addition, a system of alliances among the Western democracies was needed to contain

Soviet power. As George Kennan argued, it was "essential to us, as it was to Britain, that no single Continental land power should come to dominate the entire Eurasian land mass."[2] The dramatic growth in the world economy and the avoidance of war among the great powers, despite inefficiencies and misadventures, are testimony of the success of the American strategic vision. Containment had the effects that Kennan forecast, albeit more slowly than he expected: "the emergence of divisions within the international Communist movement, the erosion of communism and the resurgence of nationalism, and the exhaustion of communism as an ideology."[3] But success bred a new problem.

Today, a half century after World War II, many have begun to question the American postwar strategic vision. In the view of historian John Gaddis, "the geopolitical ice is shifting beneath our feet these days in unexpected ways."[4] The most dramatic change has been in Soviet behavior. In particular, Mikhail Gorbachev's 1988 announcement of major unilateral cuts in conventional Soviet forces and, in 1989, the holding of the first real Soviet elections in seventy years made it more difficult for Western leaders to sustain the image of a Soviet threat that needs to be contained. In 1989, the *New York Times* pronounced the Cold War over, and George Kennan told Congress that the Soviet Union "should now be regarded as another great power, like other great powers."[5] The Soviet Union's leading Americanologist, Giorgi Arbatov, wrote that the Western press had discovered that Gorbachev's removal of the Soviet stereotype as "the enemy" was his best secret weapon for changing the West.[6]

The decline in Soviet power and the changes in Soviet policy have highlighted other trends, including the erosion of the political division of Europe and the rise of Japanese economic power. Early in the 1980s, the Reagan administration welcomed Japan's increased power as a contribution to containment of the Soviet threat. But by the end of the decade, 56 percent of the American public believed that "economic competitors like Japan pose a greater threat to our national security than military adversaries like the Soviet Union."[7] In this respect, the contrast between the beginning and the end of the 1980s was indeed dramatic.

FOUR VISIONS OF THE FUTURE

Despite a widespread sense that the world is changing and that containment is no longer a sufficient strategy, there is little agreement on appropriate visions of the future or on strategies to deal with the new conditions they will assume. Predictions and preferences often become intertwined in the opposing visions. The four major visions of the future speak of bipolarity, multipolarity, regional blocs, and polyarchy. Although none of them is likely to provide a true picture of the future, each does provide important clues.

BIPOLARITY

Some analysts believe that the future will see a continuation (or restoration) of bipolarity. For conservatives, this vision rests on a mistrust of the Soviet Union and a reluctance to part from what has been successful in the past. For others, it is based on the belief that bipolarity has proven to be a uniquely stable distribution of power in the nuclear age.[8] Management of a balance of power with complicated nuclear deterrence systems has benefited from the simplifying calculus of bipolarity. But how well will states handle a nuclear balance if they have to consider many powers simultaneously? Whether bipolarity is the reason the world has avoided nuclear war is debatable, but even if true, it still cannot answer whether bipolarity will continue in the future.

Gorbachev's reforms in the Soviet Union may be reversible, and he could be removed from power as Khrushchev was before him. But Gorbachev's successor would not likely choose to erase completely the recent changes in the Soviet Union, for this would probably accelerate rather than stem the decline of Soviet power. As we saw in chapter 4, the Soviet lag in adapting to the third industrial revolution and in developing an information-based economy are the results of problems deeply rooted in the Soviet political economy. Any conservative resurgence that did not address these problems might temporarily restore a sense of Soviet threat among the Western democracies (unless, perhaps, the resurgence were Russophilic and inward-oriented), but it would not preserve bipolarity in the longer term. It is more likely that elements of bipolarity will continue, particularly at the military level, and that concerns will remain about the reversibility of Soviet intentions. But these elements alone are unlikely to be sufficient to restore containment as the central strategic concept for the coming decade.

MULTIPOLARITY

A number of observers assume that since the future world will not be fully bipolar, it can best be described as multipolar. Some theorists argue that the flexible shifting of alliances associated with the classical multipolar balance of power will be a new source of stability in global politics.[9] In 1971, Richard Nixon argued that "it would be a better and safer world if we have a strong healthy United States, Europe, Soviet Union, China and Japan, each balancing the other."[10] More recently, Henry Kissinger predicted the erosion of the dominance of the two superpowers in the 1990s: "You will have the U.S., Soviet Union, China, India, Europe. All of which will be simultaneously economic, political and military powers."[11]

However, as suggested in part II, the development of a true multipolarity of five countries (much less a sixth, India), with similar levels of power resources in several categories, is not likely to occur in the coming decades. As Stanley Hoffmann observed, "old-fashioned multipolarity resulted from the distribution of coercive power, but this polycentrism results from the devaluation of coercive powers."[12] According to *The Economist*, " 'multipolarity' is not only bad English, it is sloppy thinking,"[13] covering a multitude of different visions. At one extreme, multipolarity merely refers to the diffusion of power. At the other, it refers to a number of roughly equal powers, able and willing to shift alliances frequently to maintain their equilibrium. As argued in chapter 6, some of these countries are likely to be deficient in significant power resources, so the analogy to a classical military, multipolar balance of power is highly misleading. Even if such a situation did come about, the effect of rapidly shifting alliances on nuclear stability would certainly be open to question. As one Asian leader put it, "if America stops being the anchorman, if the Japanese start feeling they have to provide for their own security, it would be a disaster. . . . The Chinese fear a Japan with nuclear bombs even more than the Russians fear a Germany with nuclear bombs."[14]

REGIONAL BLOCS

Another vision of multipolarity is confined to the economic area and envisages a world of three large regional trading blocs: Europe (with an African appendage), the American Hemisphere, and East Asia.[15] Given the difficulties of coordinating global economic policies and the already existing tendencies toward managed trade, proponents of this vision argue that management of the world economy would be easier, as well as simpler for the United States, if negotiations were carried out among three regional blocs.

While regional trade may indeed increase, this vision abstracts too completely from the broader geopolitical context. Even if global free-trade interests in Europe no longer existed, Europeans would be unlikely to want an economic "fortress Europe" precisely because they would not wish to become a military fortress. Many Europeans want to keep an American security guarantee, and they fear that bloc protectionism might upset that situation. Moreover, Asians would not want to be confined to an Asian bloc that included Japan and excluded the United States. In the Chinese view, "the question of where Japan is heading has aroused grave concern in the international community." A Japanese century or "a Pacific era with Japan as the center" is unacceptable.[16] Japanese leaders are well aware of such concerns and Japanese business does not want to be cut off from the important markets of the United States and Europe. Thus, it is unlikely that either Europe or Japan would move toward a three-bloc trading world unless protectionist policies in the United States pushed them in that direction.

POLYARCHY

The fourth major vision of the future is polyarchy—"a situation of many communities, spheres of influence, hegemonic imperiums, interdependencies, [and] trans-state loyalties . . . that exhibits no clearly dominant axis of alignment and antagonism and has no central steering group or agency."[17] Seyom Brown argues that this polyarchic world might be less anarchic and violent than the decline of states into a new feudalism, where different communities engage in a wide variety of conflicts within and across state borders. But political configurations would be complex and unpredictable in such a world. Conflicts would be resolved primarily on the basis of ad-hoc bargaining among combinations of groups varying from issue to issue. The most powerful political entities in a polyarchic world would be "those that are major participants in the widest variety of coalitions and joint or multilateral ventures. . . . They would have the largest supply of usable political currency—in effect promissory notes for support on one issue in return for support on another."[18]

The vision of polyarchy is consistent with the diffusion of power and the increase of interdependence described in chapter 6, but it goes much further in its portrait of eroded hierarchy. It overstates the decline of the nation-state as the dominant institution in world politics. However, even if the vision is accurate, it portrays a world in which the United States would still remain powerful relative to other states. The diversity and scale of U.S. power resources would ensure that the United States would be involved in more political games, and thus have more promissory notes to transfer among issues than other states.

AMERICAN INTERESTS AND A NEW
STRATEGY

None of these four major visions of the future is an
accurate or even a desirable prediction. Yet none can
be completely ruled out, for the coming decades may
see elements of them all. To some extent, their evolution depends on technological and political changes
beyond American control. But, as the largest and most
powerful state at the end of the twentieth century,
American choices will make a difference. A hostile or
obstructive response to Gorbachev's initiatives might
delay somewhat the erosion of bipolarity. A protectionist trade policy could enhance the prospect of a three-
bloc world. Protectionism coupled with American
withdrawal from its alliances could stimulate Japanese
and European fears that would increase the prospects
of real multipolarity. Although polyarchy rests in part
on the diffusion of power to nonstate actors and small
states, its implications for stability and welfare will
depend heavily on whether the largest state takes a lead
in organizing collective action among other states or if
it simply allows a new feudalism to develop.

Not all observers agree that an American leadership
position is so important. Economist David Gordon, for
example, argues that the United States should heed
John Maynard Keynes' advice to Britain in the 1930s to
be self-sufficient. Gordon says that "we should not seek
and do not need to be number one. . . . We should
begin instead to work toward greater independence
from the world economy, seeking self-sufficiency."[19]
Similarly, journalist Alan Tonelson argues that American security and prosperity can be achieved in a "19th
century-like world" with means "that fall short of

today's internationalist formula of debilitating U.S. military expenditures on its allies' security."[20]

Why, then, should Americans worry about preserving and mobilizing their power resources for leadership? The simplest answer is that today's world is no longer like that of the nineteenth century, or even the 1930s. Drawing back from current international commitments would not stop technological change, hinder the development and global extension of an information-based economy, or change the high degree of dependence on transnational actors. Terrorism, drug traffic, AIDS, global warming, and other problems will intrude. Further, there are no purely domestic solutions to such transnational problems; rather, collective international action will be a critical part of their solution. Absence of leadership by the largest country would reduce the ability of all states to deal with such problems of interdependence. Polyarchy might develop more quickly and be far less benign if the United States does not continue to develop and mobilize resources for international leadership. Managing interdependence is a major reason for investing American resources for international leadership and must be central to a new strategy.

However, certain geopolitical aspects of the world at the end of the twentieth century do resemble the nineteenth century as well as the 1930s. The lessons learned from these earlier periods indicate that if the strongest state does not lead, the prospects for instability increase. The Cold War may be over in the sense that a large part of the ideological hostility has drained out of the U.S.–Soviet relationship and that the Soviet Union is becoming "just another great power." But the reduced role of ideology does not mean the end of great power politics, nor does it allow states to be indifferent to the military balance of power.

The United States will have a continuing interest in European security for several reasons. First, the continued presence of a military giant like the Soviet Union poses what might be termed an existential threat to Western Europe. Because Soviet intentions could change, the mere existence of such impressive and proximate military capabilities cannot be ignored. While European integration will eventually allow Europe to do more for its own defense, a credible American guarantee helps to balance Soviet power. Second, the question of Germany's division has thus far been managed successfully by wedding the Federal Republic firmly to Western Europe and by treating reunification as a cultural and social rather than a political issue. This strategy enjoys the support of a large majority of German (and West European) opinion. Thus, an American withdrawal that exacerbated fears of German reunification or led to German feelings of insecurity might undermine these sources of postwar stability. The effect of the two German states drawing closer will depend on the international context. The American security presence has had a reassuring effect[21] that will be needed for a considerable time to come. In addition, the situation in Eastern Europe could become politically explosive as those economically weak nations move toward greater national assertiveness. The United States has an interest in a secure and prosperous Western Europe that gradually draws the East European economies and societies toward pluralism. The primary role may rest with the Europeans, but if the United States divorced itself from the process, it might find the future geopolitical situation far less stable.

The United States also has geopolitical interests and a major role to play in the stability of the balance of power in the Pacific. Today, the United States is the only country with both major economic and military power resources in the region. Other Asian powers desire a continued American security presence because they fear a remilitarized Japan. The domestic political consensus in Japan, however, is currently opposed to militarization of its policy. As we saw in chapter 5, the prevailing view is that Japan should not aspire to replace the United States but should work closely with it as a "vice-president" in the international system. The United States' interests in the stability of the Asian balance and in obtaining Japanese help on transnational issues are best served by continuing its alliance and security presence in the region.

Thus, a successful strategic vision for the coming decades must take into account the geopolitical continuities as well as the new dimensions of transnational interdependence discussed in chapter 6. In the geopolitical realm, it will be critical to help manage the decline of the Soviet Union's empire in Eastern Europe in a way that allows evolution without violence or disruption of the process of change in the Soviet Union itself. A successful strategy must also provide reassurance of Western European security and encourage the solution to the German problem that caused three wars within seventy years. In Asia, a successful strategy must manage the impressive rise of Japanese economic power and channel it into global institutions rather than destabilizing regional military investments.

Without a stable global military balance and geopolitical framework, the processes of economic and social evolution could be disrupted. But maintaining the military balance is not sufficient. The United States will also have to invest more heavily in resources for managing transnational interdependence. In the long term of many decades, a new strategic vision may simply concentrate on managing interdependence, but its shape will depend on many unknowns as world politics evolve. The next decades are likely to be periods of transition; a successful U.S. strategy will have the dual goals of managing the geopolitical balance of power inherited from the past, as well as the emerging inter-dependence that will increase in the future. Managing complex interdependence may someday replace balance of power, but a successful strategy for the transition must integrate four components: (1) restoring the domestic base of economic strength along the lines discussed in chapter 7; (2) maintaining a geopolitical balance of military power; (3) managing an open in-ternational economy that preserves the goal of global comparative advantage without sacrificing long-term domestic interests; and (4) developing a variety of mul-tilateral regimes and institutions to organize the collec-tive action of states for coping with the transnational agenda.

GEOPOLITICAL BALANCE

The two critical tasks in maintaining the balance of power will be managing the decline of the Soviet Empire and updating the democratic alliances in a post–Cold War climate. Some see the Soviet decline as proof of the success of the harsh policies of the first Reagan administration. They propose a strategy of further weakening of the Soviet Empire by continuing the Reagan Doctrine of counterintervention in the Third World, and of military expenditures that stress the

Soviet economy and deprive the Soviets of their military advantages.[22] Aside from whether public opinion would sustain such a policy, it entails a number of risks. It is likely to divert economic resources from domestic policies that would enhance American economic competitiveness; it promises to create friction with the Allies; and it might lead to risky behavior by the Soviets. As Austria-Hungary showed in 1914, political leaders trying to stave off decline often make fatal mistakes.

Since the Soviet Union will remain the one country that could destroy us, a better strategic vision is to pursue a normal relationship—one that can be summed up as "peaceful competition and cooperation." In the words of a joint U.S.–Soviet report, this means

> regularization of the competition to constrain forces that threaten war and to channel efforts toward joint gains and cooperation. Steps can be taken to demilitarize the competition, to hold regular political discussions of regional issues, to extend confidence-building and accident-prevention measures, and to develop institutions for cooperation to meet transnational threats.[23]

This vision rests on the opinion that the sources of Soviet change lie largely within the Soviet Union. The United States cannot do much to help except at the margins, but at least it can try to avoid harming the process.[24] Establishing an international climate that allows Soviet leaders to focus on domestic reform would be a major U.S. contribution. This does not mean subsidizing the Soviet economy, for that would reduce their incentive to move toward market forces. "Market-oriented reform in communist countries will contribute to economic pluralism and diversity which are likely (though not certain) to promote political pluralism and perhaps a gradual transformation."[25] Further, this does not mean that the United States would merely accept agreements that it would not want to live with if Gorbachev's reforms were reversed.

The United States should encourage the development of economic relations with the Soviet Union on normal commercial terms (outside a narrowly bounded group of technologies that could substantially cut our lead times in critical military areas). It should also encourage economic and social contacts that advance Soviet evolution toward market rationality and political pluralization. Some worry that such changes could rescue the Soviet Union from its fate, and strengthen it so that it will again threaten the United States. But precipitous Soviet decline is even riskier. Moreover, perestroika will not succeed quickly, and if it is achieved along with increasing glasnost and democratization, the United States will face a less threatening Soviet Union than it faced in the Cold War.

The normalization of U.S.–Soviet relations will also help to diminish the threat posed by nuclear weapons. After all, the Soviet nuclear threat arises more from political hostility than from the weapons themselves (for instance, most Americans do not worry about French nuclear weapons). In the coming decades, such an approach holds more promise than alternative visions of premature nuclear abolition, which could actually increase risks in the short run. But the level of nuclear and conventional arsenals can be reduced, and steps can be taken to diminish reliance on nuclear weapons in order to reduce the chance of accident or escalation should a political crisis arise. Constant communication, restructured forces, and an emphasis on "lengthening the fuse" that connects political crises to the ultimate arsenals will be the best alternatives for the strategic relationship in the transitional decades.[26]

A major problem in past relations between the United States and the Soviet Union has been competition in the Third World. Here the future goal should be consultations to reduce the degree of intervention. It is safe to predict that there will always be turmoil in the Third World. Communication advances and social modernization stir populations from old patterns and lead to strong pressures on weak political institutions. The best approach would allow the forces of nationalism to work for rather than against the United States. Nationalism is the most effective counter to Soviet expansionism, even though nationalist regimes are sometimes anti-American. The United States is bound to be confronted with governments that call themselves Latin American Marxists, African Socialists, or Asian Communists. With some exceptions, the United States can be relaxed about the domestic social changes that such governments proclaim, so long as the changes do not ally the countries with the Soviet Union in ways that alter the world balance of power or that contribute to disorder, terrorism, and proliferation.

The distinction between domestic and international concerns is never absolute, and Americans cannot be indifferent to gross violations of human rights abroad. Nonetheless, by keeping this broad distinction in mind, the United States will be better able to thread its way through social complexity and Third World change without backing itself into a corner that benefits the Soviet Union or complicates bilateral relationships. In some instances, the UN Security Council and UN peacekeeping forces may be diplomatic alternatives to outside intervention. In this sense, the two superpowers may develop a joint interest in reviving the postwar design for an effective Security Council, which was abandoned in the ideological climate of the Cold War.

A particularly sensitive area for U.S.–Soviet relations is Eastern Europe, which the Soviet Union occupied at the end of World War II and has since regarded as essential to its military security. The Eastern European countries are suffering from the inefficiencies of their imported economic systems and, to varying degrees, smoldering with nationalist resentment over Soviet constraints on their freedom. Explosions in Hungary in 1956 and in Czechoslovakia in 1968 were put down by Soviet troops. Increasingly, however, the Soviets have realized the greater difficulty and higher costs of controlling Eastern European economies and governments. They also realize that their regional hegemony is eroding. Soviet policy has begun to tolerate pluralism in Eastern Europe, but they worry about countries leaving the Warsaw Pact and about hostile operations near Soviet borders. The best way to handle the social evolution in Eastern Europe is for the United States to encourage those countries to negotiate various economic agreements with the European Community, and to provide assistance that moves them toward market-oriented economies. At the same time, the United States can diminish Soviet anxiety about precipitous change in the security framework in Europe through negotiations toward the reduction and restructuring of conventional forces in the context of the Conference on Security and Economic Cooperation in Europe, and through prudence in rhetoric.[27]

Updating the alliances of the democratic industrialized nations is another critical component of a transitional strategic vision. The United States has a strong interest in maintaining the democratic alliances, but with diminished threat and rising economic friction, that task will be more difficult. Gorbachev's honey may prove a more powerful solvent of NATO unity than Andrei Gromyko's vinegar. Public opinion in Western Europe shows a diminished sense of military threat and an increased concern for other issues, such as ecological problems. Despite such greening of European politics, most Europeans still favor maintaining membership in NATO. Friction over burden-sharing, military exercises, and tactical nuclear-force modernization, however, threatens to erode that support.

Updating the NATO alliance has three dimensions. The first relates to the traditional function of deterrence. A residual concern about Soviet military power will keep NATO important to many European political leaders. For the past twenty years, support for deterrence has rested on the Harmel formula (named after a former Belgian foreign minister), which couples NATO's defense with efforts to promote détente. With a reduced military threat, arms-control negotiations will be an even more crucial part of the NATO consensus and a way to help manage change on the continent. American leaders must realize that failure on this front could harm NATO far more than military modernization might improve it. Second, updating the NATO alliance calls for strengthening West European defense cooperation within NATO. As one observer put it, a West European security identity should be part of a new Harmel formula: "Moves toward such a European identity are probably the most effective new contribution which Europe can make towards strengthening the alliance."[28] Sharing leadership with a strengthened Europe is a means of maintaining a beneficial institutional power resource. Finally, the NATO alliance can be updated by broadening its concerns beyond the purely military. As an institution, NATO has a specific function, but the alliance of democratic nations is concerned with broader threats, including such transnational issues as ecological degradation and terrorism. Summit meetings of political leaders and meetings of parliamentarians can deal with military issues in the context of the broader agenda of public concerns in the Western democracies.

Preservation of the U.S. alliance with Japan is also an important American interest. Japanese public opinion has been less mollified by the new Soviet policies, partly because of a territorial dispute over four small Japanese islands seized by the Soviet Union at the end of the war. The Japanese might be appeased if the Soviets returned the islands, but that would not remove Japan's interest in avoiding the political problems associated with maintaining its military security without an American alliance. Congress recently passed a resolution urging Japan to spend 3 percent of its GNP on defense. The idea was that since the United States is hobbled by defense spending, Japan should be similarly hobbled.[29] However, rather than pressing Japan to spend more on its military forces, the United States should adopt the Japanese concept of "comprehensive security" and press Japan to contribute 2.5 percent of its GNP to that broader goal. Since Japan now devotes 1.5 percent of its GNP to its military (by NATO accounting rules), this could mean that Japan would spend at least an additional 1 percent of its GNP on the budgets of international institutions, UN peacekeeping, and economic assistance to developing countries. In return, the United States should be willing to support an increase in Japan's voice and vote in international institutions. In addition, within the military area, the United States should encourage evenly balanced joint projects in order to assure access to Japanese technology and to symbolize the beneficial interdependence in the security area.

AN OPEN INTERNATIONAL ECONOMY

A critical strategic choice will be between what Edward Luttwak calls "a collective prosperity strategy that would promote further trade liberalization, and a trading-bloc strategy that would 'sell' access to the U.S. market by competitive bidding, . . . mainly between East Asians and Europeans."[30] Maintaining an open international economy will be difficult in a world where "development states" follow neo-mercantilist practices. The success of Japan in using government protection to develop new industries has been followed by Korea and others. The United States does not want to let foreign governments subsidize and target important industries, destroying them one by one and making the U.S. economy look like swiss cheese. At the same time, however, the United States also does not want protectionism to spread, as this tends to make an economy less efficient. Foreign competition is an effective antidote to the cozy and debilitating domestic arrangements that were called economic sclerosis in chapter 7. Non-tariff restrictions were applied to 12 percent of American imports in 1980 and rose to 21 percent in 1984; the rise is estimated to have cost American consumers between $30 and $50 billion. For example, economists estimate that each job saved in the U.S. automobile industry by reducing foreign competition adds $105,000 annually to America's total expenditure on cars.[31] An open international economy also contributes to global economic growth, which has political and security implications not only for the industrialized countries but also for the developing countries that otherwise would be inadvertently penalized by the spread of trade barriers.

The classical argument for free trade does not rest on reciprocity. When Britain abolished its corn-law tariffs in 1846, it did so unilaterally. Thus, if a country chooses to subsidize its exports, that is like a gift to the importing country's consumers. But modern voters are often more concerned about their roles as producers than as consumers. Even as consumers, they would suffer if a foreign government used subsidies to capture market share, destroy local industry, and raise prices. Moreover, certain goods, such as microchips, may have security implications or spin-off benefits for other parts of the economy, which economists call "externalities." Thus, to ignore the effect of trade on the sectoral composition of the U.S. economy is to ignore the benefits of such externalities. As noted in chapter 2, Edwardian Britain should have devoted more attention to certain new industrial sectors, but it was prevented from doing so by the dominance of classical liberal ideology.[32] On the other hand, when governments pick and protect winners (or losers), they may do more poorly than markets and even worsen the situation. Moreover, every industry is likely to plead special circumstances, and national security too easily becomes the first refuge of protectionist scoundrels. Once protection is granted, it is difficult to remove and may lead to cycles of tit-for-tat retaliation.

At times, limited retaliation to the restrictive practices of other countries may be necessary to open their markets, but a general policy of managed or bilaterally balanced trade is mistaken. Concern for the effects of trade on the sectoral composition of the economy is appropriate on security grounds and in economic theory, but any action should be a move toward an ideal of increasing global comparative advantage over time.[33] Government action is appropriate when there are major and clear security effects, or when a new industry with enormous potential spin-offs is in its infancy. Even in such instances, however, subsidy of public goods like basic or industrial process research is better than protection. If protection is granted because of political pressures for early development or adjustment of declining industries, it should be conditional on specific improvements and limited in time. Trade policies will always remain imperfect compromises in democratic nations, but a guiding vision and some basic principles can help to preserve the benefits of an open international economy.

Fortunately, trade is not the only dimension of an open international economy. Current annual global trade of roughly $3 trillion is a small fraction of the annual financial flows across national borders. In 1987, foreign investment in the United States came to $1.5 trillion of stocks, bonds, and other assets, up from $107 billion in 1970. Of the 1987 total, $262 billion represented direct investment, up from $13 billion in 1970. Capital also flows in the other direction: American firms have invested a fifth of their capital overseas with a book value in 1987 of $308 billion.[34] When the market share of American multinational corporations operating overseas is added to exports from the United States, American-owned corporations' share of world markets has changed very little since the 1950s.[35] A considerable fraction of international trade takes place among the subsidiaries of transnational corporations on the basis of corporate global planning. When tariff barriers are erected, direct investment by these corporations helps to alleviate the effects of protectionist measures.

Ironically, opinion polls show that the American public generally views foreign direct investment in the United States as a problem. Although direct investment helps to bring productive activity and jobs back to the United States, 40 percent of the American public favors a ban on foreign investment.[36] Foreign firms employ only 3 percent of American workers (8 percent in manufacturing) and own less than 1 percent of American land, yet there is growing fear of their political influence and control.[37] There is little systematic evidence to support these fears.[38] To the contrary, direct foreign investment in factories or land provides a tangible hostage within American governmental jurisdiction, and a foreign identity is a distinct liability in the battle of lobbyists. Thus, maintaining an open attitude toward foreign investment will be an important aspect of maintaining an open economy.

Direct American investment abroad helps to transfer resources and skills to developing countries, but it is not enough alone to induce growth in the developing world. Since the long-term American interest lies in the rapid growth of Third World countries and improving the ability of their governments to deal with transnational issues, additional measures are needed. Alleviation of the debt problem that curbs growth in many developing countries is essential. Curtailment of the American budget deficit would reduce U.S. absorption of Japanese savings, which could then be available for investment in poor countries. In addition, the United States must increase its development assistance (which declined from 1981 to 1988) and keep its markets open to the exports of developing countries. As shown in chapter 6, the poverty and weakness of underdeveloped countries can return to haunt the United States in unexpected ways in an age of interdependence.

INSTITUTIONS TO GOVERN INTERDEPENDENCE

Maintaining an open international economy will require more attention to institutions for managing economic interdependence, the final component of the strategy for transition to interdependence. Large governments are losing their ability to control private actors that work easily across national borders. The recovery of governmental power, while never complete, can be enhanced by coordinated action among governments. To develop such coordination, the United States will have to invest more heavily in a variety of multilateral institutions than it has in the past decade.

During the 1980s, the Americans rightly concluded that American leadership had to be more assertive but wrongly concluded that leadership meant acting unilaterally. According to *The Economist,* the Reagan administration misread history: "unilateralism was not the way America did business with its allies in its most powerful days in the 1950s. That was when the United States was most involved in multilateral institutions like the World Bank and the IMF."[39] But more important than the Reagan administration's initial resistance to international policy coordination and institution-building was its return to more traditional policies in the face of reality. A world in which Mexico or Brazil might default on massive debts to U.S. banks proved too risky to America's financial health. Financial stability required the intervention of the IMF, whose resources the administration, in a shift of policy, then persuaded Congress to increase. In another shift, when the Reagan administration thought through the security implications of the spread of nuclear weapons, it moved to maintain the international nonproliferation regime. Similarly, when the Iran-Iraq War raised the prospect that the Persian Gulf might be closed, administration planners became more interested in the emergency coordination role of the International Energy Agency (IEA) in Paris. Likewise, AIDS increased American interest in the World Health Organization in Geneva.

The grudging acceptance of international institutions illustrates the impossibility of following a strategy of global unilateralism to guide U.S. foreign policy in an era of interdependence. Even officials who expect little from international institutions have discovered their value in achieving American purposes. Self-interest in an interdependent world, rather than a desire to improve the world or an ideology of collectivism, accounts for this discovery. Global unilateralism may lead to occasional foreign-policy triumphs, but it is an inadequate answer to the host of problems that can be addressed only through international cooperation.

As a great power with a stake in world order, the United States has a strong interest in developing and supporting international regimes; that is, the sets of rules and institutions that govern areas of interdependence. Such regimes vary greatly in their scope and membership, dealing with issues ranging from monetary issues, international trade, and management of natural resources to cooperation against terrorism, control of armaments, environmental pollution, and the manage-

ment of particular geographic areas.[40] In recent decades, for example, a number of these regimes have
served U.S. interests by helping to inhibit the spread of
nuclear weapons, limiting trade protectionism, and organizing the rescheduling of loans to less-developed countries. The existence of an international regime that
discourages proliferation of nuclear weapons has greatly
aided American policy in this area and has made the world
a safer place. The Non-Proliferation Treaty (NPT),
opened for signature in 1968, and the UN International
Atomic Energy Agency (IAEA), created in 1957, are part
of the reason that nuclear weapons have spread so slowly,
to less than one-third the number of countries predicted
by President John Kennedy in 1963. During the last decade, The General Agreement on Tariffs and Trade
(GATT) has not kept liberalism in trade from weakening
under the pressures of economic distress and rapid
changes in comparative advantage. But reflections on
what happened in the 1920s and 1930s suggest that without this essentially liberal regime, trade protectionism
might well be spiraling out of control.

However, not all international institutions contribute
effectively to the management of collective problems.
Some rules enjoy less support than others and some
organizations are ineffective. Certain international organizations have degenerated into large unwieldy theaters
for irresponsible voting blocs. In such instances, a
smaller group of governments may need to withdraw or
work around the fossilized institutions. But those that
do work well help governments in four major ways.
First, they facilitate burden-sharing. Governments often
will contribute to a common objective only if others do
the same, and states find it harder to evade their obli-
gations when a great power can point to clear rules and

procedures. International regimes establish a set of standards that can be applied to all states, large or small. Second, they provide information to governments. Shared information is essential for effective action, particularly on issues that cross national boundaries easily, such as controlling the spread of communicable diseases, allocating telecommunications frequencies, and limiting pollution of the atmosphere and oceans. Information-sharing also encourages cooperation on other issues by governments that might otherwise act alone. Important agreements may result when information reveals substantial shared interests. International regimes make other governments' policies more predictable, and therefore more reliable. They also can provide information indirectly; for example, by giving government officials access to each other's policy-making processes through negotiations and personal contacts, by which they can anticipate more confidently their partners' reactions to hypothetical future events.

The third benefit of international regimes is that they facilitate diplomacy by helping great powers keep multiple and varied interests from getting in each other's way. As interdependence links issues, countries become more likely to trip over their own feet. The United States discovered more than fifty years ago that reciprocal trade agreements with one country could harm trade with many others; it became impossible to deal effectively with each issue except in a framework of rules (institutionalized in unconditional most-favored-nation treatment), within which particular negotiations could be carried on. Likewise, when the United States unilaterally proclaimed its decision to exercise jurisdiction over fishing and offshore oil activities near U.S. coasts in 1945, other countries made an escalating series of contradictory demands for control of a wide variety of ocean resources. Well-designed regimes introduce some order into such situations by clustering issues under sets of rules.

Finally, as discussed in chapter 7, international rules and institutions introduce greater discipline into U.S. foreign policy. International rules help reinforce continuity and a long-term focus, in contrast to what typically prevails in democratic politics. They also set limits on constituency pressure in Congress. For example, when domestic vintners sought to exclude European wines, U.S. wheat farmers, worried about retaliation, were able to defeat this move in part by invoking the rules of GATT.

In short, international regimes will be a crucial component of the American strategic vision for the transition to interdependence. Under such circumstances, the United States must rely on institutional power to organize collective actions to deal with interdependence.

Certainly, not all international rules and institutions are in the American interest. Some may be beyond repair. In some cases, the United States may want to establish smaller groups with higher standards. Some trading partners may be willing to agree to a greater reduction of nontariff barriers than all members of the GATT could agree upon. Sorting out U.S. interests as they relate to each international organization will require more attention in the future.

Importantly, the dichotomy between unilateral and multilateral action is not as sharp as it first appears. The United States is bound to follow mixed strategies in this transitional period. Some multilateral arrangements will be ad hoc or will involve only a few countries. And, though it may seem paradoxical, unilateral action can sometimes play a useful role in building international institutions, as exercising leadership often calls for someone to act first. Nonetheless, any such unilateral action must be structured so that it does not prevent others from joining, and it must be consistent with long-term U.S. goals for international organizations.

A special form of unilateral action is military force. Judiciously used or threatened, military force can play a critical role in maintaining international order. For instance, the knowledge that great powers can, at least in principle, assert their right of passage through contested waters is a useful background to American bargaining over the law of the sea. Indiscriminate use of force, however, can prove too costly in relation to the particular interests pursued; trying to seize oil fields in response to an oil crisis could cause an economic as well as a political crisis. But the U.S. naval force was a welcome stabilizing presence in the Persian Gulf when the Iran-Iraq War threatened to spill over. In other cases, such as environmental pollution and international monetary issues, force is largely irrelevant, and diplomatic hints of force may generate resentment that interferes with American objectives. In instances related to terrorism, drugs, or weapons proliferation, force may play an essential role. A key consideration is always that force should be coupled with legitimacy. If a military action is widely regarded at home and abroad as justifiable, the cost of employing force can be reduced. In the coming transitional decades, as Robert Tucker argues, "force [will remain] an indispensable instrument of order and . . . circumstances may require its unilateral employment."[41] But unilateral initiative does not mean lack of consultation or absence of concern about the opinion of others.

American leadership remains essential to the future world order. In a study of the economic summit meetings held since 1975, Robert Putnam and Nicholas Bayne discovered that "when American leadership within the summit context has faltered, no other country has been able to pick up the slack." But, they warn, the United States was unable to impose cooperation unless it acted in concert with at least one other major partner.[42]

CONCLUSIONS

Americans are rightly concerned about the changing position of the United States in world politics. However, to describe the problem as American decline is misleading. This view directs attention away from the real causes that lie in long-term changes in world politics and suggests remedies that would weaken rather than strengthen America's standing. Withdrawal from international commitments, for example, would reduce U.S. influence without necessarily strengthening the domestic economy. Indeed, given recent experience, what the United States might save in international expenditure would probably increase domestic consumption rather than investment.

Although the 1990s will require Americans to cope with the debts of the previous decade, the world's wealthiest nation should still be able to pay for both its international commitments and its domestic investments. Americans can afford both social security and international security. America is rich but acts poor. In real terms, GNP is more than twice what it was in 1960, but Americans today spend much less of their GNP on international leadership. The prevailing view is "we can't afford it" despite the fact that U.S. taxes are a smaller percent of GNP than in other OECD nations. This suggests a problem of domestic political leadership in power conversion rather than long-term economic decline. The ultimate irony would be for Americans to perceive these short-term problems as indicators of long-term decline and respond by cutting themselves off from the sources of their international influence. This need not be the case if Americans react appropriately to global changes.

As has happened many times in the past, the mix of resources that produce international power is changing. What may be unprecedented is that the cycle of hegemonic conflict with its attendant world wars may not repeat itself. The United States today retains more traditional hard power resources than any other country. It also has the soft ideological and institutional resources to retain its leading place in the new domains of transnational interdependence. In this sense, the situation for the United States at the end of the twentieth century is quite different from that of Britain at the century's beginning. Thus, loose historical analogies and falsely deterministic political theories are worse than merely academic; they may divert Americans from addressing the true nature of their situation. The problem for U.S. power in the twenty-first century will not be new challengers for hegemony but the new challenges of transnational interdependence.

The United States has both the traditional hard power resources and the new soft power resources to meet the challenges of transnational interdependence. The critical question is whether it will have the political leadership and strategic vision to convert these power resources into real influence in a transitional period of world politics. The implications for stability in the nuclear era are immense. A strategy for managing the transition to complex interdependence over the next decades will require the United States to invest its resources in the maintenance of the geopolitical balance, in an open attitude to the rest of the world, in the development of new international institutions, and in major reforms to restore the domestic sources of U.S. strength. The twin dangers that Americans face are complacency about the domestic agenda and an unwillingness to invest in order to maintain confidence in their capacity for international leadership. Neither is warranted. The United States remains the largest and richest power with the greatest capacity to shape the future. And in a democracy, the choices are the people's.

NOTES

PREFACE TO THE PAPERBACK EDITION

1. Speech in Amman, Jordan, quoted in "Kuwait: How the West Blundered," *The Economist*, 29 September 1990, p. 19.
2. Vaclav Havel, address to the United States Congress, *Congressional Record*, 21 February 1990.
3. Paul Kennedy, "Fin-de-Siècle America," *New York Review of Books*, 28 June 1990, p. 32.
4. Jacques Attali, *Lignes d'Horizon* (Paris: Foyard, 1990).
5. Kennedy, "Fin-de-Siècle America," p. 31.
6. Ibid., p. 32.

INTRODUCTION: THE DEBATE ABOUT DECLINE

1. Henry R. Luce, "The American Century," *Life*, 11 February 1941, pp. 61–65.
2. William McNeill, "Toynbee Revisited," *Bulletin of the American Academy of Arts and Sciences* 41 (April 1988): 23.
3. Eugene V. Rostow, "Thinking about the Future of International Society," *Daedalus* 96 (3 [Summer 1967]): 922.
4. Samuel P. Huntington, "Political Development and the Decline of the American System of World Order," *Daedalus* 96 (3 [Summer 1967]): 927.
5. "The Decline of U.S. Power," *Business Week*, 12 March 1979, p. 37. *Business Week* dated the onset of decline as early as the Suez crisis in 1956.
6. "Strategic Shift: U.S. Redefines Its Views on Security To Put More Emphasis on Global Economic Factors," *Wall Street Journal*, 11 August 1988, p. 16.

7. "Closer Ties Bind U.S. and Japanese," *New York Times*, 23 February 1989, pp. Al, A10; Martilla and Kiley, Inc. (Boston), *Americans Talk Security*, no. 8, August 1988, and no. 6, May 1988.

8. Lester Thurow, *The Zero Sum Solution* (New York: Simon & Schuster, 1985), p. 67; "Is America a Global Power in Decline?" *Boston Globe*, 20 March 1988, p. A22.

9. Terry Boswell and Albert Bergesen, eds., *America's Changing Role in the World System* (New York: Praeger, 1987), pp. 6, 3.

10. Immanuel Wallerstein, "The United States and the World 'Crisis,'" in Boswell and Bergesen, eds., *America's Changing Role*, p. 17.

11. Paul Kennedy, *The Rise and Fall of the Great Powers: Economic Change and Military Conflict from 1500 to 2000* (New York: Random House, 1987), p. 444. See also p. 515.

12. Paul Kennedy, "Does America Need Perestroika?" *New Perspectives Quarterly* 5 (Spring 1988): 6.

13. David P. Calleo, *Beyond American Hegemony* (New York: Basic Books, 1987), pp. 9, 123.

14. Walter R. Mead, *Mortal Splendor: The American Empire in Transition* (Boston: Houghton Mifflin, 1987), p. 10.

15. Christopher Layne, "Realism Redux: Strategic Interdependence in a Multipolar World," *SAIS Review* (Summer–Fall 1989): 19–44; and Alan Tonelson, "America in a Multipolar World—Whatever That Is," *SAIS Review* (Summer–Fall 1989): 45–60.

16. Herbert Block, *The Planetary Product in 1980: A Creative Pause?* (Washington, D.C.: U.S. Department of State, Bureau of Public Affairs, 1981).

17. Kennedy, "Does America Need Perestroika?" p. 6; David Calleo, "The End of the Hegemony of the Cheap," *New Perspectives Quarterly* 5 (Spring 1988): 32.

18. Charles Wolf, "America's Decline: Illusion or Reality?" *Wall Street Journal*, 12 May 1988, p. 22.

19. Block, *The Planetary Product*, pp. 74–75; Council on Competitiveness, *Competitiveness Index* (Washington, D.C.: 1988), app. II; Barry P. Bosworth and Robert Z. Lawrence, "America in the World Economy," *The Brookings Review* 7 (Winter 1988/1989): 43; Central Intelligence Agency, *Handbook of Economic Indicators, 1988* (Washington, D.C.: GPO, 1988), table 7.

20. Estimates of GNP rest on a number of assumptions, and historical estimates are not always reliable. For a general critique, see D. C. M. Platt, *Mickey Mouse Numbers in World History* (London: Macmillan, 1989).

21. Brooks Adams, *America's Economic Supremacy* (New York: Harper Brothers, 1900).

22. Daniel Bell, "The World and the United States in 2013," *Daedalus* 116 (3 [Summer 1987]): 1–21.

23. Kennedy, *Rise and Fall*, p. xxiii.

24. Ibid., p. 444.

25. Gordon Craig, "The Art of War," *New York Review of Books*, 28 April 1988, p. 15.

26. See Gordon Adams and David Gold, *Defense Spending and the Economy: Does the Defense Dollar Make a Difference?* (Washington, D.C.: Defense

Budget Project, 1987); and Murray L. Weidenbaum, *Military Spending and the Myth of Global Overstretch* (Washington, D.C.: Center for Strategic and International Studies, 1989). At the same time, defense spending may have negative sectoral effects such as crowding out civilian public-sector spending. See Richard DuBoff, "What Military Spending Really Costs," *Challenge* 32 (September/October 1989): 4-10.

27. "America in Decline? It's All Relative," *Boston Globe*, 30 April 1988, p. 2.

28. "Decline of U.S. Power," p. 41; "Hour of Power?" *Newsweek*, 27 February 1989, p. 15.

29. Samuel Popkin, "Fear of the Future Spurs Economic Nationalism," in American Insight Group, ed., *American Insight 1989* (Cambridge, Mass.: American Insight Group, 1989), pp. 53-58.

30. Arthur Schlesinger, Jr., *The Cycles of American History* (Boston: Houghton Mifflin, 1986), p. 5; Jaroslav Pelikan, *The Excellent Empire: The Fall of Rome and the Triumph of the Church* (New York: Harper & Row, 1987), p. 95.

31. Samuel P. Huntington, "The U.S.—Decline or Renewal?" *Foreign Affairs* 67 (Winter 1988/1989): 95.

32. Quoted in Barbara Tuchman, *The March of Folly* (New York: Alfred Knopf, 1984), p. 221.

33. George W. E. Russell, ed., *Letters of Matthew Arnold*, vol. 1 (New York: Macmillan, 1895), p. 360. I am indebted to Houchang Chehabi for this reference.

34. William Gladstone, *Gleanings of Past Years*, vol. 1 (London, 1879), p. 206.

35. Carlo Cipolla, "An Introduction," in *The Economic Decline of Empires*, ed. Carlo Cipolla (London: Methuen, 1970), p. 1.

36. Jasper Griffin, "Greeks, Romans, Jews and Others," *New York Review of Books*, 16 March 1989, p. 6.

37. Aurelio Bernardi, "The Economic Problems of the Roman Empire at the Time of Its Decline," in Cipolla, ed., *Economic Decline of Empires*, p. 77.

38. Ramsay MacMullen, *Corruption and the Decline of Rome* (New Haven, Conn.: Yale University Press, 1988), pp. 1, 5, 36.

39. Moses I. Finley, "Manpower and the Fall of Rome," in Cipolla, ed., *Economic Decline of Empires*, p. 88.

40. Charles F. Doran, *The Politics of Assimilation: Hegemony and Its Aftermath* (Baltimore: Johns Hopkins University Press, 1971), pp. 20, 133.

41. Raymond Aron, *In Defense of Decadent Europe* (South Bend, Ind.: Regnery/Gateway, 1979), p. xv.

42. Huntington, "Decline or Renewal?" pp. 76-96.

43. Susan Strange, "The Future of the American Empire," *Journal of International Affairs* 42 (Fall 1988): 14.

44. Jack S. Levy, *Wars in the Modern Great Power System, 1495-1975* (Lexington, Ky.: University of Kentucky Press, 1983).

45. Robert Gilpin, *War and Change in World Politics* (New York: Cambridge University Press, 1981), p. 211.

46. Donald Kagan, *The Outbreak of the Peloponnesian War* (Ithaca, N.Y.: Cornell University Press, 1969).

47. Gilpin, *War and Change*, p. 239.

48. Joshua S. Goldstein, *Long Cycles: Prosperity and War in the Modern Age* (New Haven, Conn.: Yale University Press, 1988), p. 17.

49. Joseph S. Nye, Jr., "Nuclear Learning and U.S.–Soviet Security Regimes," *International Organization* 41 (3 [Summer 1987]): 371–402. See also John Mueller, *Retreat from Doomsday: The Obsolescence of Major War* (New York: Basic Books, 1989).

50. John Lewis Gaddis, "The Long Peace: Elements of Stability in the Postwar International System," *International Security* 10 (4 [Spring 1986]): 99–142.

51. Naohiro Amaya, "No Glory in an Abacus," *Japan Times*, 25 October 1987, p. 3.

52. George Kennan, *Memoirs* (Boston: Little, Brown, 1967), p. 359.

53. For example, in 1988 Deputy Defense Secretary William Taft was asked why he was pressing Japan to increase its defense expenditure. "You mean," said Taft, all taken aback, "you haven't read Professor Paul Kennedy's book on the rise and fall of the great powers?" (Quoted in Murray Sayle, "The Powers That Might Be," *Far Eastern Economic Review*, 4 August 1988, p. 38.)

54. C. William Maynes, "Coping with the '90s," *Foreign Policy* 74 (Spring 1989): 43.

CHAPTER 1: POWER TRANSITIONS

1. Robert A. Dahl, *Who Governs? Democracy and Power in an American City* (New Haven, Conn.: Yale University Press, 1961). See also James March, "The Power of Power," in *Varieties of Political Theory*, ed. David Easton (New York: Prentice Hall, 1966), pp. 39–70; Herbert Simon, *Models of Man* (New York: John Wiley, 1957); and David Baldwin, "Power Analysis and World Politics," *World Politics* 31 (January 1979): 161–94.

2. See Ray S. Cline, *World Power Assessment* (Boulder, Colo.: Westview Press, 1977); Hans J. Morgenthau, *Politics among Nations* (New York: Alfred Knopf, 1955), chap. 9; and Klaus Knorr, *The Power of Nations* (New York: Basic Books, 1975), chaps. 3, 4.

3. A. J. P. Taylor, *The Struggle for Mastery in Europe, 1848–1918* (Oxford: Oxford University Press, 1954), p. xxix.

4. Edward V. Gulick, *Europe's Classical Balance of Power* (New York: W. W. Norton, 1955), pp. 248–51.

5. Kenneth N. Waltz, *Theory of International Politics* (Reading, Mass.: Addison-Wesley, 1979), p. 172.

6. Richard N. Rosecrance, *The Rise of the Trading State* (New York: Basic Books, 1986), pp. 16, 160.

7. Robert O. Keohane and Joseph S. Nye, Jr., *Power and Interdependence* (Boston: Little, Brown, 1977), chap. 1. See also R. Harrison Wagner, "Economic Interdependence, Bargaining Power and Political Influence," *International Organization* 41 (Summer 1988): 461–84.

8. Keohane and Nye, *Power and Interdependence*, pp. 27–29; Robert O. Keohane and Joseph S. Nye, Jr., "Power and Interdependence Revisited," *International Organization* 41 (Autumn 1987): 725–53.

9. Peter Bachrach and Morton S. Baratz, "Decisions and Nondecisions: An Analytical Framework," *American Political Science Review* 57 (September 1963): 632–42. See also Richard Mansbach and John Vasquez, *In Search of Theory: A New Paradigm for Global Politics* (Englewood Cliffs, N.J.: Prentice Hall, 1981).

10. Susan Strange uses the term *structural power*, which she defines as "power to shape and determine the structures of the global political economy" (*States and Markets* [New York: Basil Blackwell, 1988], p. 24). My term, *co-optive power*, is similar in its focus on preferences but is somewhat broader, encompassing all elements of international politics. The term *structural power*, in contrast, tends to be associated with the neo-realist theories of Kenneth Waltz.

11. The distinction between hard and soft power resources is one of degree, both in the nature of the behavior and in the tangibility of the resources. Both types are aspects of the ability to achieve one's purposes by controlling the behavior of others. Command power—the ability to change what others *do*—can rest on coercion or inducement. Co-optive power—the ability to shape what others *want*—can rest on the attractiveness of one's culture and ideology or the ability to manipulate the agenda of political choices in a manner that makes actors fail to express some preferences because they seem to be too unrealistic. The forms of behavior between command and co-optive power range along this continuum:

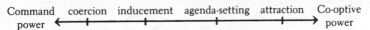

Command coercion inducement agenda-setting attraction Co-optive
power ←————+————————+————————+————————+————→ power

Further, soft power resources tend to be associated with co-optive power behavior, whereas hard power resources are usually associated with command behavior. But the relationship is imperfect. For example, countries may be attracted to others with command power by myths of invincibility, and command power may sometimes be used to establish institutions that later become regarded as legitimate. But the general association is strong enough to allow the useful shorthand reference to hard and soft power resources.

12. Robert W. Cox, *Production, Power, and World Order* (New York: Columbia University Press, 1987), chaps. 6, 7.

13. See Stephen D. Krasner, *International Regimes* (Ithaca, N.Y.: Cornell University Press, 1983).

14. David Hume, "Of the Balance of Power," in *David Hume's Political Essays*, ed. Charles W. Hendel (1742; reprint, Indianapolis, Ind.: Bobbs-Merrill, 1953), pp. 142–44.

15. Quoted in Waltz, *International Politics*, p. 166.

16. Stephen M. Walt, "Alliance Formation and the Balance of Power," *International Security* 9 (4 [Spring 1985]): 3–43. See also by Walt, *The Origins of Alliances* (Ithaca, N.Y.: Cornell University Press, 1987), pp. 23–26, 263–66.

17. A. F. K. Organski and Jacek Kugler, *The War Ledger* (Chicago: University of Chicago Press, 1980), chap. 1.

18. Stephen R. Rock, *Why Peace Breaks Out: Great Power Rapprochement in Historical Perspective* (Chapel Hill: University of North Carolina Press, 1989).

19. "New Era Declared as China Visit Ends," *International Herald Tribune*, 19 May 1989.

20. Charles F. Doran, *The Politics of Assimilation: Hegemony and Its Aftermath* (Baltimore: Johns Hopkins University Press, 1971), p. 70; Robert O. Keohane, *After Hegemony* (Princeton, N.J.: Princeton University Press, 1984), p. 32; Robert Gilpin, *War and Change in World Politics* (New York: Cambridge University Press, 1981), p. 29.

21. Bruce M. Russett, "The Mysterious Case of Vanishing Hegemony; or, Is Mark Twain Really Dead?" *International Organization* 39 (Spring 1985): 212.

22. Robert C. North and Julie Strickland, "Power Transition and Hegemonic Succession" (Paper delivered at the meeting of the International Studies Association, Anaheim, Calif., March–April 1986), p. 5.

23. Joshua S. Goldstein, *Long Cycles: Prosperity and War in the Modern Age* (New Haven, Conn.: Yale University Press, 1988), p. 281.

24. James R. Kurth, "Economic Change and State Development," in *Dominant Powers and Subordinate States: The United States in Latin America and the Soviet Union in Eastern Europe*, ed. Jan Triska (Durham, N.C.: Duke University Press, 1986), p. 88.

25. The distinction between definitions in terms of resources or behavior and the importance of indicating scope are indicated in the following table. My usage stresses behavior and broad scope.

Approaches to Hegemony

	Power Resources	Power Behavior	Scope
Political/military hegemony	Army/navy (Modelski)	Define the military hierarchy (Doran)	Global or regional
Economic hegemony	Raw materials, capital, markets, production (Keohane)	Set rules for economic bargains (Goldstein)	General or issue-specific

26. Doran, *Politics of Assimilation*, p. 15.

27. Keohane, *After Hegemony*, p. 32; Gilpin, *War and Change*, p. 144.

28. Michael Moffitt, "Shocks, Deadlocks and Scorched Earth: Reagan-

omics and the Decline of U.S. Hegemony," *World Policy Journal* 4 (Fall 1987): 576.

29. Goldstein, *Long Cycles*, p. 357.

30. Immanuel M. Wallerstein, *The Politics of the World-Economy: The States, the Movements, and the Civilizations: Essays* (New York: Cambridge University Press, 1984), pp. 38, 41.

31. Ibid.

32. Goldstein, *Long Cycles*, p. 317.

33. Halford J. Mackinder, *Democratic Ideals and Reality: A Study in the Politics of Reconstruction* (New York: Henry Holt and Co., 1919), pp. 1–2.

34. George Modelski, "The Long Cycle of Global Politics and the Nation-State," *Comparative Studies in Society and History* 20 (April 1978): 214–35; George Modelski, *Long Cycles in World Politics* (Seattle, Wash.: University of Washington Press, 1987).

35. William R. Thompson, *On Global War: Historical Structural Approaches to World Politics* (Columbia, S.C.: University of South Carolina Press, 1988), chaps. 3, 8.

36. Richard N. Rosecrance, "Long Cycle Theory and International Relations," *International Organization* 41 (Spring 1987): 291–95. An interesting but ultimately unconvincing discussion can be found in Goldstein, *Long Cycles*.

37. Paul Kennedy, *The Rise and Fall of the Great Powers: Economic Change and Military Conflict from 1500 to 2000* (New York: Random House, 1987), p. 99.

38. Jack S. Levy, "Declining Power and the Preventive Motivation for War," *World Politics* 40 (October 1987): 82–107. See also Jack S. Levy, *War in the Modern Great Power System, 1495–1975* (Lexington, Ky.: University of Kentucky Press, 1983), p. 97.

39. Pitirim Aleksandrovich Sorokin, *Social and Cultural Dynamics: A Study of Change in Major Systems of Art, Truth, Ethics, Law and Social Relationships* (1957; reprint, Boston: Porter Sargent, 1970), p. 561.

CHAPTER 2: THE BRITISH ANALOGY

1. Paul Kennedy, "Does America Need Perestroika?" *New Perspectives Quarterly* 5 (Spring 1988): 4.

2. Walter L. Goldfrank, "The Limits of Analogy: Hegemonic Decline in Great Britain and the United States," in *Crises in the World-System*, ed. Albert Bergesen (Beverly Hills, Calif.: Sage, 1983), p. 146.

3. Bruce R. Scott and George C. Lodge, eds., *U.S. Competitiveness in the World Economy* (Boston: Harvard Business School Press, 1985), p. 14.

4. Robert Gilpin, *War and Change in World Politics* (New York: Cambridge University Press, 1981), pp. 144–45.

5. Charles P. Kindleberger, *The World in Depression, 1929–1939* (Berkeley, Calif.: University of California Press, 1973), p. 305.

6. Duncan Snidal, "The Limits of Hegemonic Stability Theory," *International Organization* 39 (Autumn 1985): 579–614.

7. Arthur Stein, "The Hegemon's Dilemma: Great Britain, The United States, and The International Economic Order," *International Organization* 38 (Spring 1984): 357.

8. Timothy J. McKeown, "Hegemonic Stability Theory and Nineteenth Century Tariff Levels in Europe," *International Organization* 37 (Winter 1983): 87–88.

9. Ronald Robinson and John Gallagher, "The Imperialism of Free Trade," *Economic History Review* 6 (August 1953): 1–15.

10. McKeown, "Hegemonic Stability," p. 88.

11. Robert O. Keohane, *After Hegemony* (Princeton, N.J.: Princeton University Press, 1984), p. 37. John A. Hall similarly argues that "Britain was never a hegemon in the sense ascribed to that term by modern international relations theory" ("Will the United States Decline as Did Britain?" [unpublished paper, Harvard University, 1988]).

12. Paul Kennedy, *The Rise and Fall of the Great Powers: Economic Change and Military Conflict from 1500 to 2000* (New York: Random House, 1987), pp. 99, 118.

13. Ibid., p. 99.

14. Paul Bairoch, "Europe's Gross National Product: 1800–1975," *Journal of European Economic History* 5 (Fall 1976): 282. On this and other historical data, see the cautionary discussion in D. C. M. Platt, *Mickey Mouse Numbers in World History* (New York: Macmillan, 1989).

15. Kennedy, *Rise and Fall*, pp. 97, 139.

16. Ibid., pp. 168, 146, 145.

17. Aaron L. Friedberg, *The Weary Titan: Britain and the Experience of Relative Decline, 1895–1905* (Princeton, N.J.: Princeton University Press, 1988), p. 145.

18. Ibid.

19. Bairoch "Europe's Gross National Product," p. 282.

20. G. D. Searle, *The Quest for National Efficiency* (Oxford: Basil Blackwell, 1971), p. 6.

21. Walt W. Rostow, *The World Economy: History and Prospect* (Austin, Tex.: University of Texas Press, 1978), table II-8.

22. Friedberg, *Weary Titan*, p. 197.

23. W. Arthur Lewis, *Growth and Fluctuations, 1870–1913* (London: George Allen & Unwin, 1978), pp. 115, 133.

24. For a useful summary of the British debates, see Alan Sked, *Britain's Decline: Problems and Perspectives* (Oxford: Blackwell, 1987).

25. Henry Adams quoted in Brooks Adams, *America's Economic Supremacy* (New York: Harper Brothers, 1900), p. 12.

26. Ibid., pp. 135, 150.

27. Correlli Barnett, *The Collapse of British Power* (Atlantic Highlands, N.J.: Humanities Press International, 1986), p. 72. I am indebted to Patrick O'Brien for the estimate of expenditure.

28. Quoted in Barnett, *Collapse*, p. 71.

29. Alexis de Tocqueville, *Democracy in America* (Garden City, N.Y.:

Anchor-Doubleday, 1969), pp. 412–13.

30. Quoted in Richard H. Heindel, *The American Impact on Great Britain* (Philadelphia: University of Pennsylvania Press, 1940), p. 153.

31. Quoted in Barnett, *Collapse*, p. 50; William Gladstone, *Gleanings of Past Years*, vol. 1 (London, 1879), pp. 204–209.

32. Friedberg, *Weary Titan*, chap. 4.

33. Barnett, *Collapse*, pp. 179, 209, 232, 595.

34. Andrew B. Tylecote, "German Ascent and British Decline, 1870–1980: The Role of Upper-Class Structure and Values," in *Ascent and Decline in the World-System*, ed. Edward Friedman (Beverly Hills, Calif.: Sage, 1982), p. 47. See also the cautionary note by Noel G. Annan, "Gentlemen vs. Players," *New York Review of Books*, 29 September 1988, pp. 63–69; and the summary of cliometric research in Sked, *Britain's Decline*, chap. 2. M. J. Daunton summarizes the debate over Martin Wiener's *English Culture and the Decline of the Industrial Spirit, 1850–1980* (New York: Cambridge University Press, 1981) in the following way: "What may be accepted is his [Wiener's] general approach that the causes of decline lie beyond the sole grasp of economists" ("Gentlemenly Capitalism and British Industry," *Past and Present* 122 [February 1989]: 157).

35. David Marquand, *The Unprincipled Society* (London: Fontana Press, 1988), p. 118.

36. Scott Newton and Dilwyn Porter, *Modernization Frustrated: The Politics of Industrial Decline in Britain since 1900* (London: Unwin Hyman, 1988), p. 5.

37. Barnett, *Collapse*, p. 105.

38. David Cameron, "Distributional Coalitions and Other Sources of Economic Stagnation," *International Organization* 42 (Autumn 1988): 593–602.

39. Sked, *Britain's Decline*, p. 17.

40. Lewis, *Growth*, p. 133.

41. Friedberg, *Weary Titan*, chap. 7. See also Searle, *Quest*, chap. 1. Alan Sked places more blame on complacency (*Britain's Decline*, p. 11).

42. Heindel, *American Impact*, p. 215.

43. Friedberg, *Weary Titan*, p. 247.

44. Newton and Porter, *Modernization*, p. 19.

45. Friedberg, *Weary Titan*, p. 68.

46. Joseph Chamberlain as quoted in Friedberg, *Weary Titan*, p. vii.

47. A. J. P. Taylor, *The Struggle for Mastery in Europe, 1848–1918* (Oxford: Oxford University Press, 1954), p. xxix. For discussion of these numbers, see the exchange between Paul Kennedy and Patrick O'Brien in *Past and Present*, forthcoming).

48. Friedberg, *Weary Titan*, chap. 3; Karen Rasler and William R. Thompson, "Defense Burdens, Capital Formation, and Economic Growth," *Journal of Conflict Resolution* 32 (March 1988): 71.

49. Taylor, *Struggle*, introduction and p. 557.

50. Keohane, *After Hegemony*, p. 37.

51. Bruce Russett, "The Mysterious Case of Vanishing Hegemony," *International Organization* 39 (Spring 1985): 212.

52. Marquand, *Unprincipled Society*, p. 118.

53. Patrick O'Brien, "The Costs and Benefits of British Imperialism, 1846–

1914," *Past and Present* 120 (August 1988): 163–200. See also Lance E. Davis and Robert Huttenback, *Mammon and the Pursuit of Empire* (Cambridge: Cambridge University Press, 1986).

54. "The Soviet Economy in 1988," report by the Central Intelligence Agency and the Defense Intelligence Agency to the Joint Economic Committee of Congress (Washington, D.C.: GPO, 1989).

55. Richard Rosecrance, "Why England Slipped," *Wilson Quarterly* 11 (Autumn 1987): 104.

56. Friedberg, *Weary Titan*, p. 281.

CHAPTER 3: THE POSTWAR BALANCE OF POWER

1. Kenneth N. Waltz, *Theory of International Politics* (Reading, Mass.: Addison-Wesley, 1979), p. 168.

2. For a Soviet view, see Henry Trofimenko, "The Emergence of Mutual Security: Its Objective Basis" in *Windows of Opportunity: From Cold War to Peaceful Competition in U.S.–Soviet Relations,* ed. Graham T. Allison and William L. Ury (Cambridge, Mass.: Ballinger, 1989), pp. 167–180.

3. Paul Kennedy, *The Rise and Fall of the Great Powers: Economic Change and Military Conflict from 1500 to 2000* (New York: Random House, 1987), p. 355.

4. Ibid., pp. 368, 363.

5. Ibid., p. 369.

6. Ibid., pp. 359, 378.

7. Ibid., p. 363.

8. See George F. Kennan, *Memoirs* (Boston: Little, Brown, 1967); Charles E. Bohlen, *Witness to History, 1929–1969* (New York: W. W. Norton, 1973); Samuel F. Wells, "Sounding the Tocsin: NSC 68 and the Soviet Threat," *International Security* 4 (2 [Fall 1979]): 116–58.

9. Samuel P. Huntington, "The U.S.—Decline or Renewal?" *Foreign Affairs* 67 (Winter 1988/1989): 84.

10. Kennedy, *Rise and Fall*, p. 533.

11. Herbert Block, *The Planetary Product in 1980: A Creative Pause?* (Washington, D.C.: U.S. Department of State, Bureau of Public Affairs, 1981), p. 18; Simon Kuznets, *Economic Growth and Structure* (New York: W. W. Norton, 1965), p. 144; Council on Competitiveness, *Competitiveness Index* (Washington, D.C.: 1988), app. II.

12. Central Intelligence Agency, *Handbook of Economic Indicators, 1988* (Washington, D.C.: GPO, 1988), table 7. Official exchange rates are affected by the tradable sector of economies (about 10 to 20 percent in most large OECD countries) and by capital flows. They are sometimes volatile. Thus, exchange rates sometimes fail to give good comparisons of the underlying strengths of economies. Purchasing-power parities are used to compare real purchasing power over goods and services. However, since historical data are often based on official exchange rates, the use of purchasing-power parities

makes historical comparison difficult. It is useful to look at the data from both perspectives.

13. Oswald H. Ganley and Gladys D. Ganley, *To Inform Or To Control?* (Norwood, N.J.: Abler, 1989), p. 196.

14. Stephen S. Cohen and John Zysman, *Manufacturing Matters: The Myth of the Post-Industrial Economy* (New York: Basic Books, 1987). See also Bruce R. Scott and George C. Lodge, eds., *U.S. Competitiveness in the World Economy* (Boston: Harvard Business School Press, 1985).

15. U.S. Department of Commerce figures, which show a slight rise in the proportion of manufacturing, have been called into question by some economists. "U.S. Currency Policy Speeds Japan in Vast Economic Role," *New York Times*, 28 November 1988, p. A1.

16. Paul Bairoch, "International Industrialization Levels from 1750 to 1980," *Journal of European Economic History* 11 (1 [Spring 1982]): 275. One must be careful about these comparisons. In 1938, American industrial production was depressed from an earlier high of 39 percent share of the world total in 1928. On the other hand, post-1945 levels reflect the U.S. economy's leadership in the general move toward increasing the share of services in the gross national products of all modern economies.

17. William Thompson, *On Global War*, (Columbia, S.C.: University of South Carolina Press, 1988), p. 140.

18. Technology-intensive products are arbitrarily defined by economists as products for which research and development costs exceed 2.36 percent of the value-added. See, for example, Rachel McCulloch, *The Challenge to U.S. Leadership* (Cambridge, Mass.: National Bureau of Economic Research, 1988).

19. National Science Foundation, *International Science and Technology Data Update, 1988* (Washington, D.C.: GPO, 1989), pp. 92, 94.

20. "U.S. Declines in Electronics," *New York Times*, 5 January 1989, pp. D1–D2.

21. Richard C. Eichenberg, *Public Opinion and National Security in Western Europe* (Ithaca, N.Y.: Cornell University Press, 1989), table 3.1.

22. Committee on the Present Danger, *Has America Become Number Two?: The U.S.–Soviet Military Balance and American Defense Policies and Programs* (Washington, D.C.: The Committee on the Present Danger, 1982).

23. McGeorge Bundy, *Danger and Survival* (New York: Random House, 1989).

24. Quoted in Committee on the Present Danger, *Has America Become Number 2?* prologue, p. 3.

25. John Lewis Gaddis, "NSC 68 and the Problem of Ends and Means," *International Security* 4 (4 [Spring 1980]): 164–170.

26. James G. Blight and David A. Welch, *On the Brink: Americans and Soviets Reexamine the Cuban Missile Crisis* (New York: Hill & Wang, 1989).

27. Xing Shugang, Li Yunhua, and Liu Yingna, "Changing Balance of Soviet-U.S. Power," *Beijing Review* 19 (9 May 1983): 16.

28. See Joshua Epstein, Kim R. Holmes, John J. Mearsheimer, and Barry R. Posen, "Policy Focus: The European Conventional Balance," *International Security* 12 (4 [Spring 1988]): 152–202.

29. International Institute for Strategic Studies, *The Military Balance*,

1988–1989 (London: IISS, 1988), pp. 20, 36.

30. Franklyn D. Holzman, "Soviet Military Spending: Assessing the Numbers Game," *International Security* 6 (4 [Spring 1982]): 78–101; "Politics and Guesswork: CIA and DIA Estimates of Soviet Military Spending," *International Security* 14 (2 [Fall 1989]).

31. Kennedy, *Rise and Fall*, p. 284.

32. Arms Control and Disarmament Agency, *World Military Expenditures and Arms Transfers* (Washington, D.C.: ACDA, 1963–1989 [annual]).

33. Ruth Leger Sivard, *World Military and Social Expenditures* (Washington, D.C.: World Priorities, 1974–1987 [annual]).

34. Robert W. Cox, *Production, Power and World Order* (New York: Columbia University Press, 1987), chap. 7.

35. Robert O. Keohane, *After Hegemony* (Princeton, N.J.: Princeton University Press, 1984), p. 136.

36. Michael Mastanduno, "Trade As a Strategic Weapon: American and Alliance Export Control Policy in the Early Postwar Period," *International Organization* 42 (1 [Winter 1988]): 149.

37. Richard N. Cooper, "Trade Policy Is Foreign Policy," *Foreign Policy* 9 (Winter 1972–1973): 18–36.

38. Keohane, *After Hegemony*, p. 144.

39. Ibid., p. 142.

40. Charles S. Maier, "The Two Postwar Eras and the Conditions for Stability in Twentieth-Century Western Europe," *American Historical Review* 86 (2 [April 1981]): 333.

41. See John Lewis Gaddis, *Strategies of Containment: A Critical Appraisal of Postwar American National Security Policy* (New York: Oxford University Press, 1982); and Dean Acheson, *Present at the Creation* (New York: W. W. Norton, 1969), p. 374.

42. Maier, "Two Postwar Eras," p. 333.

43. Alan S. Milward, *The Reconstruction of Western Europe, 1945–51* (London: Methuen, 1984), pp. 469, 476.

44. Robert Gilpin, "The Politics of Transnational Economic Relations," *International Organization* 25 (3 [Summer 1971]): 415.

45. Arthur Stein, "The Hegemon's Dilemma," *International Organization* 38 (Spring 1984): 382.

46. Robert O. Keohane and Joseph S. Nye, Jr., *Power and Interdependence* (Boston: Little, Brown, 1977).

47. Keohane, *After Hegemony*.

48. Mastanduno, "Strategic Weapon," p. 123.

49. Maier, "Two Postwar Eras," pp. 342–43.

50. Hugh Thomas, *Suez* (New York: Harper & Row, 1966), p. 145; David Deese, "Oil, War and Grand Strategy," *Orbis* 25 (4 [Fall 1981]): 543–44.

51. Joseph S. Nye, Jr., "Transnational Relations and Interstate Conflicts: An Empirical Analysis," *International Organization* 28 (4 [Autumn 1974]): 961–96.

52. See Kennan, *Memoirs*; Harry S. Truman, *Memoirs* (Garden City, N.Y.: Doubleday, 1955); Dwight D. Eisenhower, *Mandate for Change, 1953–1956*

(New York: New American Library, 1965).

53. Richard K. Betts, *Nuclear Blackmail and Nuclear Balance* (Washington, D.C.: The Brookings Institution, 1986), p. 17.

54. Ibid., p. 217.

55. Blight and Welch, *On the Brink*; Joseph S. Nye, Jr., "Cuban Graffiti," *The New Republic*, 13 March 1989, pp. 16–18.

56. Betts, *Nuclear Blackmail*, pp. 21, 214, 129, 213. For an even more skeptical view of the influence derived from nuclear weapons in the earlier period, see Bundy, *Danger and Survival*.

57. Herbert K. Tillema, *Appeal to Force: American Military Intervention in the Era of Containment* (New York: Thomas Crowell, 1973), chap. 5. Tillema's cases include thirty-one cases where a Communist government threatened to come to power in a country of special interest to the United States; thirteen cases of a Communist government threatening other countries; thirty-five threats by Communist governments in Communist-threatened regions; eight situations of armed conflicts threatening territories on the margins of Communist states; nine cases of conflict in Communist-governed states; and fifty-three situations where U.S. military intervention might have been expected as a partisan or peacekeeping measure.

58. Ibid., p. 177.

59. Gregory F. Treverton, *Covert Action: The Limits of Intervention in the Postwar World* (New York: Basic Books, 1987).

60. Barry Blechman and Stephen Kaplan, *Force without War: U.S. Armed Forces as a Political Instrument* (Washington, D.C.: The Brookings Institution, 1978), chap. 4.

61. Ibid., pp. 123–24.

62. Gary C. Hufbauer and Jeffrey J. Schott, *Economic Sanctions Reconsidered* (Washington, D.C.: Institute for International Economics, 1985), p. 80.

63. *Aviation Week and Space Technology* 130 (12 [20 March 1989]): 187–89.

64. Daniel Deudney, "Whole Earth Security: A Geopolitics of Peace," Worldwatch paper 55 (Washington, D.C.: Worldwatch Institute, 1983), p. 17.

65. Bela A. Balassa and Marcus Noland, *Japan in the World Economy* (Washington, D.C.: Institute for International Economics, 1988), p. 3. Even if German reunification combined East and West Germany's GNP, the fourth-place rank of total German GNP would not be altered.

66. Donald Klein, "The Alleged Death of 'Pax Americana'," *Boston Globe*, 4 January 1988, p. 13.

67. The balance of military alliances is shown in the following table:

	Share of World Military Expenditure		Share of World Military Personnel		Number of Major Warships	
	1975	1985	1975	1985	1974–1975	1988–1989
NATO	38.1%	41.1%	20.1%	19.5%	412	503
Warsaw Pact	39.3	36.6	21.1	20.2	225	297

SOURCE: International Institute for Strategic Studies, *The Military Balance* (London: IISS, 1973–1988 [annual]); Arms Control and Disarmament Agency, *World Military Expenditures and Arms Transfers* (Washington, D.C.: ACDA, 1975–1989 [annual]).

CHAPTER 4: COMMUNIST CHALLENGERS

1. Loren R. Graham, "Science and Policy and Organization," in *The Soviet Union Today*, ed. James Cracraft (Chicago: University of Chicago Press, 1983), p. 211.

2. Valery Giscard d'Estaing, quoted in "The '90s and Beyond: Domestic Problems Crimp Global Leadership Roles of Communist Giants," *Wall Street Journal*, 6 February 1989, p. A4.

3. The split began in the late 1950s, but the open polemics did not occur until 1963. See Walter Clemens, *The Arms Race and Sino-Soviet Relations* (Stanford, Calif.: Hoover Institution on War, Revolution, and Peace, Stanford University, 1968).

4. James G. Blight and David A. Welch, *On the Brink: Americans and Soviets Reexamine the Cuban Missile Crisis* (New York: Hill & Wang, 1989).

5. General Dimitri Volkogonov, interview with author, Moscow, January 1989.

6. Phillip A. Karber, "The Military Impact of the Gorbachev Reductions," *Armed Forces Journal International* 126 (6 January 1989): 54–55.

7. Charles Wolf, Jr., "The Costs of the Soviet Empire," *Science* 230 (29 [Nov. 1985]): 997–1002.

8. Alexander Yakovlev, "The Political Philosophy of Perestroika," in *Perestroika 1989*, ed. Abel Aganbegyan (New York: Scribner's, 1988), p. 36.

9. Quoted in Stephen Sestanovich, "Gorbachev's Foreign Policy: A Diplomacy of Decline," *Problems of Communism* 37 (1 [Jan.–Feb. 1988]): 2–3.

10. Marshall Goldman, *Gorbachev's Challenge* (New York: W. W. Norton, 1987), pp. 14–15. See also Ed A. Hewett, *Reforming the Soviet Economy* (Washington, D.C.: The Brookings Institution, 1988), chap. 2.

11. "Soviet Economic Improvement Below Expectations," *New York Times*, 24 March 1987, p. A8.

12. Quoted in "CIA Cites Doubts On Soviet Economy," *New York Times*, 2 November 1988, p. A9.

13. Goldman, *Gorbachev's Challenge*, chap. 2.

14. Ibid., p. 15.

15. Abel Aganbegyan, "Economic Performance," in Aganbegyan, ed., *Perestroika 1989*, p. 101.

16. "Life beyond the Kremlin," *New York Times*, 30 May 1988, pp. 7–8.

17. "Soviets Launch Computer Literacy Drive," *Science*, 10 January 1986, pp. 109–10; "Glasnost: Soviet Computer Lag," *Science*, 26 August 1988, p. 1034.

18. Nikolai Schmelov, "Advances and Debts," [trans. Timothy J. Smith] *Novy Mir* (June 1987): 12.

19. Loren R. Graham, "Gorbachev's Great Experiment," *Issues in Science and Technology* 4 (2 [Winter 1988]): 27.

20. Quoted in Sestanovich, "Gorbachev's Foreign Policy," p. 3.

21. "Oil's Decline Seen Curbing Soviet Plans," *New York Times*, 10 March 1986, p. D10.

22. Graham, "Gorbachev's Great Experiment," p. 25. See also David Holloway, "Science and Power in the Soviet Union," in *Science, Politics and the*

Public Good, ed. Nicolaas Rupke, (New York: Macmillan, 1988), p. 144.

23. Graham, "Science and Policy," p. 212.

24. "Russian Influence in Science Diminishing," *Science,* 16 March 1984, p. 1155.

25. See Abraham S. Becker, *Sitting on Bayonets: The Soviet Defense Burden and the Slowdown of Soviet Defense Spending* (Santa Monica, Calif.: Rand Corporation, 1985). The April 1989 CIA estimate was 15–17 percent of GNP (*The Soviet Economy in 1988,* report by the Central Intelligence Agency and Defense Intelligence Agency to the Joint Economic Committee of Congress [Washington, D.C.: GPO, 1989]). William Safire cites a figure of 25 percent of GNP ("Raise and Call," *New York Times,* 1 June 1989, p. A23). A prominent Soviet economist I interviewed in 1989 estimated 18 percent. Frank Holzman (cited above) accepts the official figure of 9 percent. I am indebted to Stephen Meyer of MIT for discussion of these numbers.

26. Gorbachev quoted in *Washington Post,* 1 January 1989; see also Jan Vanous, ed., *PlanEcon Report* 4 (19 August 1988); Leonid Abalkin quoted in "Advisers Soviet Deficit Figure is Triple Kremlin's," *New York Times,* 26 January 1989, p. A3; see also "Russia's Last Chance," *The Economist,* 11 March 1989, pp. 85–86. In personal interviews, some Soviet economists have suggested an inflation rate of 10 percent.

27. Nicholas Eberstadt, *The Poverty of Communism* (New Brunswick, N.J.: Transaction Books, 1988), pp. 52, 217.

28. "Kremlin Resumes Issuing Key Data," *New York Times,* 28 October 1986, p. A7.

29. "Questions Raised on Soviet Economy," *New York Times,* 2 November 1988, p. A9; Central Intelligence Agency, *Revisiting Soviet Economic Performance under Glasnost* (Washington, D.C.: GPO, 1988).

30. Nicholas Eberstadt, "The Soviet Economy: Worse Than We Thought," *New York Times,* 23 November 1988, p. A23.

31. Anders Aslund, "The CIA vs. Soviet Reality," *Washington Post,* 19 May 1988, p. A25.

32. Henry S. Rowen and Vladimir G. Treml, "Gorbachev and the Ailing Russian Bear," *Wall Street Journal,* 21 April 1986, p. 22.

33. Mikhail Gorbachev, speech to Soviet writers, quoted in "Gorbachev on the Future: 'We Will Not Give In,' " *New York Times,* 22 December 1986, p. A20.

34. Aganbegyan, *Perestroika 1989,* p. 102.

35. Quoted in "Key Parts of Soviet Plan for Change," *New York Times,* 5 July 1988, p. A13.

36. Quoted in "Radical Plan to Balance Soviet Budget," *New York Times,* 9 June 1989, p. A6.

37. Quoted in Goldman, *Gorbachev's Challenge,* p. 244.

38. Seweryn Bialer, "Gorbachev's Program of Change: Sources, Significance, Prospects," in *Gorbachev's Russia and American Foreign Policy,* ed. Seweryn Bialer and Michael Mandelbaum, (Boulder, Colo.: Westview Press, 1988); Jack Snyder, "The Gorbachev Revolution: A Waning of Soviet Expansionism?" *International Security* 12 (3 [Winter 1987/1988]): 93–131.

39. "Soviet Aides Press Plan To Cut Subsidies Despite Concern about

Public Reaction," *Wall Street Journal*, 8 December 1987, p. 33.

40. Goldman, *Gorbachev's Challenge*; Thane Gustafson, *Selling the Russians the Rope? Soviet Technology and U.S. Export Controls* (Santa Monica, Calif.: Rand Corporation, 1981).

41. Hewett, *Reforming*, p. 367.

42. Quoted in Condoleezza Rice, "Gorbachev and the Military," *Harriman Institute Forum* 2 (April 1989): 2.

43. "Questions on the Nationalities Question: A Round Table," [Moscow] *New Times* (2 May 1989): 24–26.

44. Alexander Motyl, "The Sobering of Gorbachev: Nationality, Restructuring and the West," in *Inside Gorbachev's Russia*, ed. Seweryn Bialer (Boulder, Colo.: Westview Press, 1989), p. 169.

45. Paul Dibb, *The Soviet Union: The Incomplete Superpower* (New York: Macmillan, 1986), pp. 48–49.

46. Yegor K. Ligachev briefly challenged the new thinking in foreign affairs in 1988, but his views did not prevail ("Gorbachev Deputy Criticizes Policy," *New York Times*, 7 August 1988, p. A11).

47. Paul Bairoch, "International Industrialization Levels," *Journal of European Economic History* 11 (2 [Fall 1982]): 304; Herbert Block, *The Planetary Product in 1980: A Creative Pause?* (Washington, D.C.: U.S. Department of State, Bureau of Public Affairs, 1981), p. 86.

48. Dwight H. Perkins, "China's Economic Policy and Performance during the Cultural Revolution and Its Aftermath," in *Cambridge History of China*, vol. 15 (forthcoming).

49. Dwight H. Perkins, "Reforming China's Economic System," *Journal of Economic Literature* 26 (June 1988): 632.

50. U.S. Commission on Integrated Long-Term Strategy, *Sources of Change in the Future Security Environment* (Washington, D.C.: GPO, 1988), pp. 2–9.

51. James R. Van de Velde, letter to the editor, *New York Times*, 2 February 1988.

52. Harry Harding, *China's Second Revolution* (Washington, D.C.: The Brookings Institution, 1987), pp. 33, 12.

53. Tu Wei-Ming, "A Confucian Perspective on the Rise of Industrial East Asia," *Bulletin of the American Academy of Arts and Sciences* 42 (October 1988): 32–50. For a skeptical view of the influence of Confucian values, see Ping-Ti-Ho, "Economic and Institutional Factors in the Decline of the Chinese Empire," in *The Economic Decline of Empires*, ed. Carlo Cipolla (London: Methuen, 1970), p. 277.

54. Dwight H. Perkins, *China's Modern Economy in Historical Perspective* (Stanford, Calif.: Stanford University Press, 1975), pp. 4, 134, 117.

55. Harding, *Second Revolution*, pp. 30–33.

56. Perkins, "China's Economic Policy," p. 21.

57. Harding, *Second Revolution*, p. 129.

58. Charles E. Morrison and Robert F. Dernberger, *Asia-Pacific Report, 1989* (Honolulu: East-West Center, 1989), pp. 48, 62.

59. Central Intelligence Agency, *China's Economic Policy and Performance in 1987*, report to the Joint Economic Committee of the Congress

(Washington, D.C.: GPO, Apr. 1987).

60. Harry Harding and Ed A. Hewett, "Socialist Reforms and the World Economy," in *Restructuring American Foreign Policy*, ed. John D. Steinbruner (Washington, D.C.: The Brookings Institution, 1989), p. 170.

61. CIA, *China's Performance*, p. 5.

62. David Zweig, "Reforming China's Political Economy," *Harvard International Review* 11 (2 [Spring 1989]): 4; Dorothy Salinger, "Economic Reform in China," *Harvard International Review* 11 (2 [Spring 1989]: 18.

63. "So That the Sky Won't Fall Down," *The Economist*, 18 June 1988, p. 33.

64. *Statistical Yearbook of China* (Peking: compiled by the State Statistical Bureau, People's Republic of China, 1986), p. 732.

65. International Institute for Strategic Studies, *The Military Balance, 1983-1984* (London: IISS, 1983), p. 90.

66. CIA, *China's Performance*, p. 18.

67. For a more buoyant view of China's nuclear program, see Chong-Pin Lin, "From Panda to Dragon," *National Interest* 15 (Spring 1989): 49-57.

68. Marta Dassu, *The Problem of Reconversion of the Military Industry: The Case of China* (Rome: CeSPI Occasional Paper no. 2, 1988), pp. 21, 25.

69. "So That the Sky Won't Fall Down," *The Economist*, p. 33.

70. Harding and Hewett, "Socialist Reforms," p. 175.

71. Ibid.

CHAPTER 5: ALLIED CHALLENGERS

1. Public Agenda Foundation, "National Survey No. 12: Changing Perceptions of the Soviet Union, American Use of Force, and Nuclear Weapons," in *Americans Talk Security: A Series of Surveys of American Voters' Attitudes Concerning National Security Issues*, 9 January 1989.

2. Herman Kahn, *The Emerging Japanese Superstate: Challenge and Response* (Englewood Cliffs, N.J.: Prentice Hall, 1970).

3. Samuel P. Huntington, "The U.S.—Decline or Renewal?" *Foreign Affairs* 67 (Winter 1988/1989): 93.

4. Ibid.

5. Robert Z. Lawrence and Charles L. Schultze, eds., *Barriers to European Growth* (Washington, D.C.: The Brookings Institution, 1987), pp. 1, 4.

6. Michel Albert and James Ball, *Toward European Economic Recovery in the 1980s: Report to the European Parliament* (New York: Praeger, 1984), pp. 8-9.

7. Harvard Business School, "EEC Competitiveness in the World Economy" [case no. 9-386-134] (Boston: HBS Case Services, 1987), p. 9.

8. Jacques Pelkmans and Alan L. Winters, *Europe's Domestic Market* (London: Routledge, Kegan Paul, 1988), pp. 2, 6.

9. Harvard Business School, "EEC Competitiveness," pp. 5-6.

10. "Who Turned out the Lights?" *The Economist*, 4 February 1989, p. 72.

11. Pari Patel and Keith Pavitt, "Measuring Europe's Technological Performance," Sussex University, Social Policy Research Unit, paper no. 30, 1986, p. 68.

12. Albert and Ball, *Economic Recovery*, p. 39.

13. Carlo DeBenedetti, quoted in "Welcome to Their Party," *Wall Street Journal*, 30 December 1988, p. A6.

14. "The Costs of Non-Europe" by P. Cecchini, summarized in Michael Emerson, "1992 As Economic News" (Brussels, manuscript, 1988); see also European Community, *Europe without Frontiers: Completing the Internal Market* (Luxembourg: European Community, 1988), p. 13.

15. "European Drive towards Larger Groupings 'Flawed,'" *Financial Times*, 30 January 1989, pp. 1, 4.

16. Quoted in "Divided over Unification," *Washington Post* (national weekly edition), 14 November 1988, p. 18.

17. Quoted in "The Slanging Match Resumes," *The Economist*, 28 January 1989, p. 49.

18. Ibid.

19. "Whoa, Europe," *The Economist*, 5 November 1988, p. 12.

20. Ernst Haas, *The Uniting of Europe: Political, Social, and Economic Forces, 1950-1957* (Stanford, Calif.: Stanford University Press, 1958); Joseph S. Nye, Jr., *Peace in Parts: Integration and Conflict in Regional Organization* (Boston: Little, Brown, 1971).

21. European Community, *Europe without Frontiers*, p. 25.

22. Alberto Giovannini, "Can We Copy the European Monetary System?" *National Bureau of Economic Research Reporter* (Winter 1988/1989): 9; Peter Ludlow, *Beyond 1992: Europe and Its Western Partners* (Brussels: Centre for European Policy Studies, 1989), pp. 20–25.

23. Committee for the Study of Economic and Monetary Union, "Report on Economic and Monetary Union in the European Community," (Brussels, manuscript, April 1989).

24. See Alain Minc, *La Grande Illusion* (Paris: Bernard Grasset, 1989). For a more balanced view, see Stanley Hoffmann, "The European Community and 1992," *Foreign Affairs* 68 (Fall 1989): 27–47.

25. See Josef Joffe, "America: Europe's Pacifier," *Foreign Policy* 54 (Spring 1984): 64–82; and Stanley Hoffmann, *Janus and Minerva* (Boulder, Colo.: Westview Press, 1987), chaps. 9, 12.

26. Arthur Hartley, "After 1992: Multiple Choice," *National Interest* 15 (Spring 1989): 39.

27. "L'Europe des Nouvelles Patries," *The Economist*, 5 November 1988, p. 52.

28. Hartley, "After 1992," p. 31.

29. "Hour of Power?" *Newsweek*, 27 February 1989, p. 15.

30. Herman Kahn and B. Bruce-Briggs, *Things to Come* (New York: Macmillan, 1972), p. ix.

31. Daniel Burstein, *Yen! Japan's New Financial Empire and Its Threat*

to America (New York: Simon & Schuster, 1988), p. 292.

32. "Closer Ties Bind U.S. and Japanese," *New York Times*, 23 February 1989, pp. A1, A10.

33. "Views of Japan: Results of a Five-Nation Survey," [Tokyo] *Economic Eye*, September 1988, p. 26.

34. Quoted in Akihiko Tanaka, "When a Hegemony Falls," *Look Japan* 34 (October 1988): 15; Hayashi Kenjiro, "Passing the Torch of World Leadership," *Japan Echo* 12 (4 [1985]): 10; Shinji Fukukawa, "Japan's Choices," *Look Japan* 34 (November 1988): 4–6; Kamo Tokehiko, "The Collapse of Pax Americana," *Japan Echo* 8 (4 [1981]): 87–95.

35. Takashi Inoguchi, "Japan's Images and Options: Not a Challenger, but a Supporter," *Journal of Japanese Studies* 12 (Winter 1986): 118.

36. Joel Kotkin and Yoriko Kishimoto, *The Third Century: America's Resurgence in the Asian Era* (New York: Crown, 1988); "Japan's Mirror to Our Times," *Boston Globe*, 30 October 1988, pp. A1, A17.

37. Paul Bairoch, "International Industrialization Levels from 1750 to 1980," *Journal of European Economic History* 11 (Spring 1982): 301–5.

38. Edward J. Lincoln, *Japan: Facing Economic Maturity* (Washington, D.C.: The Brookings Institution, 1988), p. 14f.

39. "Feeling Poor in Japan," *The Economist*, 11 June 1988, p. 33.

40. Bela A. Balassa and Marcus Noland, *Japan in the World Economy* (Washington, D.C.: Institute for International Economics, 1988), p. 157; "From Superrich to Superpower," *Time*, 4 July 1988, pp. 28–31; *New York Times*, 20 July 1988; Harold Brown, *U.S.-Japan Relations* (New York: Carnegie Council on Ethics and International Affairs, 1987), p. 4.

41. R. Taggart Murphy, "Power without Purpose: The Crisis of Japan's Global Financial Dominance," *Harvard Business Review* 67 (2 [March–April 1989]): 72–74.

42. Burstein, *Yen!* p. 91.

43. "Trench Warfare?" *The Economist*, 7 January 1989, p. 76.

44. Masaru Yoshitomi, of Japan Economic Planning Agency, quoted in *Japan Times*, 21 December 1988; Kazuo Nukazawa of Keidanren, quoted in "U.S. Currency Policy Is Helping Build Japan into an Economic Giant," *New York Times*, 28 November 1988, p. D13.

45. Hiroshi Takeuchi, quoted in Kotkin and Kishimoto, *Third Century*, p. 121.

46. Editorial, *Japan Economic Journal*, 17 December 1988, p. 6.

47. *The Nation* [Bangkok] quoted in "Japan's Political Role Expands," *Daily Yomiuri*, 7 November 1988, p. 6.

48. Clyde Haberman, "The Presumed Uniqueness of Japan," *New York Times Magazine*, 28 August 1988, p. 42.

49. Murray Sayle, "The Powers That Might Be," *Far Eastern Economic Review*, 4 August 1988, p. 43.

50. Joseph S. Nye, Jr., "Japan," in *Energy and Security*, ed. David Deese and Joseph S. Nye, Jr. (Cambridge, Mass.: Ballinger, 1980); Keizai Koho Center, *Japan 1989* (Tokyo, 1989), p. 59.

51. Naohiro Amaya, "No Glory in an Abacus," *Japan Times*, 25 October 1987, p. 3.

52. Kenneth Pyle, "Japan, the World and the Twenty-First Century," in *The Political Economy of Japan*, vol. 2, ed. Takashi Inoguchi and Daniel Okimoto (Stanford, Calif.: Stanford University Press, 1988), pp. 453–56.

53. Former MITI vice-minister Naohiro Amaya, quoted in ibid., p. 451.

54. "Japan's Military Spending is Hit From Both Sides," *Washington Post* (national weekly edition), 30 May 1988, p. 21; Japan Defense Agency, *Defense of Japan* (Tokyo: Defense Agency, 1988).

55. Steven K. Vogel, *Japanese High Technology, Politics and Power* (Berkeley, Calif.: Berkeley Roundtable on the International Economy, Research Paper no. 2 [mimeograph], 1989), p. 2.

56. Margaret Shapiro, "Japan Tries to Balance No-War Ethics, Arms Buildup," *Washington Post*, 1 May 1988, pp. A21 and A28; Motoo Shiina, interview with author, Tokyo, March, 1989.

57. Shimizu Ikutaro, "The Nuclear Option: Japan Be a State!" *Japan Echo* 7 (3 [1980]): 35.

58. Haberman, "Presumed Uniqueness," p. 43.

59. Paul Kennedy, *The Rise and Fall of the Great Powers: Economic Change and Military Conflict from 1500 to 2000* (New York: Random House, 1987), p. 538.

60. Richard Rosecrance, *The Rise of the Trading State* (New York: Basic Books, 1986); John Mueller, *Retreat from Doomsday* (New York: Basic Books, 1989).

61. Henry Rosovsky, speech to U.S.–Japan Program, Harvard University, 13 December 1988.

62. Chalmers A. Johnson, *MITI and the Japanese Miracle: The Growth of Industrial Policy, 1925–1975* (Stanford, Calif.: Stanford University Press, 1982).

63. "Strategy for Asia," *Daily Yomiuri*, 8 June 1988, p. 6.

64. Peter Drucker, "Japan's Choices," *Foreign Affairs* 65 (5 [Summer 1987]): 939. See also Clyde Prestowitz, *Trading Places* (New York: Basic Books, 1988).

65. Kenichi Ohmae, *Beyond National Borders* (Homewood, Ill.: Dow Jones-Irwin, 1987), p. 127.

66. Barry P. Bosworth and Robert Z. Lawrence, "America in the World Economy," *Brookings Review* 7 (Winter 1988/89): 45.

67. Balassa and Noland, *World Economy*, chap. 4.

68. Naohiro Amaya, "The Japanese Economy in Transition," *Japan and the World Economy* 1 (Oct. 1988): 107–8.

69. Drucker, "Japan's Choices," p. 931. See also Ohmae, *National Borders*, chap. 2.

70. Amaya, "Japanese Economy," p. 109; Fred Hiatt, "Japan: Is the Sun Setting on an Era of Economic Expansion?" *International Herald Tribune*, 16 September 1989.

71. Susan J. Pharr, "Japan and the World: The Debate in Japan," *Harvard International Review* 10 (April–May 1988): 35–38.

72. "The Opening of Japan," *The Economist*, 17 December 1988, p. 69. In part, however, this reflects the fall in oil prices, which reduced the share of raw materials in Japan's import bill.

73. National Science Foundation, *International Science and Technology*

Update, 1988 (Washington, D.C.: GPO, 1989), p. 94.

74. Ibid., pp. 6, 74, 62.

75. Robert D. Putnam and Nicholas Bayne, *Hanging Together: Cooperation and Conflict in the Seven-Power Summits* (Cambridge, Mass.: Harvard University Press, 1987), p. 246.

76. Kathryn Graven, "Toyota Tech," *Wall Street Journal*, 31 March 1989; Michael Dertouzos, Richard Lester, and Robert Solow, *Made in America* (Cambridge, Mass.: MIT Press, 1989), p. 85.

77. Kent Calder, "Japanese Foreign Economic Policy Formation: Explaining the Reactive State," *World Politics* 40 (4 [July 1988]): 517–41; Nakatani Iwao, "Can Japan Support the World Economy?" *Japan Echo* 14 (4 [1987]): 16.

78. Quoted in "Japan Carving New Global Role and a Niche as Peacemaker," *Boston Globe*, 25 July 1988, p. 9.

79. James Fallows, "For Those Who Have a Yen for the Japanese Way: Think Twice," *Washington Post* (national weekly edition), 20 February 1989, pp. 23–24; Haberman, "Presumed Uniqueness," p. 53.

80. Mikio Kato et al., "The Memory of and Some Conditions for Internationalization," *NIRA Research Output* 1 (1 [1988]): 52–56.

81. Ohmae, *National Borders*, p. 128. For opposite views of the rate of change, see Karel van Wolferen, *The Enigma of Japanese Power* (London: Macmillan, 1989) and Bill Emmott, *The Sun Also Sets* (New York: Simon and Shuster, 1989).

82. "A Survey of Japan," *The Economist*, 5 December 1987, p. 34.

83. Akio Morita and Shintaro Ishihara, *The Japan That Can Say "No"* (Tokyo 1989, unauthorized translation); Ayako Doi, "Japan: Now Is the Season for America-Bashing," *International Herald Tribune*, 17 July 1989, p. 6.

84. "A Survey of Japan," *The Economist*, 5 December 1987, p. 4.

CHAPTER 6: THE TRANSFORMATION OF POWER

1. Samuel P. Huntington, "The U.S.—Decline or Renewal?" *Foreign Affairs* 67 (Winter 1988/89): 76–96; Karen House, "The '90s and Beyond," *Wall Street Journal*, 21 February 1989.

2. Seyom Brown, *New Forces in World Politics* (Washington, D.C.: The Brookings Institution, 1974), p. 186.

3. Henry Kissinger, *A New National Partnership* (Washington, D.C.: U.S. Department of State, Office of Media Services, 1975), p. 1.

4. Joseph S. Nye, Jr., "Can America Manage Its Soviet Policy?" in *The Making of America's Soviet Policy*, ed. Joseph S. Nye (New Haven, Conn.: Yale University Press, 1984), pp. 325–54.

5. Joseph S. Nye, Jr., "Neorealism and Neoliberalism," *World Politics* 40 (January 1988): 235–51; Kalevi J. Holsti, *The Dividing Discipline: Hegemony and Diversity in International Theory* (Boston: Allen & Unwin, 1985); Stanley

Hoffmann, *Janus and Minerva* (Boulder, Colo.: Westview Press, 1987), chap. 18; Michael Doyle, "Kant, Liberal Legacies, and Foreign Affairs," *Philosophy and Public Affairs* 12 (Summer 1983): 205–35.

6. See Robert O. Keohane and Joseph S. Nye, Jr., eds., *Transnational Relations and World Politics* (Cambridge, Mass.: Harvard University Press, 1970).

7. Robert Gilpin, *War and Change in World Politics* (New York: Cambridge University Press, 1981), p. 227.

8. "The World's 50 Biggest Industrial Corporations," *Fortune*, 1 August 1988, p. D3.

9. Susan Strange, *States and Markets* (New York: Basil Blackwell, 1988), p. 71.

10. This point was made to me by the late John Holmes.

11. Robert O. Keohane and Joseph S. Nye, Jr., *Power and Interdependence* (Boston: Little, Brown, 1977), chap. 1.

12. Frank Fukuyama, "The End of History?" *National Interest* 16 (Summer 1989): 18.

13. Stanley Hoffmann, *Primacy or World Order* (New York: McGraw-Hill, 1978), suggests the alternative metaphor of multiple chessboards.

14. In the past, I have used the concept of entropy (the loss of ability to do useful work) to describe this diffusion. The analogy to physics is imperfect, however, because politics is not a closed system. For example, collective actions of states can change their environments and reverse some entropic trends. J. S. Nye, "American Power and Reagan's Policy," *Orbis* 26 (Summer 1982): 391–411.

15. "New Atlantic Cable Makes More Calls Possible," *New York Times*, 14 December 1988, pp. A1, D6.

16. Raymond Vernon and Debora L. Spar, *Beyond Globalism: Remaking American Foreign Economic Policy* (New York: Free Press, 1989), pp. 99–100.

17. William Woodruff, *America's Impact on the World* (New York: John Wiley, 1975), p. 101.

18. "The City in Second Place," *Financial Times*, 12 May 1989, p. 20.

19. "American Carmakers: Taking Root and Blooming," *The Economist*, 15 April 1989, p. 79.

20. *International Herald Tribune*, 8 April 1989; *International Herald Tribune*, 11 May 1989.

21. On nationalism and social mobilization, see Karl W. Deutsch, *Nationalism and Social Communication* (Cambridge, Mass.: MIT Press, 1953).

22. Joseph F. Clare, Jr., "Whither the Third World Arms Producers?" in *World Military Expenditures and Arms Transfers, 1986* (Washington, D.C.: ACDA, 1987), p. 27.

23. "CIA Sees a Developing World with Developed Arms," *New York Times*, 10 February 1989, p. A3.

24. Center for the Study of Foreign Affairs, "India and China: Comparing Two Developing Powers Out Twenty Years," Bulletin no. 3, Foreign Service Institute, Washington, D.C., November 1988.

25. The power resources that underlie command power behavior can have intangible aspects (e.g., a reputation for ruthlessness can enhance military

power). There are some tangible aspects to the resources that underlie co-optive power behavior (e.g., broadcast systems) but most of the power resources are intangible.

26. David Baldwin, "Power Analysis and World Politics: New Trends Versus Old Tendencies," *World Politics* 31 (2 [January 1979]): 161–94.

27. Strange, *States and Markets*, p. 29.

28. Susan Strange, "Finance, Information and Power" (Paper presented at the meeting of the International Studies Association, London, March 1989), p. 1.

29. Lars Mjoset, "The Performance of Britain and the U.S. as Great Powers in a Situation of World Economic Unequal Development and Catching Up" (Paper presented at the meeting of the International Studies Association, London, March 1989), p. 48. However, if negative aspects of popular culture (such as drugs or violence) alienate foreign elites, this advantage in popular culture cuts two ways.

30. Stephen Gill, "U.S. Hegemony: Its Limits and Prospects in the Reagan Era," *Millennium* 15 (3 [Winter 1986]): 321.

31. Strange, *States and Markets*, p. 131.

32. Peter Katzenstein, "The New Institutionalism and International Regimes: The Changing Position of Japan and West Germany in International Politics" (unpublished manuscript, 1989).

33. Strange, *States and Markets*, p. 237.

34. "The World's 50 Biggest," *Fortune*, p. D1.

35. Steven Kobrin, "Enforcing Export Embargoes through Multinational Corporations," *Business in the Contemporary World* 1 (Winter 1989): 31–42.

36. Susan Strange, "The Future of the American Empire," *Journal of International Affairs* 42 (1 [Fall 1988]): 5.

37. For figures on American cultural attraction, see "Exporting American Culture," *Public Opinion* 9 (1 [February–March 1986]): 30–35.

38. "Relations with U.S. Seem Badly Hurt by Crushing of Democracy Protests," *New York Times*, 11 June 1989, p. 16.

39. Ivan Vallier, "The Roman Catholic Church: A Transnational Actor," in Keohane and Nye, eds., *Transnational Relations and World Politics*, pp. 129–52.

40. Hamid Mowlana, *Global Information and World Communication* (New York: Longman, 1986), pp. 48, 82, 94; Thomas Guback, "International Circulation of U.S. Theatrical Films and Television Programming," in *World Communications: A Handbook*, ed. George Gerbner and Marsha Siefert (New York: Longman, 1984), p. 155.

41. Strange, *States and Markets*, p. 133.

42. Joel Kotkin and Yoriko Kishimoto, *The Third Century: America's Resurgence in the Asian Era* (New York: Crown, 1988), p. 196.

43. Ralf Dahrendorf, personal communication with author, May 1989.

44. "Relations with U.S. Seem Badly Hurt," *New York Times*, p. 16.

45. Strange, *States and Markets*, p. 133.

46. Michael L. Dertouzos, Richard K. Lester, and Robert M. Solow, *Made in America* (Cambridge, Mass.: MIT Press, 1989), p. 131.

47. Strange, *States and Markets*, p. 127.

48. Keohane and Nye, *Power and Interdependence*, chap. 7.

CHAPTER 7: DOMESTIC CHALLENGES

1. Paul McCracken, "Lick the American Disease before It's an Epidemic," *Wall Street Journal*, 16 January 1989.

2. Peter G. Peterson, "The Morning After," *Atlantic Monthly*, October 1987, p. 43.

3. Richard D. Lamm, "Crisis: The Uncompetitive Society," in *Global Competitiveness*, ed. Martin K. Starr (New York: W. W. Norton, 1988), pp. 13, 15.

4. Further, some of these social problems do not show a steady U.S. decline. Crime rates are closely correlated with the proportion of young males in the population, and some types of crime have declined from their high point in the early 1980s. The rate of high school dropouts also declined, and the 39-percent use of illegal drugs among high school students in 1988 was down from a peak of 54 percent in 1979. Optimists and pessimists may disagree on whether the social glass is half full or half empty, but it is hard to make the case for a monotonic cultural decline. (Bureau of the Census, *Social Indicators* [Washington, D.C.: GPO, December 1980], pp. xxiv–xxvi; Bureau of the Census, *Statistical Abstract of the United States, 1988* [Washington, D.C.: GPO, 1987], pp. 154, 137–40; "Student Survey Detects Decline in Use of Crack," *New York Times*, 1 March 1989, p. A16.)

5. Lamm, "Crisis," pp. 33–34; "User-Friendly Technical Fixes," *New York Times*, 15 June 1988, p. D2; "Can America Compete?" *Business Week*, 20 April 1987, p. 45; Council on Competitiveness, *Competitiveness Index*, (Washington, D.C.: 1988), p. 4.

6. Daniel Yankelovich and Sidney Harman, *Starting with the People* (Boston: Houghton Mifflin, 1988), p. 240.

7. Mancur Olson, *The Rise and Decline of Nations* (New Haven, Conn.: Yale University Press, 1982), p. 4. Olson does not explicitly address the aggregate U.S. experience.

8. David Cameron, "Distributional Coalitions and Other Sources of Economic Stagnation," *International Organization* 42 (2 [Autumn 1988]): 561–604; Mancur Olson, ed., "Symposium: Mancur Olson on the Rise and Decline of Nations," *International Studies Quarterly* 27 (1 [March 1983]): 3–37.

9. "America's Shrinking Middle," *The Economist*, 12 November 1988, p. 84. See also Charles Wolf, Jr., "The Rise of Market Forces," in *Thinking about America*, ed. Annelise Anderson and Dennis L. Bank (Stanford, Calif.: Hoover Institution, 1988), p. 181.

10. "America's Trade Policy: Perestroika in Reverse," *The Economist*, 25 February 1989, p. 59.

11. Robert E. Lipsey and Irving B. Kravis, *Saving and Economic Growth: Is the United States Really Falling Behind?* (New York: The Conference Board, 1987), pp. 9, 12, 20, 25, 72–73.

12. Kenneth Flamm and Thomas L. McNaugher, "Rationalizing Technology Investments," in *Restructuring American Foreign Policy*, ed. John Steinbruner (Washington, D.C.: The Brookings Institution, 1989), p. 119.

13. "Rethinking Technology's Role in Economic Change," *Science*, 20 May 1988, p. 977.

14. Ralph Gomory and Roland W. Schmitt, "Science and Product," *Science*, 27 May 1988, p. 1131.

15. Quoted in Michael Dertouzos, Richard Lester, and Robert Solow, *Made in America* (Cambridge, Mass.: MIT Press, 1989), p. 129.

16. Paul Gray, interview, "A View from the MIT Pressure Cooker," *Wall Street Journal*, 14 March 1989, p. B11.

17. Catherine Morrison et al., *Keys to U.S. Competitiveness* (New York: The Conference Board, 1988), p. ix.

18. Samuel Popkin, "Fear of the Future Spurs Economic Nationalism," in American Insight Group, eds., *American Insight, 1989* (Cambridge, Mass.: American Insight Group, 1989), pp. 53–58.

19. Cited in Dertouzos, Lester, and Solow, *Made in America*, p. 50.

20. Laura d'Andrea Tyson, "Competitiveness: An Analysis of the Problem and a Perspective on Future Policy," in *Global Competitiveness*, ed. Martin Starr (New York: W. W. Norton, 1988), p. 97.

21. For a criticism of the concept, see Barry P. Bosworth and Robert Z. Lawrence, "America's Global Role: From Dominance to Interdependence," in Steinbruner, ed., *Restructuring American Foreign Policy*, pp. 84–86.

22. Stephen S. Cohen and John Zysman, *Manufacturing Matters* (New York: Basic Books, 1987).

23. "User-Friendly Technical Fixes," *New York Times*, p. D2; Lipsey and Kravis, *Saving and Economic Growth*, p. 18.

24. "America's Shrinking Middle," *The Economist*, p. 85.

25. Lawrence Mishel, "Of Manufacturing's Mismeasurement," *New York Times*, 27 November 1988; "High Technology Is Hampering the Service Industries," *New York Times*, 29 June 1987, p. D6; "Manufacturing Vigor Overstated," *New York Times*, 28 November 1988, p. D7. On the other hand, some economists believe that productivity figures since 1973 underestimated true productivity by as much as a third. See "Productivity's Progress," *Wall Street Journal*, 25 September 1989, p. A14; also George Hatsopoulos, Paul Krugman, and Lawrence Summers, "U.S. Competitiveness: Beyond the Trade Deficit," *Science* 241 (15 July 1988): 299–307.

26. Bosworth and Lawrence, "Global Role," p. 33.

27. Lipsey and Kravis, *Saving and Economic Growth*, p. 80; William Baumol, "A Modest Decline Isn't All That Bad," *New York Times*, 15 February 1987, p. F2.

28. For a more complete list and discussion, see Dertouzos, Lester, and Solow, *Made in America*, chap. 2.

29. Nathan Rosenberg, *Technology and American Economic Growth* (New York: Harper & Row, 1972), p. 177.

30. Harvey Brooks, "The Technological Factor in U.S. Competitiveness," Science, Technology and Public Policy Program, discussion paper 89–03 (Cambridge, Mass.: John F. Kennedy School of Government, Harvard University, 1989); John A. Alic, "From Weakness or Strength" (unpublished paper, John F. Kennedy School of Government, Harvard University, March 1989).

31. National Science Foundation, *International Science and Technology*

Update, 1988 (Washington, D.C.: GPO, 1987), pp. 88, 90, 92.

32. Cited in Dertouzos, Lester, and Solow, *Made in America*, p. 67.

33. "Science and Technology: The Gap Is Shrinking Fast," *New York Times*, 5 April 1988, pp. C1, C6.

34. "Novel Technique Shows Japanese Outpace Americans in Innovation," *New York Times*, 7 March 1988, pp. A1, A13.

35. "Can America Compete?" *Business Week*; "For Growth, Cut Butter not Guns," *New York Times*, 6 December 1988, p. A35.

36. Brooks, "U.S. Competitiveness," p. 10.

37. Dertouzos, Lester, and Solow, *Made in America*, p. 116; Alic, "Weakness." See also Ashton Carter, "Anatomy of the Dual-Use Relationship," Science, Technology and Public Policy Program, discussion paper 89-05 (Cambridge, Mass.: John F. Kennedy School of Government, Harvard University, October 21-22, 1988).

38. "Federal Policies in Transition," *Science*, 23 December 1988, p. 1621; Bobby Inman, "Why We're Slipping—and What's To Be Done," *Washington Post*, 4 October 1988, p. A11.

39. Keizai Koho Center, *Japan 1988* (Tokyo, 1988), p. 93.

40. "U.S. Students Near Foot of Class," *Science*, 11 March 1988, p. 1237; "Science Achievement in Schools Called Distressingly Low," *Science*, 30 September 1988, p. 1751; "A Modest Decline Isn't All That Bad," *New York Times*, 15 February 1989, p. F2; "Reagan's Education Secretary Will Continue under Bush, but Will Reagan's Policies?" *New York Times*, 7 December 1988, p. B16.

41. Frank Doyle and Rocco Siciliano, "A New America: The Dramatic Changes Affecting the Work Force of the 21st Century," *Business in the Contemporary World* 1 (Spring 1989): 50.

42. Cited in Julie Amparano Lopez, "System Failure," *Wall Street Journal*, 31 March 1989, p. R12.

43. Cited in Dertouzos, Lester, and Solow, *Made in America*, pp. 85, 136, 137.

44. Brooks, "U.S. Competitiveness," p. 14; Betty Vetter, "How Many PhDs Is Enough?" *AAAS Observer*, 6 January 1989, p. 10; "In Math, the Language of Science, Americans Grow Even Weaker," *New York Times*, 30 October 1988; National Science Foundation, *International Science and Technology Data Update* (Washington, D.C.: GPO, 1987), p. 37.

45. "Smaller Savings for Rainy Days," *The Economist*, 19 March 1988, p. 76.

46. Bosworth and Lawrence, "Global Role," p. 17.

47. Lipsey and Kravis, *Saving and Economic Growth*, pp. 28-34.

48. Bela A. Balassa and Marcus Noland, *Japan in the World Economy* (Washington, D.C.: Institute for International Economics, 1988), chap. 4. Moreover, figures indicating that the United States became a net international debtor in 1985 are based on a massive undervaluation of U.S. assets. If direct investments and gold holdings were valued at current market values rather than artificial book values, the United States' situation was not so dire ("Gaining a New Perspective on U.S. 'Debtor' Status," *Rand Research Review*

12 [Fall 1988]: 14).

49. George Hatsopoulos, Paul Krugman, and James Poterba, *Overconsumption: The Challenge to U.S. Economic Policy* (New York: The American Business Conference, 1989), pp. 5–17.

50. "The Savings Rate Keeps Shrinking," *New York Times*, 28 April 1989, p. D1.

51. Bosworth and Lawrence, "Global Role," pp. 17–18.

52. Herbert Stein, "A Credit Card Economy . . . And Why Not?" *Wall Street Journal*, 7 September 1988, p. 26.

53. Joseph White and Aaron B. Wildavsky, "How to Fix the National Deficit—Really," *Public Interest* 94 (Winter 1989): 3–24. Compare to Benjamin Friedman, *Day of Reckoning: The Consequences of American Economic Policy under Reagan and After* (New York: Random House, 1988).

54. "And Now a Pause for Some Wishful Thinking," *The Economist*, 4 February 1989, pp. 21–22. See also Lawrence H. Summers, "The Budget Deficit Problem: 1989," *Tax Notes: Special Report*, 6 March 1989.

55. Francis Bator, "Must We Retrench?" *Foreign Affairs* 68 (2 [Spring 1989]): 93–123.

56. Edward S. Corwin, *The President: Office and Powers, 1787–1957: History and Analysis of Practice and Opinion* (New York: New York University Press, 1957), p. 200.

57. Dexter Perkins, "What Is Distinctly American about the Foreign Policy of the United States?" in *Foreign Policy and the American Spirit: Essays*, ed. Glyndon Van Dusen and Richard Wade (Ithaca, N.Y.: Cornell University Press, 1957), pp. 3–15.

58. James Schlesinger, *America at Century's End* (New York: Columbia University Press, 1989), p. 87.

59. I. M. Destler, Leslie H. Gelb, and Anthony Lake, *Our Own Worst Enemy: The Unmaking of American Foreign Policy* (New York: Simon & Schuster, 1984).

60. Philip G. Cerny, "Political Entropy and American Decline," *Millennium* 18 (1 [Spring 1989]): 50.

61. Quoted in Richard Rose, *The Postmodern President: The White House Meets the World* (Chatham, N.J.: Chatham House, 1988), p. 289.

62. Ibid.

63. Cerny, "Political Entropy," p. 55.

64. Joseph A. Schumpeter, *Capitalism, Socialism, and Democracy* (New York: Harper Brothers, 1950), pp. 81–86.

65. "Japan's Technology Gap," *The Economist*, 15 April 1989, p. 18.

66. James M. Fallows, *More Like Us: Making America Great Again* (Boston: Houghton Mifflin, 1989), p. 43.

67. Naohiro Amaya, "The Japanese Economy in Transition," *Japan and the World Economy* 1 (October 1988): 107.

68. Takashi Inoguchi, "Four Japanese Scenarios for the Future," *International Affairs* 65 (1 [Winter 1988/1989]): 27.

69. Gallup Poll (Los Angeles, Calif.: Times-Mirror Corporation, 3 Feb. 1989), p. 85.

70. Fallows, *More Like Us*, p. 47.

71. "The Myths of Corporate Japan," *The Economist*, 27 May 1989, p. 16.

72. Jessica Tuchman Matthews, "Redefining Security," *Foreign Affairs* 68 (2 [Spring 1989]): 162–77.

73. Richard N. Cooper, "Government Should Spend More—Not Less," *Washington Post*, 9 February 1981, p. A13.

74. Overseas Development Council, *Foreign Aid Review* (Washington, D.C.: GPO, 15 Dec. 1988), p. 1.

75. Herbert Stein, "Tax the Rich, They Consume Too Much," *New York Times*, 23 October 1988, p. F2.

76. *New York Times*, 14 February 1989; "A Portrait of America's New Competitiveness," *The Economist*, 4 June 1988, p. 57; "U.S. Chips Are Quietly Cracking the Japanese Market," *Wall Street Journal*, 22 March 1989, p. B4; "The U.S. Gets Back in Fighting Shape," *Fortune*, 24 April 1989, pp. 42–48.

77. Cited in Dertouzos, Lester, and Solow, *Made in America*, pp. 8, 126.

78. Lipsey and Kravis, *Saving and Economic Growth*, pp. 78–82.

CHAPTER 8: FUTURE WORLDS AND AMERICAN CHOICES

1. Edward S. Corwin, *The President: Office and Powers, 1787–1957: History and Analysis of Practice and Opinion* (New York: New York University Press, 1957), p. 200.

2. George Kennan, *American Diplomacy, 1900–1950* (New York: New American Library, 1951), p. 10.

3. Graham T. Allison, "National Security Strategy for the 1990s," in *America's Global Interests: A New Agenda*, ed. Edward K. Hamilton (New York: W. W. Norton, 1988), p. 210.

4. John Lewis Gaddis, "How the Cold War Might End," *Atlantic Monthly*, November 1987, p. 88.

5. Thomas L. Friedman, "Soviet Strife, U.S. Caution," *New York Times*, 12 April 1989, p. A1; George R. Kennan, "The Soviet Union Today Is Only Another Great Power," *International Herald Tribune*, 11 April 1989, p. 6.

6. Giorgi Arbatov, "The Limited Power of an Ordinary State," *New Perspectives Quarterly* 5 (2 [Summer 1988]): 31.

7. John Martilla, "American Public Opinion," in Hamilton, ed., *America's Global Interests*, p. 268.

8. Kenneth Waltz, "The Origins of War in Neorealist Theory," *Journal of Interdisciplinary History* 18 (4 [Spring 1988]): 615–28.

9. Karl W. Deutsch and J. David Singer, "Multiple Power Systems and International Stability," *World Politics* 16 (April 1964): 390–406.

10. Quoted in Seyom Brown, *New Forces, Old Forces, and the Future of World Politics* (Glencoe, Ill.: Scott Foresman, 1988), p. 234.

11. "Kissinger's World View," *Christian Science Monitor,* 6 January 1989, p. 19.

12. Stanley Hoffmann, *Gulliver's Troubles* (New York: McGraw-Hill, 1968), p. 34.

13. "America, Asia and Europe," *The Economist,* 24 December 1988, p. 33.

14. Ibid., p. 41.

15. Lester Thurow, quoted in *International Herald Tribune,* 31 January 1989, p. 1.

16. Wan Guong, "China's Foreign Policy Goals," *Harvard International Review* 11 (2 [Spring 1989]): 30.

17. Brown, *New Forces,* p. 242.

18. Ibid.

19. David M. Gordon, "Do We Need To Be No. 1?" *Atlantic Monthly,* April 1986, p. 100.

20. Alan Tonelson, "The End of Internationalism?" *New Republic,* 13 February 1989, p. 25.

21. Josef Joffe, "America: Europe's Pacifier," *Foreign Policy* 54 (Spring 1984): 64–82.

22. Kurt M. Campbell, "Prospects and Consequences of Soviet Decline," in *Fateful Visions: Avoiding Nuclear Catastrophe,* ed. Joseph S. Nye, Jr., Graham T. Allison, and Albert Carnesale (Cambridge, Mass.: Ballinger, 1988), pp. 153–69; Joseph S. Nye, Jr., "Gorbachev's Russia and U.S. Options," in *Gorbachev's Russia and U.S. Foreign Policy,* ed. Seweryn Bialer and Michael Mandelbaum (Boulder, Colo.: Westview Press, 1988), pp. 385–408.

23. "Windows of Opportunity," joint statement of the John F. Kennedy School, Harvard University, and the Soviet Academy of Science, reprinted in Graham T. Allison and William Ury, eds., *Windows of Opportunity* (Cambridge, Mass.: Ballinger, 1989). See also Abraham Becker and Arnold Horelick, *Managing U.S.–Soviet Relations in the 1990s* (Santa Monica, Calif.: Rand Corporation, 1989).

24. Ed A. Hewett, "An Idle U.S. Debate about Gorbachev," *New York Times,* 30 March 1989, p. A25.

25. Charles Wolf, Jr., "The Rise of Market Forces," in *Thinking about America: The United States in the 1990s,* ed. Annelise Anderson and Dennis L. Bark (Stanford, Calif.: Hoover Institution, 1988), p. 188.

26. Nye, Allison, and Carnesale, eds., *Fateful Visions,* chaps. 2, 10.

27. This follows the proposal of Valery Giscard d'Estaing, Henry Kissinger, and Yasuhiro Nakasone to the Trilateral Commission (*International Herald Tribune,* 11 April 1989, p. 1).

28. François Heisbourg, "Now for NATO's Next 40 Years," [London] *Times* 4 April 1989, p. 12.

29. James M. Fallows, "Let Them Defend Themselves," *Atlantic Monthly,* April 1989, p. 17.

30. Edward Luttwak, "Do We Need a New Grand Strategy?" *National Interest* 15 (Spring 1989): 13.

31. Gary Hufbauer, quoted in "Burger Flippers Take the Heat," *New York Times,* 26 April 1989, p. D2; "Assessing Reaganomics: The Trouble with

Theories," *The Economist*, 21 January 1989, p. 75.

32. Aaron L. Friedberg, *The Weary Titan: Britain and the Experience of Relative Decline, 1895–1905* (Princeton, N.J.: Princeton University Press, 1988), chap. 2.

33. Roger B. Porter and Raymond Vernon, *Foreign Economic Policymaking in the United States* (Cambridge, Mass.: John F. Kennedy School of Government, Harvard University, 1989), p. 12. There may be no single stable point of global comparative advantage based on fixed factor engagements, and in some industries, comparative advantage may be created by government intervention. This may provide a ground for specific responses but not for a wholesale move to a philosophy of managed trade.

34. Norman Glickman and Douglas Woodward, *The New Competitors: How Foreign Investors Are Changing the U.S. Economy* (New York: Basic Books, 1989), pp. 5, 9.

35. Robert E. Lipsey and Irving B. Kravis, *The Competitiveness and Comparative Advantage of U.S. Multinationals, 1957–1984* (Cambridge, Mass.: National Bureau of Economic Research, reprint 964, 1987).

36. "Japanese Foreign Direct Investment: Love and Hate in America," *The Economist*, 19 March 1988, p. 74.

37. Glickman and Woodward, *New Competitors*, pp. 7, 45.

38. Ibid., chap. 9. For an opposing view, see Martin Tolchin and Susan Tolchin, *Buying into America: How Foreign Money Is Changing the Face of Our Nation* (New York: Times Books, 1988).

39. "The World America Created," *The Economist*, 24 December 1988, p. 33.

40. The following discussion draws on Robert O. Keohane and Joseph S. Nye, "Two Cheers for Multilateralism," *Foreign Policy* 60 (Fall 1985): 148–67.

41. Robert W. Tucker, "Using Force against Libya," *New York Times*, 11 January 1989, p. A23.

42. Robert D. Putnam and Nicholas Bayne, *Hanging Together: Cooperation and Conflict in the Seven-Power Summits* (Cambridge, Mass.: Harvard University Press, 1987), p. 273.

INDEX

Index